CONTENTS

FOREWORD

Since I first mentioned my plan for this book, I have regularly confronted the question *why*. Most people anticipate a writer's next work based on her or his past work, but history has given us plenty of wild surprises, like the wide range of George Bernard Shaw's plays. I guess I fit into that tangle a bit, but the question is nonetheless legitimate. Why *was* this supposedly nice Jewish *chachem* ("a clever, wise, or learned person," according to Leo Rosten), a woman who was fairly well known as a liberal-integrationist-feminist writer and sometimes integrationist and feminist activist, suddenly choosing to write about a black preacher who harshly and aggressively opposes everything she believes in?

With all the people and subjects in the world to write about, why do I choose Louis Farrakhan?

But those questioners know that I have had a lifelong interest in the course of the black fate in America, and I could not for long be put off by the man who is clearly going to write a large piece of this American opera, the man who will be winning many kudos in the black world. Who better to write about than the person you are predicting will be, in a few years, the main man in black America?

These thoughts took on a special, almost mystical feeling as I read the 1996 memoir of Raul Hilberg, a personal hero, the man who had brought us in 1961 the most comprehensive report of the Holocaust in *The Destruction of the European Jews.* I was suddenly and inexplicably forced to examine a piece of myself that I had never questioned. Hilberg's book, *The Politics of Memory: The Journey of a Holocaust Historian* (published by my own publisher, Ivan R. Dee), confronted me, as some books can, with the contrast between our lives, and in that contrast I saw myself in a new light. Most of European-born Hilberg's life has been devoted to the study and propagation of how and why the European Jews were exterminated, but his basic concern has been the anatomy of his own people, and he has often pitted himself "against the main current of Jewish thought."

In the same years, having been born in the same period in the United States, and sharing many of Hilberg's intellectual, emotional, and ethical instincts, for reasons not altogether beyond me I concentrated instead on the history and fate of American blacks.

Why, at nineteen years old, having experienced the dreadful revelations of what had recently befallen the European Jews, did I decide to commit myself somehow to improve the fate of American blacks? Along with many other Jews. Some have tried to offer a simple answer. We were overwhelmed with a sense of guilt that we had survived when so many had perished; we could do nothing about the past of the Jews, so we turned to help those among us who were in such pain. I have since decided that was far too simplistic an explanation. First, American Jews still experienced all kinds of discrimination. It was not Germany, but it was still discrimination. Second, on another and more significant level, Jews had been involved with blacks since at least the turn of the century. The connections between Jews and blacks was much more complex than that simple explanation made it appear. But for years, though I always believed I led the "examined life," I never examined that piece of my life.

My absorption with blacks was mostly quiet, mostly private, except for periods of active participation, mostly from 1946 to 1950 and from 1960 to 1970, with occasional spurts along the way, and later with a wide array of writing, mostly for Chicago publications.

I was never alone. And in the last thirty years, despite all the friction that has arisen between blacks and whites, despite the enthusiasm for separatism among so many blacks, despite the anti-Semitism among so many blacks, there has remained that connection between what has become a small band of Jews, other whites, and blacks. In a sense, we try to convince ourselves that nothing has changed, that we are not pitting ourselves "against the main current of Jewish thought," as Hilberg has done, that we are simply hanging in there. Why? Why does Raul Hilberg continue to light a candle rather than curse the darkness? The answer is within us and totally outside the orbit of this preface. But that feeling of having to keep the candle lit accounts for why I wrote this book.

Every biographer of a living subject depends on the friends, relatives, acquaintances of the subject who are willing to share their thoughts with the writer. While some of the names of those who talked with me about Louis Farrakhan appear in the text, along with some of the writers I relied on, others do not, but they deserve equal acknowledgment. Their names follow, in no particular order.

Leon Forrest, writer and professor at Northwestern University, whose chapter on Elijah Muhammad in his *A Serious Voice for Freedom* (1994) was influential; Richard Cohen, *Washington Post* columnist, who, inadvertently or not, gave me a strong Jewish perspective; Clarence Wood, chairman and commissioner of the Commission on Human Relations of the City of Chicago and president of the Human Relations Foundation of Chicago, an endless source of information about race relations and the major characters on that scene in Chicago; Salim Muwakkil, senior editor of *In these Times* and *Chicago Sun-Times* columnist, former editor of *Muhammad Speaks*, and a longtime Farrakhan observer with formidable insights; the late John McDermott, founder and for many years editor of the *Chicago Reporter*, a highly regarded journal of race relations, and executive director of the local Catholic Interracial Council, who had a powerful sense of the prevailing white liberal integrationist views toward Farrakhan.

Also Lu Palmer, Chicago black radio personality, founder and chairman of the Chicago Black United Committee, a major nationalist political leader in the city and longtime supporter of the Nation of Islam; Muzette Hill, Chicago La Salle Street lawyer with Lord, Bissell, and Brook, former chair of the Cook County Bar Association, who openly states that she is more comfortable after she's gone home to her family in an all-black neighborhood, and who is a friendly admirer, though sometimes reluctant defender, of Farrakhan; Rabbi Herman Schaalman, Sholom Emanuel Congregation in Chicago, who, after several attempts at rapprochement with Farrakhan, has no further interest in the process; Capers Funnye, black Jewish rabbi of the Beth Shalom B'nai Zaken Ethiopian Hebrew Congregation on Chicago's South Side, former administrator and now board member of the Jewish Council on Urban Affairs.

And Hermene Hartman, publisher of *N'Digo*, a black Chicago tabloid specializing in profiles of successful black men and women, a close friend and admirer of Farrakhan's; Judge Eugene Pincham, formerly on both the Chicago municipal court and on the U.S. Court of Appeals for the Seventh Circuit, who, after retirement, ran for mayor of Chicago and later for Cook County state's attorney, and who strongly supports Farrakhan though he is unsympathetic to his anti-Semitism; George O'Hara, a retired white suburban businessman now running a "motivational" speakers bureau, so enthusiastic about Farrakhan's ideas that he would join the Nation "in a minute" but for his wife's objections, one of only two whites in Farrakhan's entourage, who claims to be Farrakhan's public relations man but strangely lacks information; Manning Marable, author of *Black Liberation in Conservative America* (1997), professor and director of the Institute of African American Studies, Columbia University, an integrationist, among a handful of blacks who has developed a serious critique of Farrakhan's ideas, mostly negative; Reverend Wyatt Tee Walker, charismatic leader of the large, successful Canaan Baptist Church in Harlem, inspired to become a minister after working with Martin Luther King, Jr., and a harsh opponent of Farrakhan (and the press); Mel King, chairman of the Community Fellows Program at the Massachusetts Institute of Technology, former Massachusetts legislator, former chairman of the Boston NAACP, who in the sixties knew Farrakhan well and was impressed with him as "a highly thoughtful, mild-speaking person."

Libraries and librarians, under such attack today by politicians and by their own peers to transform themselves into electronic way stations, have for centuries played a huge role in the writer's life. How to thank them enough? My thanks go to the librarians in the Library of Congress, the New York Public Library, the Chicago Public Library, Northwestern University Library, and, unexpectedly in this worldly and elite club, the suburban Evanston, Illinois, Public Library, with its large and unusual holdings and its knowledgeable and helpful librarians. I also want to mention especially the librarians at the Vivian Harsh Collection at the Carter Woodson branch of the Chicago Public Library, which houses the second largest collection of materials on and by blacks in a public library in the country.

There are others—librarians in obscure places; policemen who leveled with me; writers such as Andrew Hacker, Darryl Pinckney,

George Fredrickson, and dozens of others whose books and articles, particularly regular articles and reviews in the *New York Review of Books*, have helped so much; people at the Episcopal Church Center in Chicago, especially Richard Seidel, historian for the Center; the people in the public relations office of the Catholic Archdiocese, and others.

Then there are my precious family and dear friends, especially Lisa Cohen and Gail Barazani, who, with their endless and imaginative help and encouragement, helped me beat the cancer statistics and settle back to work again. I also want to thank Richard Gage at the Illinois Arts Council and all those kind friends without whose financial assistance this book would have been impossible.

Finally there is Ivan Dee, whose encouragement is never failing, even when he occasionally disagrees, and whose editing is consistently superb, even when I occasionally disagree.

F. H. L.

Evanston, Illinois
April 1997

LOOKING FOR FARRAKHAN

PROLOGUE

"Who hath not own'd, with rapture-smitten frame,
The power of grace, the magic of a name?"
—Thomas Campbell, *Pleasures of Hope*, 1799

Since the end of American slavery in 1865, descendants of the slaves have struggled to find a name for themselves. While their place of origin was Africa, and while "back-to-Africa" movements have occasionally appeared since the early nineteenth century, and while many American blacks carry a strong identification with Africa, most blacks have not, except for a short period in the twenties, been entirely comfortable being associated with Africa. For good reasons. As part of the effort to diminish their stature, slaveowners and even, during Reconstruction, teachers and others associated with the training of blacks regularly asserted that Africans were savages. Hope for blacks, most believed, lay in identifying with white America, not with the Africans of the past.

For many years after the end of slavery, blacks called themselves and were called *colored* (the National Association for the Advancement of Colored People was founded in 1910). At the same time they also called themselves *Negro*, originally from the Latin *niger* meaning black, and from the old, now discarded anthropological term Negroid, which referred to the alleged physical characteristics of the peoples of Africa and other nations (the National Negro Business League was founded by Booker T. Washington in 1900; Marcus Garvey founded the Universal Negro Improvement Association in 1914). The term *black* was also used (*The Souls of Black Folk* was first published by W. E. B.

Du Bois in 1903), though it was also a derisive term used by whites along with *nigger, coon, jig,* and others despised by blacks.

Negro and *colored* remained in general use until the late 1960s, when an elite of civil rights activists led a movement to change the name to *black,* insisting that the other terms had been the inventions of white people. Meanwhile, since the thirties Elijah Muhammad and his Nation of Islam had rejected *Negro,* referring to blacks as "so-called Negroes" without inventing a more satisfactory term. Writing about the Nation in the late sixties, a black historian coined the term *black Muslims,* for the group. It has been used ever since.

In the 1960s, when *black* was first hoisted as the banner name, some at first saw it as inherently prejudicial: it applied a color appellation that did not suit all those light-skinned (or white-skinned) descendants of rape during slavery who were once called *mulattoes* and other expressions, such as *quadroons,* that applied to those of lighter skin color. Those who led the movement to use *black* insisted that it simply stated the distinction between the descendants of slavers and those of slaves. Just as there are distinctions in skin color among whites, so there are among blacks, the thinking went. In a short time *black* became almost universally accepted as the name for the descendants of slaves.

In the 1970s and 1980s, following the revolutions and coming of independence to some African nations, there came a new identification with Africa. Now there were those who chose to call themselves *Afro-Americans* and even adopted African names, rejecting the names they insisted rightly they had inherited from their families' slave masters. But though some intellectuals changed their names, the idea didn't generally catch on, even with the example of the famous black poet Leroi Jones, who changed his name to Imanu Amiri Baraka, or the famous boxer Cassius Clay, who became Muhammad Ali. Afro haircuts became popular, though they were rarely if ever simply the outgrowth of hair one found in parts of Africa. This Afro worn in northern American cities was carefully shaped in the beauty salon. (It was a lot cheaper than the varieties of cornrows and other hairdos that arose later.)

In the late eighties the elite once more reconsidered. Now they didn't wish to be called *blacks* or *Afro-Americans,* they wanted to be called *African Americans,* like Italian Americans and Polish Americans.

Some of them had been to Africa and formed strong ties. A few wore African garb. Some were learning Swahili and other African dialects. You could scarcely find a straightened, curled, oiled hairdo in this group, though there was no shortage of "ordinary" black hairdos in the black neighborhoods.

The long history of blacks in America had carried so much pain and suffering, the theory went, that once again it had become necessary to try to forge a more satisfying, realistic identity. As the Chicago Reverend Nathan Jarrett explained it to me, "African American brings a conscious understanding that people must be identified with a common heritage of land, country, people, history. Because our history has been so negative in this land, our identifying with whites has led us to not respect ourselves. On the other hand, there is a rich history of African culture, so if we identify with that, it's positive. It's worth telling the story. It's worth celebrating."

Slowly *African American* became the name used generally in the media and among the educated elite.

But on the streets and in the homes, even of the elite at times, the allegedly hated name that came directly from slavery, *nigger*, continued to be commonly used, an expression of affection, anger, surprise, the whole gamut of emotion—a supposedly deeply held secret that the elite would like to forget. They would like to ban Mark Twain's *Huckleberry Finn* from the libraries because Twain refers to his African American hero as "nigger Jim."

But it shouldn't be forgotten. It is a sign of self-hatred, hatred absorbed from whites, a common phenomenon among oppressed peoples. (Along with the anti-Semites she learned it from, my mother used to call less assimilated Jews *kikes*, but unlike *nigger*, *kike* was rarely used affectionately.) It is a sign of a people who see themselves as low-down outcasts not very different from their slave ancestors. Alternatively, it might be heard as an affectionate gesture to those ancestors. "We haven't forgotten you," the term might be heard to say, as it survives all opprobrium. It might also be heard as a cry of defiance. "Yes, we're niggers, and we're as good or better than any of you." As if to say, with Lenny Bruce, if you use any "dirty" name long enough and often enough, it will lose its sting.

Perhaps following Lenny, in the last thirty years or so a number of books have been published by blacks using *nigger* in the title—three books titled *Nigger* by Dick Gregory (1970), Roger Ekins (1970), and Labi Siffre (1993), plus *The Nigger Bible*, by Robert DeCoy (1967), Mark Morant's *The Insane Nigger* (1983), and *Nigger Amos* by Horace Davis (1966). Richard Pryor, the best black comedian of modern times, caresses his manic defiance of whites, of life, and of other blacks by referring to blacks almost exclusively as *niggers*.

The struggle to find an appropriate name is not trivial. Gertrude Stein may have been wrong when she said, "Rose is a rose is a rose is a rose," following Shakespeare, who asked, "What's in a name? That which we call a rose by any other name would smell as sweet." It is the effort to change the image—the qualities by which they are known and know themselves—that has prompted this search for an appropriate name by leaders of black people. It is a struggle that emerges directly from the deep insecurities of a people almost universally rejected by white America. It is a struggle to find legitimacy and identity in a culture that has, since the first landings on this soil, since the Founding Fathers, denied legitimacy to those it forced to become Americans (if only three-fifths Americans, according to the Constitution).

Unfortunately one does not choose one's identity. Stein and Shakespeare were probably right. A name change doesn't change one's identity. It results from one's family heredity, from one's cultural, racial, and religious background. For most of us there is little we can do to create a new identity that denies our heredity and history, though of course history is filled with examples of individuals who have succeeded in making themselves into something they were naturally not. Amandine Aurore Lucie Dupin, Baroness Dudevant, exchanged her skirts for pants, took up cigar smoking, and assumed a masculine name, George Sand, to overcome the prejudice against women writers in the nineteenth century. Americans, ranging from popular entertainers to immigrants in our ever-changing, protean culture, seem to find it easy. Immigrants and despised people especially often change their names as they enter middle-class life, leaving their early backgrounds behind. How many Poles, Czechs, Russians, and Jews have shortened or changed their names in order to blend into the American scene? In my generation, many Jews also surgically altered the shapes of their noses to avoid the opprobrium of the "Jewish nose," and many Orientals went to plastic surgeons to alter their eye shapes. For many years until the sixties, blacks used a variety of tactics to whiten their skin and almost universally straightened their hair.

Louis Farrakhan is one such person. He rejected his family name, Walcott, first using simply Louis X in the tradition of the Nation of Islam, and later adopting Farrakhan when he reached the state of grace within the Nation where one can have a surname. He rejected his family's Episcopal religion for Elijah Muhammad's version of Islam, and gave up a career as a musician to become an activist in the Nation. He fled the mixed world in which he grew up, with aspirations to succeed as a musician in the wider culture, for an all-black, self-denying world that would provide him with all the psychological protection such a world offers.

What must be seen as a tragic aspect of blacks' search for an appropriate name is the condition of limbo that the search implies. "Just what are we? Where do we fit into this massive mosaic of America?" are the questions it suggests. More importantly implied is the sense of inferiority, so long bred into blacks, that persists despite clear advances made in the last thirty years. The unofficial committees that have willed the name changes have not been those who suffer in the streets of the ghettos; they are the intellectual or social leaders of the black world, the ones presumed least likely still to endure the feelings of inferiority that beset blacks. Nevertheless, even among these more privileged people that feeling is made manifest by this search for a new name that will confer a more substantial status on blacks, a source of greater pride, a pride of place that seems to elude so many of even the most accomplished blacks as they make their way in the world.

In his 1990 book *The Content of Our Character*, the conservative intellectual Shelby Steele discusses this search for enhanced pride. "This self-conscious reaching for pride through nomenclature," Steele says, "suggests nothing so much as a despair over the possibility of gaining the less conspicuous pride that follows real advancement. In its invocation of the glories of a remote African past and its wistful suggestion of homeland, this name denies the doubt black Americans have about their contemporary situation in America. There is no element of self-confrontation in it, no facing of real racial vulnerabilities, as there was with the name 'black.' I think 'black' easily became the name of preference in the sixties, precisely because it was not a denial but a confrontation of inferiority anxiety, with the shame associated with the color of black. There was honest self-acceptance in this name, and I think it diffused much of our vulnerability to the shame of color. Even between blacks, 'black' is hardly the drop-dead fighting word it was when I was a child. Possibly we are ready now for a new name, but I think 'black' has been our most powerful name yet because it so frankly called out our shame and doubt and helped us (and others) to accept ourselves. In the name 'African-American' there is too much false neutralization of doubt, too much looking away from the cauldron of our own experience. It is a euphemistic name that hides us even from ourselves."

I find myself resisting *African American* because the African origins of American blacks are almost lost in history. The use of *African American* is part of an elite's search for an identity that reaches beyond and before slavery, an attempt to find a history and a culture that removes the stain of enforced servitude for three hundred years. It is part of a movement that is engaged in studying African history and culture, of wearing African garb, of learning African languages, of creating a nationalist credo to provide an identity that wipes out the identity of a people emerging from a slave culture and one that creates an identity separate from America, separate and distinct. The black identity as an American is fraught with too much pain and suffering. An escape is necessary, an escape from what W. E. B. Du Bois described in 1903 as an escape from a double-consciousness—"this sense of always looking at one's self through the eyes of others, of measuring one's soul by the tape of a world that looks on in amused contempt and pity. One ever feels his twoness,—an American, a Negro: two souls, two thoughts, two unreconciled strivings; two warring ideas in one body, whose dogged strength alone keeps it from being torn asunder." That double-consciousness is no less present in 1997 than it was in 1903. The choice of the name *African American* attempts to shed that burden, but, as Steele said, "It is a euphemistic name that hides us even from ourselves."

This escape from the reality of American black life is what Louis Farrakhan and other lesser-known black nationalists nurture in their teachings and preachings. This escape prompted all the back-to-Africa movements that are at the core of current black nationalist thinking, and later of Elijah Muhammad's adapting that early thinking to his own. Such an escape is not to be sneered at or patronized. It represents the desperate longings of a despised people to find legitimacy and justice in their lives, but it is an attempt at escape that is self-denying and fruitless. Nationalists reject the goal of integration, the goal of the major civil rights organizations since the turn of the century, insisting that in integration lies only more injustice and discrimination. Yet it is only integration into the larger society that can bring full participation and justice.

For years the leaders of the Nation of Islam called their brethren "so-called Negroes"; but the current usage in the Nation is *black*, almost as if to defy the leadership of what the Nation views as the lost people of their race.

Having lived through much of the history I recall here, and having been dismayed and pained by much of it, it isn't easy to decide what name I will use to write about the subjects of this book. I hope it signifies no particular attachments that, on one score at least, my choice lies with Louis Farrakhan. I agree with Shelby Steele that, to date, *black* represents the sharpest, clearest delineation of the identity of the current heir of the American slave.

Part One

ANTECEDENTS

1.

In his leadership of the Nation of Islam, Louis Farrakhan represents the most recent link in a complex historic chain of almost two centuries, though the links do not always closely resemble one another. He brings together strains of the "back-to-Africa" movement that began in the early nineteenth century; strains of the Tuskegee self-help movement that began about seventy years later, after Emancipation; and religious movements that include various mixtures of Christianity and Islam along with the potent notion of race pride. From their earliest years in America, when most blacks still lived in slavery, despair over the conditions of black lives had burst periodically into efforts to relieve those conditions. While slave revolts occasionally erupted in the South, former slaves in the North—freed slaves, escaped slaves, and those who had been born free after their mothers had been freed—before Emancipation forged the first organizational links in the chain that led, after Emancipation, to the emergence of organizations that led to the creation of the Nation of Islam and to its most recent incarnation in the leadership of Louis Farrakhan.

The first back-to-Africa movement was the effort of freed slaves. By the time of the Civil War there were nearly half a million free blacks in the United States (there were nearly four million slaves at the time), most of whom lived in poverty, with none of the privileges and rights of their white neighbors. The attraction to Africa was ambivalent for many of these people, most of whom were already more than third-generation Americans, more American than most whites. And they had grown up being taught by whites that the pagan masses of Africa were savages, a notion described by Mark Twain in his journals as one of the "many humorous things in the world . . . the white man's notion that he is less savage than the other savages." Surely Twain found it even funnier that the blacks in this country, whose origins were in Africa, often took to heart the white man's notions. Right from the start, no doubt as a result of white influences, the back-to-Africa movement was suffused with a Christian missionary zeal aimed at "civilizing" the savages. On the other hand, Africa was the black homeland and represented psychological comfort and security to American blacks. For an energetic and rebellious few, the choice between life in their African homelands and life as despised and rejected citizens in the United States was clear.

Beyond ambivalence, there was also outright opposition to the back-to-Africa movement, first by the abolitionists, notably Frederick Douglass, then later, after Emancipation, by the Tuskegee self-help movement led by Booker T. Washington, and then by the integrationist movement led by W. E. B. Du Bois. But in the 1920s the emigration movement briefly took on mass appeal, with Marcus Garvey. And in the 1970s there was again talk of emigration to Africa. Throughout these years only a handful actually crossed the ocean. Even Garvey himself never set foot on the land he considered God's.

2.

Although most of Africa itself in the nineteenth century was slowly coming under colonial occupation—often brutal occupation—by the Europeans and English, it sometimes seemed more hospitable to American blacks. Most of them lived under the most repressive and brutal slave system the world had known. Even for freed blacks, life was harshly discriminatory. In an account of a journey to Africa in 1859, entitled *A Pilgrimage to My Motherland: An Account of a Journey Among the Egbas and Yarubas of Central Africa in 1859–1860*, Robert Campbell, a Jamaican free black who was educated and lived in Philadelphia and held a prestigious job there—one of the black intelligentsia of the time, an early statistician—wrote, "If I am still asked what I think of Africa for a colored man to live and do well in, I simply answer that with as good prospects in America as colored men generally [have], I have determined with my wife and children, to go to Africa to live, leaving the inquirer to interpret that reply for himself."

As early as 1811 a rare wealthy free black, Paul Cuffee (who had taken that name as a variation on an African name, Kohfee, a Ghanian name), of New Bedford, Massachusetts, who had managed to acquire a small fortune in shipping, sailed one of his ships to Sierra Leone on the west coast of Africa, an English colony. Before the British put down their colonial flag in 1796, a British abolitionist society had founded Freetown in Sierra Leone in 1787, a small settlement for freed American slaves and those rescued from slave ships. So it was to Sierra Leone that Cuffee sailed to found his "Friendly Society from America." When he returned to the States he organized a party of emigrants, and the next year he carried, at his own expense, thirty-eight people back to start his colony in Sierra Leone. But the effort seems to have failed, and when Cuffee returned to the United States he proposed that a black colony be established on its southern coast.

Meanwhile among whites there had been talk since the late seventeenth century of creating a colony in Africa for freed blacks. Some of these designs, often among abolitionists, were altruistic—to provide a safe, nondiscriminatory haven for freed blacks and thereby to atone for slavery. But much of the talk was far from altruistic. Many discussions, such as those in Virginia in 1691, when the Virginia legislature passed a law requiring slaveowners to remove any freed slaves from the area, were means to rid the country of freed blacks because it was feared their presence might incite rebellion on the plantation. At one point, early in the eighteenth century, after successful slave revolts and a fight for independence in Haiti at the turn of the century, it was suggested that a penal colony for rebellious slaves be established in Africa.

Such ideas drifted around until 1816, when a group of white liberal clergy and some freed blacks, with the support of Henry Clay, speaker of the House of Representatives, formed the American Society for Colonizing the Free People of Color in the United States, which came to be known as the American Colonization Society. The Society aimed to found a colony for freed blacks in Africa, based on the American government model.

The plan appeared to be altruistic, but, according to *Africa 1995*, "However noble these efforts might have appeared at the time, an underlying reason for the action might be found in Clay's own words in which he counseled that such colonization would 'draw . . . off' free blacks. The response by the founder of the Society, Rev. Robert Finley, was 'We shall be clear of them.' "

With great mixed motives, then, the Society petitioned Congress in 1819 to provide funds to establish a colony. After considerable debate Congress allocated $100,000 to transport back to Africa blacks rescued from illegal slave ships and those brought over since 1808, when the U.S. slave trade had been outlawed. But no money was allotted for the purchase of land until 1822, when, after several failed attempts by the Society to establish colonies in Sierra Leone, the United States paid $300 to local African chieftains for the area that came to be known as Liberia.

While white missionaries and politicians were debating the merits of an African colony for freed blacks, the freed blacks were listening and talking among themselves. Whatever the motives of the whites may have been, and whether the blacks knew of these mixed motives, the idea of a colony in Africa appealed strongly to small numbers of freed blacks. Thus they welcomed the government's offer. By 1830 about a thousand people had settled in Liberia. In 1847 the Free and Independent Republic of Liberia was declared, with the capital, Monrovia, named for President James Monroe. While Liberia immediately received diplomatic recognition from other nations, it was only in 1862, under Abraham Lincoln during the Civil War, that the United States finally recognized it. Small wonder, because in fact Liberia was—and remains—the unofficial colony of the United States.

The forty or so years before the Civil War saw a steady, though small, flow of emigrants to Liberia. Eventually there were about 15,000 American settlers who in some respects were not much different from other colonists who came to Africa: they largely seized control and ruled over what was then about a million indigenous people. Today the population exceeds 2.5 million.

In his 1974 book *Marcus Garvey and the Vision of Africa*, the historian John Henrik Clarke describes an 1852 meeting of an Emigration Convention at which one of its foremost leaders, a widely respected intellectual, sometimes called "the father of black nationalism," Martin

R. Delany, urged emigration to Africa to establish a colony in what is now Nigeria. Delany said, according to Clarke, "Settle them in the land which is ours, and there lies with it inexhaustible resources. Let us go and possess it. We must establish a national position for ourselves and never may we expect to be respected as men and women until we have undertaken some fearless, bold and adventurous deeds of daring, contending against every consequence." That this educated, sophisticated, free black, himself subject to severe discrimination and very much aware of the privations of most of his fellow blacks, had such dreams of the rawest kind of colonization forces us to ask whether such ideas are bred into our nature or whether the conditions under which most American blacks had lived left them no alternative but to ape their masters. Or was Delany simply naive? Did he think he could "go and possess" a piece of Africa without harming the natives who lived there? Did he think those "fearless, bold and adventurous deeds of daring, contending against every consequence" didn't include a battle to subdue the people whose land he was urging his people to take? In fact, for many years the Liberian colonists remained on the coast, not venturing into the heavy jungles of the interior, thus not disturbing the people who lived there. Relations between the ruling American blacks and the indigenous peoples remained reasonably peaceful. Then, early in the twentieth century, the Firestone Tire and Rubber Company discovered Liberia, and the United States decided that the country was well situated for a variety of military operations and communications installations. These helped the ruling American blacks but provided nothing for the indigenous peoples.

In the 1920s this reasonably well-settled country, though completely undeveloped, poverty-stricken, and illiterate, and ruled uneasily by the American immigrant minority at the behest of the United States, was thrown into turmoil by allegations that the government—those freed slaves—had participated in the slave trade. A Liberian government commission in 1929, finally investigating the charges, found evidence that the government had indeed been involved in the widespread shipment of what was euphemistically called "contract labor" to neighboring colonies ruled by whites. The government, under a new president (though still a descendant of Americans), survived but was generally unstable until the election in 1944 of William V. S. Tubman, still another American. Tubman introduced important political and economic improvements during his long reign from 1944 to 1971, but conditions in Liberia were not notably altered. At Tubman's death in 1971, his vice-president, William R. Tolbert, was named to the presidency and then reelected in 1975. Tolbert was the first Liberian president to be a native of the land.

In 1979 the government was forced to announce to its very poor population a rise in the price of rice, the country's staple food. Rioting followed. In a military coup led by native Liberians who were hostile to Americans, Tolbert and hundreds of government officials were killed. The ensuing years were filled with government anarchy and continual strife, both between native strongmen vying for power and between natives and Americans—brutal armed strife, like what was then happening in so many other countries in Africa. It seems that the experience of living under brutal treatment in the United States and then being nominally controlled by the American government for many years created the same kind of preparation for democratic government as did living under the brutal treatment of the European colonizers of Africa. The fulfillment of the hopes of those early freed slaves for an escape from tyranny didn't last as long as the slave trade did.

While some American blacks were forging what they believed was the country of their salvation in Africa, many others strongly disagreed with them. Most important among them was Frederick Douglass, the famous abolitionist leader who had escaped from slavery in 1838 and nine years later had been enabled to buy his freedom. In his speeches and writings, especially his widely read abolitionist newspaper, *North Star*, which he published in Rochester, New York, from 1847 to 1863, Douglass continually opposed the back-to-Africa movement, insisting that it detracted from the more important movement to free American slaves.

3.

The Civil War and the promises to blacks engendered by Reconstruction temporarily put an end to the back-to-Africa movement, though there were several loosely proposed plans to create a separate state in the United States for the freed slaves. Emancipation and then Reconstruction created such great hopes among the freed slaves that talk of emigration to Africa was all but forgotten. But the end of Reconstruction in 1875 saw the destruction of those promises with a wave of violence against blacks throughout the South. Semislave economic arrangements for blacks were restored, and restrictive state legislation removed the rights conferred by Emancipation and Reconstruction. Gradually voting rights disappeared, total segregation was established, and even the mildest suspicion of transgression could lead to fierce retribution. Economic life for blacks was reduced to the most menial jobs at the lowest wages. Education, one of the great promises of Reconstruction, a promise valued by the former slaves almost above all, was devastated, reduced to a shadow of its former self, though several colleges established with help from the federal government and abolitionists did survive. Now the former slaves had, just as they had before, no benefits of citizenship, but they also were without even the minimal protections of the slave master. They were at the mercy of any white Southerner who chose to malign blacks in any way. The Ku Klux Klan, which had been organized to fight Reconstruction in 1866, was officially disbanded in 1869, but its members continued to terrorize blacks.

As a consequence, interest in Africa began to rekindle, mainly in the thoughts of Bishop Henry McNeal Turner, the twelfth bishop of the African Methodist Episcopal (AME) church, who was appointed by Lincoln in 1863 as the army's first black chaplain. Born into slavery in Abbeville, South Carolina, in 1834, Turner had been freed because he was the son of an African king, but he was denied schooling under South Carolina laws that outlawed education for blacks. After struggling secretly to gain his schooling, he was hired by a group of local white lawyers who took him under their wing and taught him the law, along with a general education. He joined the white Methodist Episcopal church in 1851 and two years later was licensed to preach. Not long after, he withdrew from the white church to join the AME church, and thereupon he served in black churches in Baltimore and Washington. In 1880 he was named bishop.

Turner was an idealistic, highly religious man who had been reasonably well treated by whites and had entertained the belief that, with emancipation, blacks would be given a rightful place in society. Terribly disillusioned at the demise of Reconstruction, he turned his eye to Africa to become for many years the leading advocate for the back-to-Africa movement. In 1891, with visions of creating new colonies there, he established missions of the church in Sierra Leone, Liberia, and South Africa. But though he preached widely of the improved quality of life to be had in Africa and was widely applauded and loved, he was not successful in drawing many Americans into the fold. Whether because of the deep discouragement and fear left by slavery and the aftermath of Reconstruction; or whether, despite the horrifying events that followed Reconstruction, the former slaves nurtured some faith they might yet prosper in the United States; or whether, because they had been taught that Africa was a primitive land they had been rescued from, Turner's urgings brought only slight success. Despite the conditions in the South in the aftermath of Reconstruction, blacks hoped they might yet attain equal rights. Turner discouraged that hope. Like many others, he also believed that Africans were not quite civilized; his missions were more specifically designed to bring Christianity and "civilization" to African "savages" than were the earlier back-to-Africa movements—not exactly the kind of approach that was likely to succeed among many ordinary people.

Despite the wholesale depreciation of Africa by whites, and though not many blacks actually went to Africa, blacks nevertheless held a strong identification with those lands, both as homelands and, as colonization took root, home to fellow sufferers from white oppression. Almost all of Africa lay under the rule of Europeans—often cruel—which contributed further to a reluctance to emigrate. Many of the black intelligentsia worked for the freeing of the African colonies. A variety of societies were formed to this end, and in 1900 W. E. B. Du Bois led an American delegation to the first Pan-African Congress in London to "start a movement looking forward to securing of all African races living in civilized countries their full rights and to promote their business interests," and "to act as a forum of protest against the aggression of the white colonizers." Not a very forceful document, this aims statement was designed to attract the attention and support of the white liberals of the Western world. On the other hand, it was the public pronouncement of a weak, powerless group that expressed a great deal of courage and optimism.

4.

There now arrived on the American scene a man who opposed all thoughts of emigration or even of active resistance to the powers of white domination and discrimination. In response to the horrors of race hatred and persecution, he organized an anti-anti-movement. Born a slave in about 1858 in Virginia, Booker T. Washington founded his Tuskegee Institute in Tuskegee, Alabama, in 1881. There he urged blacks to turn their energies inward, toward themselves, toward creating for themselves some safety and security in America by perfecting manual skills they could sell to the white man or turn into their own profitable businesses. Thrift, patience, and industrial training were the answer to the black's problems, he said. Learn a trade—become a skilled plumber, carpenter, millhand, housekeeper, dressmaker; become efficient farmers and workers to qualify in the white-owned business world. The Tuskegee Institute was designed to teach a wide variety of skills, from homemaking to farming. Washington was urging, in effect, a temporary second-class place in American society, the best that he believed could be attained for many years to come.

"No race that has anything to contribute to the markets of the world is long in any degree ostracized," he told an audience containing some blacks but mostly whites in a speech at the opening of the 1895 Atlanta Exposition. "It is important and right that all privileges of the law be ours, but it is vastly more important that we be prepared for the exercise of these privileges. The opportunity to earn a dollar in a factory just now is worth infinitely more than the opportunity to spend a dollar in an opera house." The honor of addressing such a celebrated event, so unexpectedly given to a black, to speak at a huge city gala that attracted officials from all over the country, was won by Washington after many similar speeches in the fourteen years since he had founded Tuskegee. He was the supreme gift to the white establishment: the black leader who urged his followers to accept their offering gratefully.

Africa was, in Washington's mind, a foolish dream. One should dream, certainly, but right now it was more important to make one's way in the world. For that one must always recognize that one must prove his good judgment, and his disciplined ways, and his accomplished skills, and his undivided loyalty, so that the white man will extend to him the rights of citizenship. Reading Washington's autobiography, *Up from Slavery*, one sees that Washington sincerely believed his prescription would eventually pay off for blacks who followed him.

Ironically Washington was able to establish Tuskegee Institute in 1881 because the blacks in Macon County, in which Tuskegee was located, still had the vote and were able to use it to extract state money to start the school. They exchanged their vote in 1880 for a former Confederate colonel, W. F. Foster, running for the state legislature on the Democratic ticket, mostly shunned by blacks, for a promise from him to push for a state appropriation to open a school for blacks in the county. Foster won, Tuskegee was established. It wasn't long before such bargaining was denied the rest of Southern blacks as they lost the vote in the white backlash against Reconstruction. In line with his theory that blacks could regain the vote only by catering to whites, Washington urged his followers to ignore voting rights. Still, at the turn of the century he himself appealed to state legislatures to revise their constitutions to give the vote equally to educated blacks and whites while denying it to *all* illiterates.

Washington's 1901 autobiography betrays his wholesale dependence on the kindness of whites to provide political opportunities for blacks. He says, "I think . . . that the opportunity to freely exercise such political right will not come in any large degree through outside or artificial forcing, but will be accorded to the Negro by the Southern white people themselves, and that they will protect him in the exercise of those rights. Just as soon as the South gets over the old feeling that it is being forced by 'foreigners,' or 'aliens,' to do something which it does not want to do, I believe that the change in the direction that I have indicated is going to begin." There were, in fact, at the turn of the century when he wrote this book, not even vague signs that such changes were likely. It is difficult to decide whether Washington uttered such statements because he believed them or in order to placate whites, which was true of many of his public utterances.

In his Atlanta Exposition speech, he said the words that would endear him to the white leadership of the nation and forever after be taken to characterize his views: "In all things purely social we can be as separate as the five fingers, and yet one as the hand in all things essential to mutual progress." That Exposition speech, according to his own account, made him a hero among whites in America. It enabled him to raise money to support several branches of the Tuskegee Institute and to expand and improve the facilities of the main campus. The white establishment adopted him as a great leader. He dined with presidents. And after initial resistance to his ideas by blacks who felt the trade-off of civil and political rights and higher education for economic security wasn't worth it, he found a good deal of acceptance among blacks and for many years was recognized as the major leader of blacks and a friend to whites.

Although Washington publicly continued to assert the benefits of second-class citizenship until his death in 1915, there is evidence that his views over the years became more complex. He helped fund the integrationist W. E. B. Du Bois's research and helped obtain libraries for several black liberal arts colleges. In his later years he apparently changed his mind about the efficacy of agitation over questions of social equality, and he secretly filed lawsuits against segregated facilities and against discriminatory behavior.

Yet Washington was never a favorite of the black intelligentsia. In 1903, in *The Souls of Black Folk*, W. E. B. Du Bois made clear his anger at Washington for advocating the submission of blacks to second-class citizenship. " . . . It is utterly impossible, under modern competitive methods, for workingmen and property-owners to defend their right and exist without the right of suffrage," Du Bois wrote. "He . . . counsels a silent submission to civic inferiority such as is bound to sap the manhood of any race in the long run." Despite such harsh criticism from black intellectuals, Washington remained a moving force, establishing branches of Tuskegee and speaking widely until he died in 1915. His reputation persisted more or less intact until the 1950s, when Southern blacks rejected what was sometimes called "gradualism," the heart of Washington's credo, and turned to a variety of direct tactics to attain their civil and political rights. But in the North, as early as the 1920s, there were some blacks for whom American civil and political rights were unimportant. What was important was the ability to build a separate black world.

5.

The beginning of the new century had brought an attempt to break the black chain with the past, to break the chain that depended on sentiments either of emigration or of second-class citizenship. Instead the new outlook reflected the call of Frederick Douglass. Now there was a flowering of civil rights organizations, most notably the Niagara Movement, that culminated in the founding in 1909 of the National Association for the Advancement of Colored People (NAACP), setting the stage for the long struggle for civic equality and integration. These groups, who collectively came to be known as the New Negro, led by Du Bois and his colleagues, followed Frederick Douglass's lead in opposing the back-to-Africa movement as a distraction from the more important goal of freedom in America, this time not from slavery but from discrimination and violence against former slaves. Du Bois and his people, together with white liberals who joined their cause, clearly set their eyes against Washington's imaginings about the white man's generosity and looked to a struggle for full and equal citizenship.

Du Bois had begun his career as a scholar, not as an activist. Born free in Great Barrington, Massachusetts, in 1868, he went south to Nashville to attend the black Fisk University. After graduation from Fisk in 1888, he returned to New England and spent four years at Harvard, then two years at the University of Berlin in graduate studies, concentrating on black history and sociology. In 1897 he returned to the South, this time to teach at another black university, Atlanta University in Atlanta, Georgia. Du Bois had devoted his adult life to scientific study, believing that his work would lead to greater economic and political freedom for blacks. Life in the South at the turn of the century proved a great antidote to his ideas, so that by the time he published *The Souls of Black Folk* in 1903 he believed that whatever truth might emerge from the scientific study of blacks would not "encourage [or] help social reform." He had become an activist.

While Booker T. Washington was regarded as the preeminent black leader, *The Souls of Black Folk* created a great stir among blacks and led many to turn to Du Bois for a new kind of leadership. He had written, "The time is come when one may speak in all sincerity and utter courtesy of the mistakes and shortcomings of Mr. Washington's career, as well as of his triumphs. . . . So far as Mr. Washington preaches Thrift, Patience, and Industrial Training for the masses, we must hold up hands and strive with him, rejoicing in his honors and glorying in the strength of this Joshua called of God and of man to lead the headless host. But so far as Mr. Washington apologizes for injustice, North or South, does not rightly value the privilege and duty of voting, belittles the emasculating effects of caste distinctions, and opposes the higher training and ambition of our brighter minds—so far as he, the South, or the Nation, does this—we must unceasingly and firmly oppose them. By every civilized and peaceful method we must strive for the rights which the world accords to men. . . ."

A few years later Du Bois helped found the Niagara Movement, went on to help found the NAACP, and became the editor of the organization's magazine, *Crisis*. As such he became the best-known and most respected advocate for black civil and social rights in the first half of the twentieth century. While Du Bois and his associates had opponents, those most fiercely allied against him were the separatists, Marcus Garvey, Noble Drew Ali in the 1920s, and, following them in later decades, Elijah Muhammad.

6.

After the end of Reconstruction, with hope they might find a better life, more ambitious, courageous, and hopeful blacks formed a small but steady stream out of the South. They sought jobs, better living conditions, an escape from the escalating violence, and, most important, relief from the Jim Crow laws and attitudes that had overtaken their lives. In the North and the West, they had heard, there were no Jim Crow laws. Blacks could vote, sit anywhere on buses, get hired on jobs, live in something beside shacks, go to school beyond the fourth grade, walk down the street without having to step off the curb for a white person, were called "mister" rather than "boy," used the same public washrooms as whites, and on and on. Most important, lynchings, in some years a daily occurrence in the South, were unheard of elsewhere. Between 1910 and 1920, especially in response to offers of jobs during World War I, more than 300,000 blacks moved north, mostly to Chicago, New York City, and Detroit, but also to almost every Northern industrial city. In the twenties the number grew to an estimated 1.3 million. A smaller number scattered across the West, with 250,000 migrating to the West Coast in the 1940s. The National Urban League, which today has branches in major cities, was founded as the National League on Urban Conditions among Negroes in New York City in 1910 by the white liberal Ruth Standish Baldwin, widow of the owner of the Long Island Railroad, and a black, George Edmund Haynes, who had been secretary for the International Committee of the Young Men's Christian Association, to help Southern immigrants find jobs and housing and adapt to urban life.

Life in the North was clearly better for blacks, though much of the dream turned out to be a sham. Blacks lived huddled in ghettos and paid high rents for sometimes terrible tenements. The jobs for which they were hired were low level, manual labor. Women were almost completely confined to the same jobs many of them had done in the South, housecleaning. Blacks were excluded from most public accommodations. Probably one of the most notorious such exclusions was the one at Harlem's famous Cotton Club in the twenties, when the great masters of black music on the bandstand, entertaining the audience, were the only blacks allowed into the club—and they had to use the back door. But the Cotton Club was only one of many clubs, restaurants, and bars that closed their doors to black customers while the black help used the back door. Blacks also found that in the North they were harassed and beaten by police. And the schools that black children attended were "separate and unequal."

Nevertheless those blacks who came north in ever larger numbers—especially the millions who responded to promises of jobs during two world wars—chose not to return home. Whatever went on in those cities—housing segregation, job discrimination, exclusion from public accommodations, segregated schools, police brutality—life was safer and more comfortable in the North. There were no lynchings, far less discrimination, and, though they may have been inferior to white schools, real schools nonetheless. Occasionally blacks would confront a burned-out home or a burning cross when they tried to move into a white neighborhood, but in most Northern cities the boundaries of the black ghettos crept outward. As blacks moved in, the process often involved whites leaving neighborhoods in response to what was called block busting, realtors' practice of driving whites out with threats of lower property values in order to resell their properties to blacks at inflated prices.

While blacks in the North lived their lives in fear of humiliation, just as Southern blacks did, it was a matter of degree. The South was much worse. And while some blacks in the South prospered—doctors, lawyers, schoolteachers, shop owners—far more prospered in the North. Every large Northern city developed a tiny black upper class and a larger black middle class. Some got rich in the numbers racket (the then illegal lottery) and other criminal activities, though blacks were rarely included in the more lucrative criminality in the cities. But most earned respectable livings as railroad workers, packinghouse workers, steelworkers, and in many other jobs that, though often menial, paid wages unheard of in the fields of the South.

A few blacks managed to start small businesses, some of which, especially a few insurance companies, went on to make their owners rich. By the 1940s most large Northern ghettos had thriving business and cultural communities, partly owned by whites but also owned by blacks. A few of the young managed to get to state colleges which were open to them by law or to the few white private colleges that welcomed them or to those black colleges that survived Reconstruction in the South. Some in the next generation managed to send their children to college, and some became doctors, dentists, and lawyers who, though most were barred from serving the larger community, nevertheless grew wealthy serving their own communities.

Perhaps as important as the minimal physical comforts, safety, education, and prosperity blacks gained in the North was the fact they could vote. In most cities they were not strong or populous enough to elect their own representatives. From 1903, when the last Reconstruction black congressman was defeated, until 1928 there were no blacks in Congress. Then, in 1928, Chicago blacks, living massively cramped in one district and thrilled to have the vote, organized to elect William Dawson a congressman. Dawson held the field to himself until 1944 when Harlem elected Adam Clayton Powell, one of the most ardent black spokesmen the race has had.

In most elections after 1928, Chicago blacks were able to elect a congressman to represent them, and later city councilmen, though their representatives were mostly corrupt and venal. But until the

Voting Rights Act of 1965 blacks had only a few representatives in Congress (mostly elected from large Northern urban ghettos with a concentrated black vote) and no elected municipal or state officials. Nevertheless the fact of the vote itself was enough to give blacks hope for the future. Stokely Carmichael and Charles V. Hamilton wrote in 1967 in *Black Power: The Politics of Liberation in America*, "The *act* of registering to vote . . . gives one a sense of being. The black man who goes to register is saying to the white man, 'No.' He is saying, 'You have said that I cannot vote. You have said this is my place. This is where I should remain. You have contained me and I am saying, "No" to your containment. I am stepping out of bounds.' . . . This is what [the act of registering to vote] does. The black person begins to live."

But I am getting ahead of my story. The first twenty or so years of the migration north saw very little of that affluence that developed between the wars. In those years blacks lived in poverty and strong intolerance but nevertheless in greater peace than they had enjoyed in the South. In 1915 that peace was shattered when the Ku Klux Klan reorganized. This time it followed blacks out of the South to establish groups in many major Northern cities. Violence broke out against blacks, especially as white workers began to see them as a threat to their jobs. In East St. Louis, Illinois, a bloody riot in 1917 took forty black lives.

In World War I thousands of black men had fought for what they believed was freedom and democracy. President Woodrow Wilson had promised that, "with thousands of your sons in the camps and in France, out of this conflict you must expect nothing less than the enjoyment of full citizenship rights—the same as are enjoyed by any other citizens." Hopes rose. Instead the president sat silent as black soldiers recently returned from the war, still in uniform, were hung from trees. Formerly integrated federal agencies were resegregated by Wilson, the apostle of peace and brotherhood in the larger world.

Before the war ended, in fact, Wilson sent Dr. Robert Russa Moton, successor to Booker T. Washington, to France to warn black soldiers against great expectations when they returned. In Europe the army issued what became a notorious order forbidding black soldiers to fraternize with white women, after it became clear that such matches were welcomed by European women. This was scarcely a lesson the army wanted its black soldiers to learn.

The war ended. In 1919, as the war economy was collapsing and whites as well as blacks were losing their jobs, the Klan and other white-supremacy groups began to make themselves heard. Black soldiers were leaving the army disappointed and angry. Riots broke out in twenty-six cities over a six-month period. The flame was ignited in Longview, Texas, where whites became enraged when blacks sent a telegram to the *Chicago Defender*, the most popular black newspaper in the country, describing a lynching in the town. Despite the fact that whites engaged frequently and openly in lynching blacks, apparently they resented it when news of the lynchings became public property— especially black property, black Northern property. So they burned down half the black section of town. But things had changed since the end of the war: blacks fought back.

The worst of the riots occurred in Chicago, home to the largest black population in the North. On a hot day in late July 1919, after several riots had already occurred around the country and had been widely publicized in the black press, the story circulated that a black teenager had swum over the color line at a South Side beach. Allegedly he was stoned by whites; blacks then fought, and the boy was drowned. Blacks were enraged, especially young veterans. They attacked whites. Whites then went to war against blacks, for thirteen days raging through the streets of the black community, throwing stones, beating people, shooting at random. Houses and businesses were bombed and burned. People were snatched from trolleys and buses and beaten. Blacks took revenge, burning and looting. The police were either inept or uninterested in stopping the terror against blacks. According to a 1922 study by the Chicago Commission on Race Relations, more than a thousand families, mostly black, were made homeless by the riot, and as many as thirty-eight people were killed with hundreds injured. Riots in other cities followed.

In this atmosphere of racial hatred and mayhem in Northern cities, two new links were forged in that historic chain of black aspiration. One was a new religious movement that offered a new racial identity; the other was a new back-to-Africa movement.

The religious movement, another forerunner of the Nation of Islam, was the Moorish Science Temple, a handmade amalgam of

Christianity, Islam, and strains of other Eastern religions, with temples in cities around the country. It was led by Noble Drew Ali, who called himself and was called the Prophet.

The new back-to-Africa movement featured what sometimes appeared to be a fairly loony Marcus Garvey successfully promoting the largest Black Nationalist movement in the world. Urging blacks to migrate to Africa, Garvey over time became an object of love and admiration, mockery and vilification, and a source of inspiration for blacks, among them Elijah Muhammad and Louis Farrakhan.

7.

If Marcus Garvey is known to whites at all, it may be only in the image seen in an oft-printed photo that shows Garvey just as he was described by W. E. B. Du Bois in 1923 in the *Century*: "a little, fat black man, ugly, but with intelligent eyes and a big head, . . . seated on a plank platform beside a 'throne,' dressed in a military uniform of the gayest mid-Victorian type, heavy with gold lace, epaulets, plume, and sword." Du Bois might have added that Garvey had bulbous cheeks and often wore a huge feathered cocked hat or sometimes, instead of a military uniform, a cap and gown of purple, green, and gold to create the appearance of a scholar.

In his intense dislike and resentment of Garvey, like most of the black intelligentsia, Du Bois would not have mentioned that his military costume, though certainly silly, was not at all unique to him. His various costumes were not much more elaborate than the costumes worn as early as 1860—and they are still worn—as part of the pomp and circumstance of the ceremonial events of many American fraternal organizations such as the Elks, the various Masonic orders, the Knights of Pythias, and so on. Like the fraternal organizations too, Garvey honored his followers with royal titles—dukes, princes—and organized and led large parades with many different costumes representing the special groups of his organization, such as the Black Cross Nurses, the Universal African Motor Corps, the Black Eagle Flying Corps, and the African League—not the sort of thing a highly serious and scholarly intellectual like Du Bois would appreciate. It was all truly pretty silly, but the common folk had long ago shown that they loved big costumed parades. Marcus Garvey understood that. Besides, he loved all that stuff himself. And he created an organization that provided it, an organization that, only three years after it was founded, claimed two million members in thirty branches. No doubt the claim was exaggerated, along with so many of Garvey's claims, but he does seem to have won a great many followers.

While this garish vision of Garvey is shared by many blacks as well as whites, many other blacks also know that behind Garvey's wildly egotistical posturing and exaggeration was a fiercely dedicated and complex man who was for many years acknowledged as the most famous "race" leader in the world. Garvey was, by all the evidence, viewed as such a danger to the status quo that he was ultimately jailed on flimsy charges of mail fraud cooked up by the Justice Department, and was deported immediately upon his release from jail.

By the time he was indicted in 1923, there was so much financial chaos in the Garvey organization that the indictment was plausibly legitimate. Garvey himself accused most of his lieutenants of fraud, and the entire black press excoriated him for what were widely viewed as fraudulent practices in the sale and use of millions of five-dollar shares in the Black Star Line, a shipping enterprise whose profits Garvey hoped would serve to achieve financial independence for many blacks at the same time it provided the transport for American blacks to Africa. But the company's financial records were in such incredible disarray that the Justice Department could find no substantial evidence. Instead of dropping the case, Justice prosecuted Garvey and three of his officers on what the jury and later the Supreme Court accepted as evidence, but what clearly seems to have had no substance. Garvey was the only one convicted. He was sentenced to five years in a federal penitentiary.

Jail didn't stop Garvey, though it did slow him. His wife, Amy Jacques Garvey, and his lieutenants worked hard to keep his organization alive. While there was certainly decline because Garvey's masterful personality had been the linchpin of the organization, the government had not succeeded in shutting him down. He received sympathy even from his worst enemies for the injustice done him. But the government had still another card to play.

President Calvin Coolidge commuted Garvey's sentence after two years and ordered his release from jail. Coolidge's reasons remain a mystery. But Garvey was immediately taken from the jail in Atlanta to a train going to New Orleans harbor, with no chance to return to his home and office in New York to get his affairs in order and make his farewells. As the Harlem *Amsterdam News*, one of the many black newspapers that had earlier condemned Garvey, reported, "Whatever his faults or virtues, governments certainly seem afraid of him. The officers of the ship that carried Napoleon to St. Helena could not have been more careful with him than the U.S. authorities are with Garvey. This one black man has succeeded in alarming the most powerful governments in the world."

Did Coolidge commute Garvey's sentence and order his immediate release just to get Garvey out of the country sooner? As for Garvey, he is quoted by Len S. Nembhard, in his *Trials and Triumphs of Marcus Garvey*, as telling the crowds that had come to the ship to see him off, "Cheer up, for the good work is just getting under way. Be firm and steadfast in holding to the principles of the organization. The greatest work is yet to be done. I shall with God's help do it." Unfortunately that optimistic farewell in December 1927 marked the end of Garvey's reign, though he made many efforts to keep it alive. Without the energy, enthusiasm, and money of Northern American blacks, Garvey's mission to create a racially pure state in Africa and to free Africans from their colonial rulers was doomed.

One might say that even if Garvey had not been the naive, overzealous, foolish man he was, and even though he had as many as a million followers who were contributing money and enthusiasm to his campaign, his mission would have been doomed because racism made victims of even those blacks whose mission it was to leave the United States. Garvey thought emigration was the answer, but in order to achieve his ends he had to rely on white businessmen, politicians, sailors, and their black lackeys, including the so-called free black government of Liberia, which Garvey dreamed of as the new black homeland for his followers. All these people he needed used him unmercifully, robbing him, cheating him, and deceiving him. They held the power, the knowledge, and the money; all Garvey had was his own zealotry and his overweening ambition, a few fanciful but not necessarily foolish schemes, and the ability to inspire perhaps a million people. One would have thought such characteristics would lead to a stunningly successful career, sort of like a Carnegie, a Ford, a Billy Sunday, or a Pat Robertson, or even, on a far smaller scale, a Louis Farrakhan. But Garvey was a little ugly black man from the West Indies who in the 1920s was unable to deal with the white commercial and political world or the sophisticated American black world.

The tributes paid Garvey today are at least in part in recognition of his suffering at the hands of those with more power and skill than he had, especially the whites he tried to do business with. In 1923, when it became clear that Garvey's future was doomed, his fierce opponent, W. E. B. Du Bois wrote in the *Century*, "He is a world figure in minute microcosm. On a larger field, with fairer opportunity, he might have been great, certainly notorious. He is today a little puppet, serio-comic, funny, yet swept with a great veil of tragedy; meaning in himself little more than a passing agitation, moving darkly and uncertainly from a little island of the sea to the panting, half-submerged million of the first world state. And yet he means something to the world. He is [a] type of a mighty coming thing. He voices a vague, formless, but growing, integrating, human mind which some day will arrest the world."

"One God! One Aim! One Destiny!" was the motto of Marcus Mosiah Garvey's Universal Negro Improvement Association (UNIA) and African Communities League, which he founded in 1914 in his native Jamaica. Garvey was born in 1887, the eleventh child of Marcus, a stone mason, and Sarah Garvey. Unable to gain much education, he nevertheless read and wrote well enough to get work in a print shop when he was still in his teens. A curious young person can often find much of interest to read in a small, independent print shop; he or she may find what some might consider inflammatory literature demanding justice for the oppressed. Garvey was inspired by some of the literature that passed through his print shop, and he went on to participate in a variety of protest activities. Wanting to see the world, especially to observe how blacks were treated elsewhere, he spent several years traveling throughout Central and South America and in 1912 went to London. There, again finding racial segregation and hostility, he published several little newspapers protesting the treatment of West Indians. Garvey met resistance from the authorities wherever he went, including from his own people in Jamaica, who had a cozy arrangement with the British whites who held power. Garvey's feelings about this arrangement of whites, "coloreds," and blacks in Jamaica was just one of the sources of wrath he was to bring down on himself from the formidable group of American black civil rights leaders, including editors and publishers, who finally helped to bring about his imprisonment. It was this group who first questioned his financial dealings and who finally asked the U.S. government to take action against him.

Light-skinned blacks in the United States have—since white masters began bestowing mixed children upon their female slaves—generally enjoyed higher status within both the black and white communities, reflecting the self-hatred of color that was engendered by whites. Yet the bottom line has always been that even with only a few drops of black blood, one is black. Some light-skinned blacks enjoy special favors from whites, but in the end they are discriminated against just like all other blacks. Light skin has often brought better jobs, more money, and fancier houses and cars, but that money has rarely bought homes in well-to-do white communities or a real share of white power. As the late Arnold M. Rose wrote in 1948, in *The Negro in America*, "The Negro leader ... can attain some degree of distinction, but always as a representative of 'his people,' not as an ordinary American. ... The Negro genius is imprisoned in the Negro problem." So while some light-skinned blacks have shunned socializing with their darker brothers and sisters, when the chips are down they are all blacks, and everybody knows it. Garvey didn't. He was a newcomer with no knowledge of American mores. Confronting a large black population as he had in his homeland, he figured the relations among American blacks were just like those in Jamaica.

At home Garvey had always faced discrimination not only from whites but from those light-skinned blacks who shared power with the few British whites who remained there. Du Bois, writing in the *Century*, described the situation well: "This is the West Indian solution of the negro problem. The mulattos are virtually regarded and treated as whites, with the assumption that they will, by continued white intermarriage, bleach out their color as soon as possible. ... Thus the privileged and exploiting group in the West Indies is composed of whites and mulattos, while the poorly paid and ignorant proletariat are the blacks, forming a peasantry vastly in the majority, but socially, politically, and economically helpless and nearly voiceless."

Garvey deeply, angrily resented and hated those "mulattos" who denied the racial heritage they shared with him and, in so doing, denied him power and privilege. He brought his hatred with him to the United States.

With no knowledge of how the color lines differed and how his hatred might be received in America, Garvey conducted a vicious and ugly campaign against light-skinned blacks, calling them traitors, "excuses to get out of the Negro Race," "time-serving, boot-licking agencies of subserviency to the whites." He shouted to his audiences, "I believe in racial purity, and in maintaining the standard of racial purity. . . . It is only the so-called 'colored' man who talks of social equality. . . . We are not seeking social equality. We want the right to have a country of our own, and there foster and re-establish a culture and civilization, exclusively ours." Unfortunately for Garvey, the ranks of black leaders were filled with light-skinned blacks.

Gradually, as black newspapers and magazines reacted to Garvey's slanders, he began to realize that he was making a mistake, but his prejudice was so ingrained that it was hard to shed. Typically he was at one point denouncing the light-skinned Booker T. Washington and Frederick Douglass as "bastards," and at the next naming his boarding-house and his first steamship after the two men.

Garvey's hatred of light-skinned blacks was only one product of a mind clearly deeply disturbed by racism that got him into trouble in the United States. Perhaps an even greater problem was his implausible alliance with the Ku Klux Klan, which resulted from his rejection of political or social reform for blacks in a white-dominated society. "Political, social, and industrial America will never become so converted as to be willing to share up equitably between black and white," he is quoted as saying in *Philosophy and Opinions of Marcus Garvey*. Believing there was no point to it, Garvey shunned efforts to change the relationships between blacks and whites. All he wanted from whites was that they not interfere with blacks' efforts to build a homeland for themselves in Africa.

This philosophy naturally endeared Garvey to the Klan and other white-supremacy groups, which offered him their support. Why Garvey did not understand how civil rights leaders and many ordinary blacks would react to his friendship with the Klan, his invitations to its representatives to speak at his Liberty Hall in New York, and his meeting in Atlanta with the Imperial Wizard of the Klan, is one of the peculiar mysteries that surround Garvey. Du Bois wrote in *Crisis*, "Marcus Garvey is, without doubt, the most dangerous enemy of the Negro race in America and the world. He is either a lunatic or a traitor."

According to his wife, Garvey hoped the Klan would help pay for the move back to Africa. He didn't approve of the Klan's violence against blacks, she said; he just didn't expect anything else from whites and hoped to be able to use them.

Garvey was certainly not a traitor. But one could conclude that he was indeed a lunatic if one looks closely at his career. On the other hand, one might see his actions in quite another way: one might call them pure opportunism. While his bitter views of light-skinned blacks and all whites were reviled by some, especially the NAACP and most of the black press, the huge membership and followers of his organization did not object. They were, like their leader, dark-skinned, uneducated, poor, the most rejected. They appreciated Garvey's raving about racial purity. In fact they thought Garvey was all he claimed for himself. They applauded when he was quoted in the *New York Times* as saying, "All true Negroes are against social equality, believing that all races should develop on their own social lines." They applauded when Major Earnest Sevier Cox, author of *White America*, a racist tract, and John Powell, the organizer of the Anglo-Saxon Clubs of America, spoke at Garvey's Liberty Hall. At least one of his followers believed so strongly in his views that she wrote to the mayor of New Orleans the following, which was reprinted March 31, 1923, in the anti-Garvey *Chicago Defender*, then the largest black paper in the country: "We like your 'Jim Crow' laws, in that they defend the purity of races and any person married to any but a Negro cannot become a member of our organization. . . . We are not ashamed of the Race to which we belong and we feel sure that God made black skin and kinky hair because He desired to express Himself in that type."

Elijah Muhammad, and Louis Farrakhan after him, venerated Garvey for many of his ideas. Although Elijah would not have said he favored Jim Crow laws, Farrakhan later even went that far.

When Garvey returned to Jamaica from a couple years in London in 1914, filled with anger over the discrimination and persecution of blacks he had witnessed wherever he went, he had dreams of a great freedom movement he would lead. He wrote in *Current History* in 1923 of finding the same situation wherever he'd gone, "the same stumbling block—'You are black.' I read of the conditions in America. I read *Up from Slavery*, by Booker T. Washington, and then my doom—if I may so call it—of being a race leader dawned upon me in London after I had traveled through almost half of Europe. . . . The Universal Negro Improvement Association and African Communities [Imperial] League was founded and organized five days after my arrival [on July 15, 1914, in Jamaica], with the program of uniting all the negro peoples of the world into one great body to establish a country and Government absolutely their own."

Unfortunately Jamaican blacks didn't respond enthusiastically to his call. As he wrote in *Current History*, "Nobody wanted to be a negro."

In 1916 Garvey followed the large numbers of West Indians who migrated to the United States in response to often exaggerated job offers in the defense industry. In New York he found himself immersed in intense ferment among blacks angry about their living conditions. The end of World War I intensified the problem as it brought massive unemployment and discrimination. It took a while for Garvey's speeches, first on street corners, later in halls, and then in his own Liberty Hall, to grab people's attention, but soon enough he was electrifying his audiences, and by 1918 he was publishing a weekly newspaper, the *Negro World*, that claimed by 1920 a guaranteed circulation of 50,000, a huge number for a black paper in that time (it was said there were 200,000 a couple of years later). It was sold all over the world, though in time its fierce antiwhite, anticolonial tone led to its being banned by the white regimes in most of Africa.

In early 1920, when Garvey issued in the *Negro World* his call for a first international convention of the UNIA, to be held in New York in August that year, just four years after he'd come to the United States, the response was overwhelming. The day after the convention opened on August 1, 1920, the *New York Times* described the huge parade that wound through Harlem and ended with a rally at Madison Square Garden of an estimated 25,000 people, the largest crowd ever seen in that hall. Princes and tribal leaders from twenty-five African countries attended. The convention adopted a Declaration of the Rights of the Negro Peoples of the World and demanded that the word Negro be spelled with a capital N for the first time. (On March 7, 1930, a decade later, the *New York Times* began using the capital N "in recognition of racial self-respect for those who have been for generations in 'the lower case.'")

The convention also named Garvey the provisional president of the African Republic, to indicate a government-in-exile. In creating a Negro homeland in Africa and freeing the rest of Africa from colonialism, Garvey was to have the help of a supreme potentate, a supreme deputy potentate, and several other similarly designated officers, each of whom was to be paid $12,000 a year, a princely sum in 1920—one of the various obligations assumed by Garvey and his followers that would eventually land him in jail.

The year before, Garvey had launched the Black Star Line of Delaware (a state known to businessmen for its less stringent requirements for incorporation) with offers to his followers all over the country and in the West Indies to turn five-dollar shares in the line into riches. He bought three practically useless, outrageously overpriced ships from unscrupulous shipowners and then spent massive sums allegedly maintaining them. In fact he was robbed by the ship's captains or others in control. One ship ended in dry dock in Cuba; a second sunk in the Hudson River in a winter storm after having been abandoned; the third, after costing the Black Star Line nearly $200,000, including repairs, in just two years, was sold at public auction for $1,625 to pay off a judgment against the line.

Despite these failures, buoyed by the convention, Garvey tried to rejuvenate the shipping company later in 1920, this time with the hope of developing trade with Africa; he tried to buy a newer, bigger ship. This time he incorporated in New Jersey in much the same way he had in Delaware. He told an enthusiastic audience on March 5, 1921, in Liberty Hall, "Today we control three-quarters of a million dollars, not three-quarters of a million on mere paper, but in property value— money that can be realized in twenty-four hours if the stockholders desire that their money be refunded to them." It seems that Garvey actually did have, if not three-quarters of a million dollars, at least enough to make a substantial deposit on a new ship. But he was not to get it because of outrageous chicanery on the part of white shipowners and traitorous Black Star officers, plus the interference of the Federal Bureau of Investigation which warned the U.S. Shipping Board, the final negotiator of all such transactions, that the UNIA had Communist ties.

While Congress fiddled with the return of the deposit money, $22,500, to stockholders and Garvey's creditors, Garvey was arrested in 1922 on charges of mail fraud, convicted, and later deported. His organization in the United States struggled to survive without him. Back in Jamaica in 1927, he was restless. After eleven years in the United States, he needed a wider canvas than little Jamaica offered. He and his wife moved to London in 1928. He scheduled a public meeting in Albert Hall, which held ten thousand. Only one London newspaper took note of the event, reporting that "each member of the audience had the choice of 50 seats."

Garvey scarcely flinched. A few months later he attracted a slightly larger audience in Paris, then went to Geneva to present a petition to the League of Nations suggesting that the mandates of former German colonies in Africa, taken away as part of the Treaty of Versailles, be given to blacks as a free state. The fact that the League ignored him did not deter Garvey. He returned to London to try again, this time more successfully.

Over the next few years Garvey's fortunes rose and fell. He spent the 1930s trying to revive his following, but those years were bleaker than usual for blacks, and Garvey could find no financial support for his efforts. He died in June 1940, only fifty-three years old. He had never set foot in his beloved Africa, and in the end his death was scarcely noted. But he was not forgotten. Only a few years later, in 1947, in his seminal history of American blacks, *From Slavery to Freedom*, John Hope Franklin wrote of Garveyism: "Its significance lies in the fact that it was the first and only real mass movement among Negroes in the history of the United States and that it indicates the extent to which Negroes entertained doubts concerning the hope for first-class citizenship in the only fatherland of which they knew."

Garvey's ideas were quoted widely throughout Africa as blacks fought for their independence. In his 1955 *Black Moses: The Story of Marcus Garvey and the Universal Negro Improvement Association*, E. David Cronon quotes from a 1948 Nigerian newspaper a poem that venerates Garvey:

"For thy redemption brave Garvey fell,
But yet in the gang of immortals,

Thy sons shall fight unseen by mortals,
And ere long regain thy pride, oh Nigeria."

Some of Garvey's ideas are deeply embedded in the Nation of Islam. Whenever there is talk of black nationalism in the United States, Africa, or elsewhere, Garvey's name is prominent. His opportunism—or what could be viewed as lunacy—and his financial disasters are forgotten, just as Elijah Muhammad's similar but more humble problems are forgotten (or denied) by his followers. Elijah's disciples, with justification, have proudly pointed out the similarity between him and Garvey.

8.

Religion, mainly Christianity, has often played a large part in black activist movements. It was no surprise that the most successful movement to overturn racial segregation in the United States was led by a Christian minister, Dr. Martin Luther King, Jr., and that the church was the focal point of that movement. Almost from the beginning of slavery, blacks began adapting the Christianity of their white masters to their own needs. Their own earlier African religious ceremonies, mostly tied to nature and what were considered by whites pagan spirits, were forbidden. Gradually, especially with the addition of their own music, Christianity began to provide relief from slave life, often the only sanctioned one.

Some, like W. E. B. Du Bois, have charged that the system of belief adapted by the slaves and retained far beyond slavery not only retarded rebellious action but in fact inhibited the social and intellectual growth of the people under slavery—as if the system of slavery itself was not responsible. Perhaps no one expressed this sentiment better than Du Bois when he wrote in *The Souls of Black Folk*: "Nothing suited his [the slave's] condition then better than the doctrines of passive submission embodied in the newly learned Christianity. The long system of repression and degradation of the Negro tended to emphasize the elements in his character which made him a valuable chattel: courtesy became humility, moral strength degenerated into submission, and the exquisite native appreciation of the beautiful became an infinite capacity for dumb suffering. The Negro, losing the joy of the world, eagerly seized upon the offered conceptions of the next; the avenging Spirit of the Lord enjoining patience in this world, under sorrow and tribulation until the Great Day when He should lead His dark children home—this became his comforting dream."

One is compelled to wonder about a Northern, highly educated freed black asking why slaves could not easily see through the defects of the only freely given pleasurable hours of their lives, with all the implications of those moments. But Du Bois went on to say that this spirit changed with the emergence of freed blacks and the development of the abolition movement. While Christianity retained its hold among many freed blacks, their ideas were expressed in a new song:

"O Freedom, O Freedom, O Freedom over me!
Before I'll be a slave
I'll be buried in my grave
And go home to my Lord
And be free."

Although Du Bois wrote about "O Freedom" in 1900, implying that it was an example of a new religious spirit that began even before Emancipation, the song had no known circulation until after the Civil War. The first published mention of it appears in a description of a black church-school in Florida in 1885, in a Boston Methodist periodical, *Zion's Herald*. But even if the song came later than Du Bois imagined, which the evidence seems to indicate (the tune in part strongly resembled "The Battle Cry of Freedom," written as a Civil War song in 1861), it certainly was symbolic of a new attitude toward religion. It was Christianity with a bold face, and if it emerged only in the 1880s, it was still a boon to blacks finding their way after slavery. But the old theme—

"Children, we all shall be free
When the Lord shall appear"

—clung strongly. Even today many black preachers haven't let go of the powerful themes of submissiveness that permeated the early Christian churches, white and black. But that theme of waiting for redemption that suffused the early Christian religion, and that survives in the fundamentalist religious groups, has over the years been strongly tempered by life in the here and now among most other Christians, and black preachers wisely combine waiting for redemption with "O Freedom." Some go much further, emphasizing freedom themes, in the image of Dr. King, serving as centers of support for their community, involved in all kinds of local problems—housing, drugs, and so on. The Inner City Church in Knoxville, Tennessee, as just one example, has a prison ministry, a radio station, a day-care center, and a community development bank. This was one of twenty-six black Southern churches fire-bombed from January 1995 through April 1996.

After slavery ended, Northern white Christian missionaries, usually abolitionists, went among the former slaves proselytizing for their own denominations, often building churches, schools, and colleges to the chagrin of Southerners who, slavery or not, did not want blacks educated. In time there arose a group of homegrown black ministers, some trained in given denominations, most self-taught. Within just a few years there were throughout the South and then later in the North a host of small and larger churches of every possible Christian denomination, many of them with no affiliation to any mainstream denomination. Many were offshoots of mainstream white churches that did not permit blacks past their front doors; others were independent churches with a Christian service adapted by individual ministers. By the 1890 census, just twenty-seven years after Emancipation, there were 24,000 black churches in the country, with an estimated enrollment of more than 2.5 million. Du Bois estimated at the turn of the century that there was, in the country, one church for every six black families. They served as a source of strength and unity for people whose families had been destroyed by slavery. By that time they were almost all either Baptist or Methodist.

It is therefore no surprise that black political reformers would include in their rhetoric some religious content. Whether Marcus Garvey opportunistically launched his own African Orthodox Church in which God, the Madonna, and Christ were all black because he believed that such nationalistic religious symbols would bring more people into the UNIA, or whether he really believed in his black Christianity as a natural extension of his nationalist themes, is not easy to conclude. It is not difficult, however, to imagine his African church as a reaction to his early Anglican religious background, dominated by the "perfidious" whites and coloreds of his homeland. But Garvey was not the first black reformer to transform Jesus into a black man. In his

Black Moses, E. David Cronon says, "This rejection of an alien deity embodying Caucasian features was not original with Garvey and was in fact a logical part of any intensely race-conscious movement of this nature." Garvey's sincerity seems quite real in the following verse from his *The Tragedy of White Injustice:*

"White men the Saviour did crucify,

For eyes not blue, but blood of Negro tie."

As Garvey was not the first black leader who professed a black Christianity, so Wallace D. Fard, the founder of the Nation of Islam and mentor to Elijah Muhammad, was not the first to offer his fellow blacks an alternative to Christianity in Eastern religion. In fact, while Fard was greatly inspired by Garvey's nationalism, he owed a greater debt to Noble Drew Ali, the Prophet, "the reincarnation of Muhammad," the first to introduce Islam to American blacks, who also proposed a new racial identity, "Asiatic," and a new homeland in Morocco, which he believed was the homeland of the "Moors."

Born Timothy Drew in North Carolina the year after the Civil War ended, Drew later went north and developed the idea that he could lead his fellow blacks out of what he saw as the trap that had been laid for them by white Christianity. When he was about forty-seven years old, in 1913, now Noble Drew Ali, he organized what he called a Moorish Science Temple in Newark, New Jersey. Exactly what the uneducated Ali knew about the Moors that convinced him that his people—those who could eventually emigrate to Morocco—should call themselves Moors, is lost to history. Perhaps he had heard about or even seen on a local stage a production of *Othello*. That Moor is certainly a grand, if tragic, figure. But the truth is that the Moors were not black, Shakespeare notwithstanding. They were among the many people of North Africa who were Caucasian. They may also have been among those Arab peoples who played a large part in the slave trade, since many of their commercial and military dealings were carried out in combination with the Arabs. The Moors had a few grand centuries of European conquest, mainly ruling Spain in the Middle Ages, leaving behind some glorious architecture, but they were finally driven out with the Jews by the Spanish Christians, in the 1492 Inquisition. They returned to North Africa, but their identity as a separate people seems to have passed into history. Their name has come to refer to any Muslim who speaks Arabic and lives in Northwest Africa, or anyone of Muslim, Jewish, or Turkish descent who lives in North Africa.

While Ali seems to have had little knowledge of history or letters, he did acquire some of the beliefs of Islam, which he mixed liberally with his own in a sixty-page booklet that he distributed to his followers. For instance, while he forbade the use of cosmetics, alcohol, and tobacco, as does Islam, he added his own injunction against meat and eggs. Women, as in Islam, were expected faithfully to obey their husbands. (In 1913 this was not an unusual injunction anywhere in the world, but it was unusual—except among Muslims and Orthodox Jews—that women were to be seated apart at church meetings.) Many of Ali's proscriptions for a holy life were later adopted by the Nation of Islam.

What seems to have attracted Ali to Islam is that it appeared to have no color lines; it did not discriminate against blacks or any other race. Ali seems to have decided that if blacks were actually descended from whatever he thought the Moors were, and if they adopted what he described as a Moorish identity and practiced what he taught as an Islamic religion, they would be free of white tyranny. In fact, like Wallace Fard's, Elijah Muhammad's, and now Louis Farrakhan's Nation of Islam, Ali's Moorish Science was a highly imaginative blend of Islam, Christianity, and the ideas of the leaders and their lieutenants.

Ali gradually built a movement of Moorish Science Temples in most major Northern cities and even a few in the South, convincing fellow blacks that by joining his temple they could escape the intolerable burdens placed upon them as "Negroes" in America. As Ali had learned a little Islamic lore, so he had learned a great many more historical Christian myths, especially the one that had been used against blacks. At the same time he knew the Islamic Koran lacked any such similar hateful myths against blacks. Specifically the Koran did not include the despised biblical "curse of Canaan [or Ham]" that white Christians had used historically to justify slavery and their postslavery treatment of blacks.

According to the third volume of the preeminent *Anchor Bible Dictionary*, "Few biblical stories are as enigmatic as Noah's curse of one of his descendants, popularly but erroneously known as 'the Curse of Ham.'" While the story has always been a strong part of biblical lore, it was a famous seventeenth-century English jurist, Edward Coke, who provided the fertile improvement on the earlier Christian version that gave it such importance in the next two centuries. Coke's version? Simply stated, what God had said in Genesis was that blacks were destined always to be slaves. Coke relied first on a widely accepted, if highly questionable, interpretation of Noah's story that made all the descendants of Noah's son, Ham, black. Then Coke used the story that says that the forebears of Ham's son, Canaan, were to be servants forever. Coke ignored a great deal of scholarly discussion about these stories and became known far and wide for his remarkable insights about these biblical injunctions—just when the English slave trade was burgeoning and when there was arising in England fierce liberal opposition to the trade and to slavery.

The curse in Genesis is actually described thus: "Ham [the son of Noah and father of Canaan] saw the nakedness of his father, . . . And Noah awoke from his wine, and knew what his younger son had done unto him, and he said, Cursed *be* Canaan, a servant of servant shall he be unto his brethren." Earlier in Genesis, God had decreed that Noah's three sons were to disperse across the earth to found the three races of man, and it was thought by some scholars that Ham's children were sent to an area now called North Africa. But biblical geographic references are not ones anyone would ever use to plan a trip. It was also thought by some that the ancient people called Hamites were the first settlers of North Africa; but, strangely enough, both whites and blacks have always been widely represented in the area generally thought of as North Africa. Interestingly, in recent years, some black scholars have argued that the ancient Egyptians were black. Of course, that's a claim that would be hard to prove to whites. How many white scholars could accept that the extraordinary civilizations of the ancient Egyptians were actually the work of blacks? In fact the respected historian Bernard Lewis recently wrote in *The Middle East: A Brief History of the Last 2,000 Years* that as late as 1863 black African slaves served in the Egyptian army.

Judge Coke's interpretation of the "curse of Canaan" spread to the American colonial South, where England sold its African captives, and soon enough became the elegant unofficial justification of slavery in churches and elsewhere across the South. It was that biblical curse that the unlettered Noble Drew Ali, whose mother had probably been a slave, rightly concluded lay at the bottom of the Christian denial of black humanity, and it was to save his people from the effects of that curse that he would give them an "Asiatic" racial and religious identity.

Ali seems to have deserved the term "Prophet." He was not much of a political leader. He did not attract a worldwide following as Garvey did and as Farrakhan has, though it was estimated he had as many as 25,000 followers when he died in 1929. But he had no business enterprises, nor did he publish a newspaper. In fact there seem to have been few written documents emerging from Ali's Moorish Science Temples. He had only these temples (rented or purchased buildings) in which his followers could congregate with designated leaders in the major Northern cities and a few Southern ones. The largest temple, and finally Ali's headquarters, was in Chicago, which contained the largest black population in the North.

Ali wasn't entirely without a sense of pizzazz; he required that all his men wear red fezes to symbolize their Eastern identity, and all his followers had to carry "Nationality and Identification Cards" that identified them as "a Moslem under the Divine Laws of the Holy Koran of Mecca, Love, Truth, Peace, Freedom, and Justice," signed by "NOBLE DREW ALI, THE PROPHET." Just to be on the safe side, he added, in capital letters, "I AM A CITIZEN OF THE UNITED STATES." But he didn't go in for parades or publicity. He was in fact agitated whenever his followers went public on the street, calling attention to their identity cards and noising about their unusual origins. Northern whites weren't much happier with "uppity" blacks than Southerners were, and the police were often called to intervene. Unlike Marcus Garvey, Ali reproached his followers: "We did not come to cause confusion," he told them. "Our work is to uplift the nation." He insisted that while Morocco was their capital, they were also citizens of North America, under the temporary rule of whites. As such they had no choice but to submit to the law until white rule fell.

This apparently simple and genuine Prophet, who believed that the white race would soon be overcome by his "Asiatics," and who honored all the prophets, including Jesus, Muhammad, Buddha, and Confucius, along with the "God of our Father, Allah," and who had been able to attract so many followers, was not able to control his dominions. First there were the melees in the streets as the men in their red fezes taunted whites, including the police, and then came the opportunists who saw a chance to make some money on this movement.

Imagine! Asiatic relics for gullible followers. Trinkets, charms, potions, pictures. The Catholic church provided a fine example. But the Catholic church controlled and supported most of its relic sales, while Noble Drew Ali apparently had no interest in them. A few people grew rich.

These get-rich schemes didn't fit the dreams and plans of the Prophet and some of his lieutenants. In a struggle for power, strongest in Chicago, someone was killed. Although he was not in Chicago at the time of the killing, the police were quick to charge Ali with the murder. But with a shortage of evidence, he was never brought to trial. He died shortly afterward in 1929, under mysterious circumstances. Some said he had died after a brutal beating by the police, others claimed he was killed by his rivals.

Unlike Garveyism, the Moorish Science Temple survived without Ali, though it declined greatly over the years and at some point split in half. The founding of the Nation of Islam in 1930, just one year after Ali died, didn't help. Wallace Fard first, then his successor Elijah, adapted Ali's ideas to create a new religious structure with a new leader who was more appropriate to the thirties but offered some of the satisfactions that Ali had offered. As C. Eric Lincoln said in 1959 in his *Black Muslims in America*, Ali's followers "feel quite at home in this new nationalism, which maintains some aspects of the familiar 'Asiatic' religion without requiring them to love the hated 'Europeans.' In fact they may now look forward to the predicted destruction of their enemies with increased assurance, for Elijah Muhammad, the Messenger—unlike Noble Drew Ali—is not a man to compromise." Nor is Elijah's successor.

Part Two

BEGINNINGS

1.

While for many of us moderns, religion remains ever a source of mystery, other millions of people are sustained in their daily lives by a great transcendent idea deriving from an allegedly holy source, from a personal God. What for many of us are strange and often beautiful myths are for millions true stories around which they plan their lives. Many of those who take their sustenance in this manner never view, as some of us do, the founders of their religions as encompassed in mystery. For these people, Christ really was the son of God and did rise again after he was crucified. Muhammad was truly chosen by Allah to be the Prophet to the world. Moses really did bring the Ten Commandments down from the mountain and lead the Jews into the Promised Land. These are facts. It makes no difference to the faithful that these events cannot be proven empirically or that very little, if anything, is known of these figures. While some church historians and theologians, along with some secular archaeologists, have done massive research to uncover the lives of the founders, for the faithful such information is irrelevant.

But these generalizations do not always apply to the visionaries of modern-day antiestablishment religious movements. The histories of, for instance, Joseph Smith of the Mormons, Mary Baker Eddy of the Christian Scientists and her famous rocking chair, or William Miller of the Seventh Day Adventists are fairly well documented by their own church historians and others. Mark Twain and Willa Cather both wrote about Mrs. Eddy. Yet the American black visionaries of off-center religious groups of this century—Noble Drew Ali of the Moorish Science Temples, and W. D. Fard, founder of the Nation of Islam—are, like the prophets of old, largely wrapped in mystery, and what is not mystery is secrecy. For example, like the celebration on December 25 of Christ's birthday, the Nation's major annual "Saviour's Day," a three-day commemoration of Master W. D. Fard's birthday on February 26, actually marks a birthday for which there is no proof. Nor is there proof of anything else about his life.

The Nation claims that a text written by Fard, called *Supreme Wisdom*, has been preserved in what, from the descriptions, is apparently a small booklet. It sounds suspiciously like it was put together by some members of the Nation long after Fard disappeared, and may or may not contain any of Fard's writings. Available only to members of the Nation, it is not discussed with outsiders. Some members are so secretive that they refuse to reveal whether any of Fard's writings even exist. After searching all the public sources and finding no evidence of any extant Fard writings, I asked a representative of the Nation's publishing company, the Final Call, if they had anything of Fard's in print that was only privately available. The woman told me about *Supreme Wisdom*, which she claimed had been in print since the early thirties but was available only to members. She couldn't tell me anything about the contents; that information was available only to members. Having already been denied access to the Nation, I didn't pursue the matter. Such secrecy among religious groups is not so unusual. Writers must guarantee that what they write will reflect positively on Christian Science and Mrs. Eddy before they can get into the massive Eddy sources.

Some known remnants of what were probably authentic Fard writings exist, but the title *Supreme Wisdom* is not among them. Still, it is possible that some of Fard's writings were preserved and, to lend them more religious authority, were given this divine-sounding title in their printing. The original titles lacked such divine authority. It is important to the success of the leaders of a religious group to be able to provide their members with evidence of the existence of their gods. That evidence appears in God's words.

A former member of the Nation, Farid Muhammad, of East-West University in Chicago, remains close to the Nation as he does also to the more traditional National Islamic Assembly. He has no copy of *Supreme Wisdom*, which leads one to believe that *Supreme Wisdom* may have been printed since the death of Elijah, when Farid left the Nation. He has the impression, he says, that the book resembles a "catechism," though he then says he thinks it consists of a small collection of physical facts such as the size of the earth, which might suggest a similarity to what we know of a document of Fard's called "Teaching for the Lost Found Nation of Islam in a Mathematical Way." When I asked the Final Call Publishing Company representative if she knew of this document, she explained that the Nation "is founded and operates entirely on mathematical ways"—but she had never heard of such a book, nor had she heard of anything else by Fard except *Supreme Wisdom*.

Supreme Wisdom, Farid says, was originally transmitted only orally, and the early followers of Fard were expected to memorize it. Its purpose, Farid believes, was to provide some little bit of "sophisticated" information to the largely illiterate people who were attracted to Fard. The so-called facts in the *Supreme Wisdom*, Farid adds, were culled from such sources as Jehovah's Witnesses and the Masons, two of the sources that Nobel Drew Ali had relied on, and therefore were also sources that Fard, who is suspected of being a former member of Ali's Temple, would have drawn from. There is evidence that some of Fard's writings were indeed transmitted only orally, and that followers were expected to memorize them. There is also evidence that Fard intended to add to the sophistication of his unlettered followers.

In his many close contacts with members of the Nation, Farid has heard a lot of rumors about *Supreme Wisdom*, but it seems that many members may have no clear grasp of it. That he seemed content with an array of assumptions about this book, with no clear idea of what it is, was fairly typical of his general attitudes toward the Nation. He would not join again, but he accepted it and asked few questions, though in his other life he is chairman of behavioral and social sciences at East-West University.

While it is certain that Fard wrote several documents outlining his theories and prescriptions for the good life, there is mixed evidence about whether they were ever printed, were booklets, or books, or perhaps just a few handwritten pages. Or whether they were secret or public documents. The only documented evidence we have is a 1937 research article published in the *American Journal of Sociology*. This was only seven years after Fard was first heard of but three years after he had disappeared, leaving no trace. These documents were treated as Fard's authentic writings and used as major resources for the article on the Nation of Islam in the *AJS* by an apparently experienced sociologist, Erdmann D. Beynon, of the University of Michigan, who published in the same year, when he was forty-five, a book about Hungarian immigrants in the United States. While his age and experience and his position in a prestigious university tend to make us want to trust Beynon's words, some points in the article make us wonder about the sophistication of sociologists at the time.

One of these Fard documents, "The Secret Ritual of the Nation of Islam," is treated typographically in the *AJS* as if it were a book, that is, set off in italic lettering. Then, in the next sentence, the author describes it as an "oral transmission." Well, was it a printed document as he indicated, or was it merely an oral document as he also said? Or had it been transmitted orally for a while and then printed? Can't tell from Beynon. He goes on to say of this "book," "The entire teaching is symbolic and can be understood only by the initiates." Does he mean "members," and if he does, where does that place him in his understanding of the document? Did the Nation, practically in its infancy in 1937, give him special training so that he could understand the obscure symbolism of this text? He gives us no hint.

Another of the Fard sources is also treated strangely: "Teaching for the Lost Found Nation of Islam in the Mathematical Way, consisting of 34 problems," seems actually to have been printed at some point but given only to registered Muslims. (With no real knowledge about them, I am treating all these sources as unpublished.) Once again, Beynon doesn't say how he gained access to this document from which he freely quotes.

From the quotes in the *AJS*, the "Mathematical Way" doesn't sound like it would have later become *Supreme Wisdom*. From the evidence of events described as having occurred over the years, it seems more likely that the original documents were either discarded sometime after 1937 by some members of the Nation who did not want them known, or they simply disappeared in the disorder that seems to have befallen the Nation in the years after Fard's disappearance. This disappearance has never been explained, but if Fard had help leaving the scene, either from his internal enemies or from the authorities, it seems reasonable that his writings would have gone with him.

Several years later, when Elijah Muhammad was firmly in control of the Nation, he apparently decided he should create a document that would follow Fard's prescription for a special religious document for members only—a kind of bible. Result: *Supreme Wisdom*. But who knows? Perhaps Elijah secreted away some documents of Fard's which he later published under a new title for his own idiosyncratic reasons. A researcher *might* find someone in Detroit who was a member of the Nation in Fard's time who could read *Supreme Wisdom* and recall whether it was something he or she could identify as Fard's. But since most of Fard's early followers were illiterate, such a search would be difficult. Memory is never very trustworthy, and loyalty can be so strong that a person who had been told for many years that these were Fard's words would be unlikely to contradict that. The question is moot anyhow, isn't it? Whatever *Supreme Wisdom* is, it contains for the Nation's members the words of their great visionary, called by them Allah, and is unlikely to receive any serious challenge anytime soon.

From other written materials of the Nation it appears that, as in ancient religions, whatever is known about the founder of the Nation of Islam is the lore spun by his disciples, in this case Elijah Muhammad, Fard's allegedly most favored lieutenant. Elijah took over the Nation when Fard mysteriously disappeared in 1934, just four years after he had first appeared on the streets of the Elmwood section of Detroit known as Paradise Valley.

Elijah said he received threats against his life by other members who were suspicious about the strange coincidence of Fard's disappearance and Elijah's ascendance, and he and his followers fled to Chicago, where he and Fard had earlier established Temple No. 2. It was several years before Elijah was able to settle down comfortably with Fard's mantle, but Elijah was soon claiming that "There is no plainer truth that could ever come to both white and Black than what Allah, in the Person of Master Fard Muhammad to Whom all praises are due forever, has delivered to me whom He chose to deliver this Message of Truth." But Fard's "Message of Truth" itself may well have vanished.

The schism in the Nation caused by Fard's disappearance was the second in just the four-year existence of the Nation. Fard was, it seems, a highly controversial character. The first schism occurred over the issue of human sacrifice, which Fard advocated, and which involved rumor, gossip, the police, and what may have been actual and intended grisly killings. A third schism occurred in 1964 when Elijah suspended Malcolm X, who may have been more influential in the Nation at that point than his mentor, though the full consequences of that schism did not emerge until after Elijah's death in 1975, when his heir, Wallace, who had been greatly influenced by Malcolm X, disbanded his father's empire and urged the members to follow him into a more traditional Islamic life. Wallace took with him many of his father's former followers, among them the world-famous heavyweight boxer Muhammad Ali. But Malcolm's bitterest enemy, Louis Farrakhan, was probably the bigger winner. Assuming the leadership of the Nation, he retained the allegiance of those members who remained committed to the traditions first proposed by Fard and carried down and elaborated by Elijah. As a result of complicated financial deals, Farrakhan also gained some of the wealth Elijah had accumulated.

2.

In his 1965 *Autobiography*, Malcolm X describes how he would sit "galvanized, hearing what I then accepted from [Elijah] Muhammad's mouth as being the true history of our religion, the true religion of the black man. Mr. Muhammad told me that one evening he had a revelation that Master W. D. Fard represented the fulfillment of the prophecy.

"'I asked Him,' said Mr. Muhammad, 'Who are you, and what is your real name?' And He said, 'I am The One the world has been looking for to come for the past two thousand years.'

"'I said to Him again,' said Mr. Muhammad, 'What is your *true* name?' And then He said, 'My name is Mahdi. I came to guide you into the right path.'"

There is no reason to believe that Fard, like a number of Muslim leaders over the centuries, did not actually claim to be the messiah, whose coming at the end of world was predicted in the sixth century. In fact, one of his followers in the thirties was quoted as saying, "When the police asked him who he was, he said: 'I am the Supreme Ruler of the Universe.'"

But who and what Wallace Fard—or Wali Fard, W. D. Fard, W. Farrad Muhammad, Mr. Farrad Muhammad, Professor Fard, Mr. F. Muhammad Al, The Prophet, or Allah—actually was has never been known. Elijah said he first identified himself as "a brother from the East." What did he look like? Was he a large aggressive spellbinder like Garvey, or was he an elegant charmer like Farrakhan, or a little nebbish-looking man like Elijah? All we have is Elijah's description to Malcolm X: he was "a small, light brown-skinned man," a description that also fits Elijah. Permit me to fantasize, based on Beynon's *AJS* article and Fard's own words: Fard is about five feet ten, thin, wiry, with long arms and legs; on a long neck sits a face filled with curiosity on one hand and irony on the other. His eyes are very dark, small, and close together. His nose is long and slightly flat, a Negroid nose that could almost pass for white, but his lips are full. His teeth are small and yellow. And he looks like a man you'd like to know, but you'd always be a little cautious with him because he appears to be a man who knows everything.

(So much for my fantasy. Early in 1996, in time for Saviour's Day, allegedly the date of Fard's birth, a photo alleged to be Fard suddenly began appearing in the *Final Call*, the Nation of Islam's newspaper. It is an obviously posed photo of an extraordinarily handsome, sensitive-looking man with thick dark hair and brows, what appears to be olive-colored skin, and "white" features. He might be viewed as a light-skinned black or a white with Mediterranean features, a native of Mecca, as he is said to have claimed at some point. He is shown wearing a suit, white shirt, and tie, holding a book that he is strongly concentrated on. Various sizes of the photo appeared in almost every issue. Is this an authentic photograph unearthed from the 1930s? Despite the fact that all his other papers disappeared? Or is it something else?)

Was Fard, as he claimed, born in Mecca, the son of wealthy parents of the same tribe as the Prophet Muhammad, and educated in England for the diplomatic corps? Or was he educated, as was also claimed, at an undesignated branch of the University of California? Or was he just like Elijah and most of the people whom he attracted to his new religion—the son of a former slave, uneducated in his early life like his friends in Detroit, come North to escape the Jim Crow South and seek his fortune, who may have taught himself to read and then managed to attain an amazing smattering of education, especially under the influence of Noble Drew Ali and his Moorish Science Temple, and no doubt hanging around the public library, and who, last and most important, was endowed with extraordinary charismatic gifts? The *Encyclopedia of American Religions* suggests that Fard had been a member of Ali's Temple. As they were first presented, Fard's ideas certainly reflected Ali's, including Ali's reliance on a variety of popular mystical sources. But within a short time Fard had traveled far beyond Ali.

Fard was clearly charismatic. The *Dictionary of Negro Biography* estimated in 1982 that "Some 8,000 are said to have become members of his first Temple of Islam." Although no date is offered, one assumes the *Dictionary* is referring to the four years during which Fard led the group. But that figure was issued in the mid-thirties by the Muslims and was probably inflated. On the other hand, the figure of five thousand issued by the Detroit police at about the same time most likely underestimated the number, thus placing the Nation's membership in the early thirties somewhere between five and eight thousand, a healthy number given the relatively small population of blacks in Detroit (about 8 percent) in the thirties and given an organization that had strict requirements for membership.

But the *Dictionary* also says, "There is little authentic information about this mystic. . . ." As the years have passed, any authenticity about Fard's background and teaching grows muddier and muddier. There is, however, no question about the authenticity of the Nation's regard for him, of his "sainted" role as the venerated founder of the Nation of Islam.

For reasons not clearly accountable, 1996 saw a renewed interest by the Nation in Fard, though there appears to be no new information (except that photo). For instance, in May of that year, Tynetta Muhammad, Elijah's common-law wife, who is now a major "philosopher" of the Nation, devoted one of her weekly *Call* columns to Fard. She said, "The world is gradually coming into the knowledge of the Divine Work and Teachings of Master W. Fard Muhammad *through the examples of the Divine Leadership of the Honorable Elijah Muhammad and his mighty Helper, the Honorable Minister Louis Farrakhan* [my italics]." She went on to tell her (quite original) story of Fard's divinity, his origins, his teachings, and his choice of Elijah "to continue this Divine Work in progress," and how Farrakhan was "God's choice in the continuance of this work in the general Resurrection of the mentally dead ex-slaves of America."

Why Louis Farrakhan should choose to resurrect Fard at this date may be entirely capricious. More likely the reason can be found in Farrakhan's continuing search for legitimacy. History lends legitimacy, authenticity. The Nation doesn't have a whole lot of history, only something over sixty years, including Fard, who has until recently not been given proper attention as its legitimate founder.

Given the secrecy of the Muslims, and the harshly negative public atmosphere surrounding the Nation for most of its life, it is not surprising that the best-known source of information about Fard dates to 1937. But while it certainly is a rich source (the only one) and has been quoted regularly, this obscure 1937 article in the *American Journal of Sociology* entitled "The Voodoo Cult Among Negro Migrants in Detroit" is not altogether trustworthy, like so many other sources of information about the founders of religions. The author seems to have been naive in his acceptance and blithe reports of some so-called facts. He seems to have lacked the critical judgment we would expect from a sociologist today. For instance, the word *voodoo* in his title derives, he states unapologetically, from the Detroit police. In regular run-ins with the Nation, the police came to call the group the Voodoo Cult because of alleged incidents of human sacrifice among them, Beynon says. He admits he didn't try to trace a connection between the Muslims and the West Indian voodoo cults or their progenitors in Africa, and in fact he says he doesn't know much about those cults. Nevertheless, for the title of his article he used the police label instead of the group's actual name, as if it had more validity.

We have to ask whether the police called the Muslims a voodoo cult because they had actually uncovered ritual human sacrifices—certainly evidence of voodoo practice—among the Muslims or whether they called them a voodoo cult because they were illiterate, uneducated, unemployed Southern blacks who were practicing a religion that was no more familiar to the police than the voodoo cults of the West Indies, about which Americans have always had a certain uninformed morbid fascination. Or were the Detroit police leery of this group because, as Beynon says, the Nation had "severed contact with the social organization of the community in which they live," completely isolating themselves from the surrounding community "as effectively as did the members of agricultural religious communities who migrated to new homes." The police have always been unhappy with groups in their midst who try to cut themselves off from their surveillance and supervision. Such an effort by a group is usually seen by the police as a threat to the stability of the community, or, said another way, a threat to their control.

But Beynon may have been confused. Fard did *teach* in his "Secret Ritual" (which, Beynon says, was never printed and "is symbolic and can only be understood by the initiates") that it was the duty of every Muslim to offer four "Caucasian devils" for sacrifice in order to guarantee his return to his home in Mecca. Fard also claimed that "Allah demands obedience unto death," therefore no Muslim would dare refuse the sacrifice of himself or a loved one. Someone could get pretty confused if the "Secret Ritual" was only transmitted orally and had to be symbolically interpreted. Was Fard really telling his followers to kill one another? Did his followers take him seriously? One might accept just a lot of excited talk as good evidence of the practice of human sacrifice. In fact, Beynon offered no evidence of Muslims killing even one Caucasian. His evidence for one actual sacrifice of a Muslim and the attempted sacrifice of another he received from the police, who reported that a sacrifice was made on an "altar" in 1932 by a man who killed his roommate in order to become, he allegedly told the police, "the Saviour of the world." The second instance was of a man who was arrested, the police said, "as he prepared the ceremonial slaying and cooking of his wife and daughter." This man allegedly told the police the killings would have "cleansed him from all sin."

Beynon says that rumors of sacrifice in the community were so widespread that the police had to intervene, forcing the Nation to resort to secrecy—an attitude it still strongly maintains—and making it impossible to know whether there were further sacrifices. Beynon quotes from a 1932 issue of the *Detroit Times* that describes how two "women welfare workers" were filled with horror when they discovered they were the intended sacrifice victims of a "fanatical" man who, according to the *Times*, was "part of an Asiatic trend among Negro dole recipients of the Elmwood District." The man allegedly told the police that "each of these was a 'no good Christian' and they would have been sacrificed if he knew where he could find them." This turned out to be the same man, Robert Harris, who supposedly sacrificed his roommate on the altar.

Maybe the police reports and the newspaper accounts were accurate. But the historical record warns us that police and newspaper distortions—even total fabrications—about events in the black community (and other poor communities as well) are notorious, even today. The infamous Rodney King case in California in 1991 opened a lot of eyes to this problem. Not so well known are the millions of dollars spent every year in settlements by police departments all over the country that are sued by victims of a police officer who has lied in his report, accusing the victim of violence that supposedly justified police brutality.

But we have to consider that those Muslim "dole recipients" in Detroit were not the most sophisticated people in the city. They just may have believed in Fard's claims for the benefits of human sacrifice and the requirement that "Allah demands obedience unto death."

Well, maybe. Some early Muslims did accept Fard's teachings about human sacrifice, Beynon reports, though they may not have actually committed any. And when one group opposed to sacrifice went off by themselves to organize another temple, they were branded by their fellow Muslims as "Rebels against the Will of Allah." But a voodoo cult the Muslims were not. It is easy to understand how the immense secrecy grew up among them, and how the fierce antiwhite sentiments that Fard used to attract his audiences became a stronger and stronger factor in the Nation.

It was in this new breakaway temple, founded by the antisacrifice Muslims, that Elijah Muhammad, who had been Fard's right-hand man, was elevated to the rank of prophet. Although Beynon does not provide dates for this event, it appears to have been sometime between Fard's disappearance in 1934 and Beynon's appearance on the scene in 1937. According to his stories, the new Detroit temple was soon abandoned by this group when they were forced to flee the city by other members who wanted nothing to do with Elijah.

3.

Some will hesitate over this theory that I cautiously present, but it seems most likely that Fard, like so many other mystics, fit the psychiatric designation of a paranoid schizophrenic with powerful delusions of grandeur. He may have been guided by the "inner voices" that accompany schizophrenia. He was said to say, "My name is W. D. Fard and I came from the Holy City of Mecca. More about myself I will not tell you yet, for the time has not yet come. I am your brother. You have not yet seen me in my royal robes." Some of his followers believed his story that he was born in Mecca, the son of wealthy parents of the tribe of Muhammad, the founder of Islam, and closely related to the kings of Hejaz, a large region of Saudi Arabia. Some also believed, as he told them, that he had been educated in England to prepare for a diplomatic career in the service of Hejaz but had abandoned all that to bring "freedom, justice, and equality" to his "uncle" living in "the wilderness of North America, surrounded and robbed completely by the Cave Man," as Fard wrote in his "Mathematical Way." Perhaps I am misled; perhaps Fard was not a paranoid schizophrenic with delusions of grandeur but only a man with a hugely grandiose sense of himself. To make the distinction may be only a matter of vivid description.

Fard may indeed have come miraculously from Mecca, in true prophet fashion, to appear suddenly in the streets of the poorest blacks in Detroit. He may have been dressed, as he is described by one of Beynon's informants, humbly as a peddler, selling, like Arab and Syrian peddlers of the time, things such as silks that he claimed to have brought from Mecca. He was apparently a strongly sympathetic figure whom people invited into their homes where they fed him and listened to his stories about the people in the East who were their kinsmen. Beynon quotes a couple of women who say that Fard easily won their confidence and captured their imagination. It seems he would eat his host's food and then admonish them not to eat such "poison."

"If you would live just like the people in your home country, you would never be such [kind of people] any more," he would tell his hosts. They were enthralled. "We all wanted him to tell us more about ourselves and about our home country and how we could be free from rheumatism, aches and pains," one of Beynon's informants told him. If they would cast off their American identity and offer their loyalty to Allah, they would get relief from their ailments as he described them— "fever, headaches, chills, grippe, hay fever, regular fever, rheumatism, also pains in all the joints . . . foot ailment and toothaches . . . pulse beat more than eighty-eight times per minute. . . ."

Fard's listeners were indeed suffering from many ailments, especially those that resulted from harsh winters in the North where heating and warm clothing were inadequate. Beynon writes: "The migrants realized that they suffered much more physical pain than they had in their old homes. They connected this suffering with the civilization of the white man to whose cities they had come. Even before they met the prophet, they had begun to blame the Caucasian for their aches and pains."

Soon enough, people began gathering at one another's homes to hear this prophet. Before long the crowds were too large for private dwellings. They pooled their pennies and rented a hall which they called the Temple of Islam, and soon word of Fard's teachings spread. He began with biblical sayings as his source. After all, this is what his listeners knew, though most of them were illiterate. He organized classes in English so they could learn to read "the proofs about themselves" in a variety of books. These included both Hendrik van Loon's *The Story of Mankind*, a highly praised children's illustrated history of the world, first published in 1921 and regularly updated until 1972, and the relatively abstruse scholarly *Conquest of Civilization* by James Breasted, a world-famous Egyptologist who founded the Oriental Institute at the University of Chicago. Fard also urged his followers to get radios so they could listen to the speeches of Judge Rutherford, the leader of Jehovah's Witnesses, and Frank Norris, a fundamentalist Baptist preacher. Malcolm X quotes Elijah as saying that Fard "knew the Bible better than any of the Christian-bred Negroes."

As his audiences grew, Fard grew more daring, more defiant, more prophetic. It was time to begin taking up Noble Drew Ali's attacks on the white man's Bible and then moving beyond Ali to attack the "white devils" themselves. They used what Fard called "trickenology" to "keep [blacks] blind to themselves so that [they] can master them . . . use them for a tool and also a slave"—phraseology that long survived Fard in the Nation.

Blacks owed no allegiance to the United States because they were citizens of "the Holy City of Mecca," Fard said. They were the "lost-found Nation of Islam in the Wilderness of North America," the descendants of the lost tribe of Shebazz, stolen by traders from the Holy City of Mecca 379 years ago. The Caucasians were the colored people who had lost their original color. The original people must regain their religion, Islam, their language, Arabic, and their culture, astronomy and higher mathematics, especially calculus. Fard introduced the Koran to his followers, Beynon says, but only in his own interpretation of the Arabic text.

This new lost-found people must obey the laws of Allah as adapted from the Koran by Fard: "avoiding all meat of 'poison animals,' hogs, ducks, geese, 'possums' and catfish"—a list that would astonish any traditional Muslim. It would also undo Southern blacks, who didn't have the proper inhibitions against such foods programmed into their genes by the great Allah but who nevertheless observed Fard's prohibitions, setting the stage for several generations of Muslims who still read Elijah's prescriptions for eating right and living well. The *Final Call* regularly reprints excerpts from Elijah's *How to Eat to Live*, based on Fard's rules. The prohibitions, of course, include the traditional Islamic ban on alcohol. A ban on smoking came later with Elijah.

Fard also insisted that his followers send their children not to the white schools but to the University of Islam, a K-12 school he created. There the children would learn "higher mathematics," astronomy, and "the general knowledge and ending of the spook civilization." The Detroit Board of Education had some problems with Fard's school and instructed the police to break it up and compel the children to return to the public schools. But the Nation resisted. Protests occurred (called riots by Beynon) in which members of the Nation "tried to storm the police headquarters," Beynon said. Soon enough, he explains, because the police feared "race riots," those who had been arrested were released with suspended sentences. The authorities thereafter ignored the school.

Although there was already a history of race riots across the country, supposedly justifying police fears, the record is clear that the violence in Detroit was initiated by whites. Beynon reports no incidents of any kind of violence among the Muslims as of 1937, except that one alleged sacrifice. But he does report that Fard established the Fruit of Islam, a military-style organization drilled in tactics and the use of guns, intended to defend the Nation against the police or other whites who might attack them. The FOI is still a potent part of the Nation.

Years later Malcolm X said in his *Autobiography* that Elijah told him that "his older children's lack of a formal education reflected their sacrifice to form the backbone for today's Universities of Islam in Detroit and Chicago." The *Final Call* periodically publishes an article raving about the success of the Nation's University of Islam.

4.

The idea that blacks bear illegitimate names, the names of their slave-owner forebears instead of their original family names, may have emerged before Fard, but it was certainly he who gave wide currency to the idea. He did not suggest the African names the slaves would most likely have had, and which many American blacks adopted after the 1960s. Fard had no interest in Africa; it was the Middle East that he looked to. He claimed Saudi Arabia, Mecca, as his own native country and that of all American blacks. This meant his followers were to have Islamic names. Where he acquired the knowledge of these names, like all his disparate pieces of knowledge, is not known, but he seems to have had an unlimited source of Islamic-sounding names.

It wasn't to be automatic, of course. You didn't receive a new Islamic name just because you signed up as a member of the Nation of Islam. You had to earn your new name and pay for it. If you carefully and faithfully followed Fard's teachings, you would find yourself restored to your original self from that false self you had had since being kidnaped from Mecca. When you were transformed, you could write a letter to Fard describing your transformation and asking him to endow you with your original name, which he would divine in his communication with the spirit of Allah. With your letter you had to enclose ten dollars, a high price for poor people to pay in the early thirties, but after all, this was your new identity.

Fard renamed many people, adding to their lives glamour they hadn't dreamed of. Beynon records that Joseph Shepard became Jam Sharieff; Lindsey Garret became Hazziez Allah; ordinary Henry Wells became Anwar Pasha. Sometimes Fard's contact with the spirit ran into bad weather. Mistakes happened, as when he gave three different surnames to three Poole blood brothers, one of whom turned out to be Elijah Muhammad. Was Fard troubled by such a mistake? Well, it must have caused him a few difficult moments. But he had a grand appreciation of the absurd. That wasn't a mistake, Fard said. Allah's spirit had wisely informed him that the three Poole brothers had three separate fathers, a fact of which they had been unaware. Beynon doesn't tell us whether Elijah and his brothers shared Fard's appreciation of the absurd. But consider for a moment this event. Fard, Elijah's mentor, had announced to the world that he and his two brothers were bastards. For Fard could not possibly have meant that in Georgia at the end of the nineteenth century, Elijah's mother, the granddaughter of a former slave, had had three legal husbands with whom she had had those three sons. And Fard never explained the rest of the family—nine more children. Fard's pronouncements contradicted Elijah's stories that he was one of twelve children born to a stubborn, principled, courageous Georgia sharecropper-preacher.

Did Elijah and his brothers get angry at Fard? We have no idea. But some members of the Nation did strongly note the coincidence between the rise of Elijah and the disappearance of Fard. Did Elijah decide not to get mad but to get even? Years later, in 1970, Elijah told Hans Massaquoi, an *Ebony* editor, that on March 19, 1934, Fard "just left, natural, like a friend leaving another friend." But, Elijah said, while Fard was preparing his exit, he finally admitted to Elijah that he was really Allah. Elijah said that Fard pleaded with him not to reveal his secret divinity "till He could teach me, so I could teach the others. Then He put me over the whole thing—the whole nation. He made me the head of the black man in America."

All we have is Beynon's description of that set of events, and it raises questions about Elijah's story to Massaquoi. Beynon says that after three years of Fard's absence, in 1937, the Nation was "tending to become more amorphous. From among the larger groups of Moslems there has sprung recently an even more militant branch than the Nation of Islam itself. This new movement, known as the Temple People, identifies the prophet, Mr. W. D. Fard, with the god Allah. To Mr. Fard alone do they offer prayer and sacrifice. Since Mr. Fard has been deified, the Temple People raise[d] to the rank of prophet the former Minister of Islam, Elijah Mohammad." (Beynon adds in a footnote that the Temple People claimed that Fard had changed Elijah's name from Karriem, the one he had originally assigned him, to Muhammad to indicate his higher status; but the other Nation members continued to call him Karriem.)

Apparently Elijah was already in Chicago in 1937, since Beynon referred to him as "a resident of Chicago." Beynon said, "He is always referred to reverently as 'the Prophet Elijah in Chicago.'" When Elijah reclaimed the title of the Nation of Islam is unclear, as is so much about those years between Fard's disappearance and the reestablishment of the Nation.

The Nation has maintained Fard's naming tradition, even if it doesn't have his imagination. Scarcely any of those colorful Islamic names exist in the Nation today. Members at first simply drop their surnames and substitute Xs or, later, two Xs or three Xs in case of duplication. Then, when the great day comes and they are entitled to a real surname, well, the lists are filled with Muhammads. Exactly how this naming process now operates is one of the secrets of the Nation.

But it is no secret that, unlike Fard, Elijah exhibited a good deal of interest in money, and the same is certainly true of Louis Farrakhan. This interest in money is said to be for the good of the Nation, to build businesses and mosques and to buy radio and television time and expand the publishing business to get the message out.

5.

In just four years, during which he had to adjudicate internal struggles, Fard established the basic structure of the Nation of Islam by which it generally continues to operate sixty years later. Over the years, first Elijah, then Malcolm, and then Farrakhan expanded and strengthened the Nation immensely, in every direction, but they have retained Fard's essential ideas.

Perhaps most interesting about Fard's influence is the sociologist Beynon's description of how the socioeconomic conditions of Fard's followers changed over the years he talked with them. He claims that when they met Fard "practically all the members of the 'cult' were recipients of public welfare, unemployed, and living in the most deteriorated areas of Negro settlement in Detroit." By 1937, after the people in the Nation had been members for various lengths of time since Fard's arrival in 1930, "there is no known case of unemployment among these people. Practically all of them are working in the automobile and other factories. They live no longer in the slum section . . . but rent homes in some of the best economic areas in which Negroes have settled. They tend to purchase more expensive furniture, automobiles, and clothes than do their neighbors." Economic conditions had slightly improved in Detroit in those years, and the recent immigrants had learned their way around a bit, but the Nation members claimed to Beynon "that they have secured work much more easily than have other Negroes." For this special dispensation, they thanked Allah.

Beynon heavily credits the ascetic way of life advocated by Fard for the Muslims' improved economic conditions. No liquor, little meat, and only one meal a day that consists mostly of fruits and vegetables can have a big impact on one's financial resources and can be crucial on the job market. Of course, Beynon doesn't tell us how many people he's talking about or how he knows whether people were telling the truth. But it seems clear from his report that rather dramatic changes did occur among the Nation's followers during the few years they were under the influence of that highly curious man. And the same claims have been made and accepted by many for Nation members ever since.

In the 1930s Fard's emphasis was on recent migrants from the South, with all the problems they brought along. In more recent years a great emphasis in the Nation has been placed on rescuing the worst victims of urban racial carnage—those in prison and on the streets.

Fard's belief that an Islamic identity could somehow alter the role of the poor black in America was part of that larger dream that blacks have held for so long, that a new name can somehow save them. But Fard taught that the label isn't what brings change, it is the will to create a new identity. In true American fashion, Fard taught that one could change oneself if one only had the will. And the bottom line, Fard knew—as leaders of successful religious groups always know—is in the magical inspiration of a leader to inspire faith to create that will. In those four short years in which he created the Nation, Fard built the foundation for a magical faith that has endured.

What parts of anger, resentment, and fear of the white and love of the black contribute to what has to be called faith among the Muslims I don't know. Probably there cannot be found in mosques all over the country any active member who does not combine these traits. But in addition, the man or woman who has now or will have an active role in the Nation also has, as Fard and his successors did, a fear and loathing and anger against his or her own fellow blacks, as taught by whites, that creates a strong feeling to be something else. It was the genius of this man whose name we don't even know that he was able to create the formula for the balancing of all these elements to constitute an enduring faith. This faith has built an organization that, despite its problems, sustains a great many people.

Part Three

FARD'S FAITHFUL

FOLLOWER, ELIJAH

MUHAMMAD

1.

Detroit, 1934. The buzzing of mosquitoes and flies resounded in the still air as folks squirmed, swatting at their arms, legs, necks, faces. There was no escape. Indoors the heat was unendurable. Outdoors the bugs were iniquitous. But the people didn't complain. What could they say? How could it help anyone, the little ones especially, to talk about how much worse it had been in Georgia? Did it help to say this wasn't what they had expected in this heaven that Detroit was supposed to be, where they couldn't sleep outside on the porch because of the bugs and couldn't sleep inside—Momma, Poppa, Uncle Ellsworth, Grandma, John Marshall, Petunia, and Elijah and his whole family in just the two downstairs rooms, and you couldn't go upstairs 'cause you'd suffocate? It certainly wouldn't help anyone to say that, next to Georgia, this Paradise Valley was truly named, but it was Sandersville, Georgia, after all, that they were comparing it to.

Momma went in to make another pitcher of lemonade. "Now mind, if anyone hears anything, I don't want to be the only one not to know." Somebody had to hear something soon. The Master wasn't like that, he wouldn't just go off like that and not tell them nothing. He never caused no one to worry about him before. Pretty soon they were going to have to maybe get a posse out. You couldn't go to the police. How could you be sure it wasn't the police who had him or maybe even killed him or just beat him up somewhere and left him for dead? It wouldn't be the first time that happened in Paradise Valley. And the Master never did get along so friendly with the police.

Every able-bodied person, even the young girls, joined the Fruit of Islam to search the streets for Master Fard. It had been six days, six long bitter hot days, each one bad enough to kill a man who had been left in some alley or empty lot seriously injured. You'd have to get water to him, a doctor. Each of the searchers carried a little bottle of water and a clean rag. But they came back after a few hours. They'd gone to the edges of the Valley. They were worn out, feeling helpless. He was nowhere to be found.

They went out again every day, going far beyond the boundaries they knew. Finally they gave up. They went to the Temple of Islam to say goodbye to their beloved leader, Master Fard, who had brought them the message of Allah. He had gone as he had come, a mystery. Perhaps they would never know. But he had brought them a new sense of life, a new purpose, a new definition of themselves that they would not soon forget, that they would remain faithful to—they promised each other that day.

Elijah Karriem, or Muhammad, as he said Fard had recently re-named him, took over the service. It was a simple Christian service like he'd seen his daddy perform in Georgia, not exactly a burial service because no one knew whether the Master was dead or not. There were some songs, not normally practiced in Fard's temple, but this was a special occasion. And the men and women sat together in families, not like they usually did when Fard preached, when it was the women on one side and men on the other. But families didn't want to separate at this time. When Elijah spoke, he said the Master had told him to take over the Nation. He said the Master had insisted on keeping it a secret while Elijah was learning all that the Master had to teach him to prepare him to take over the Nation.

2.

The story told for more than sixty years is that Fard simply disappeared. In its various versions, this story is repeated in all the standard works and by Fard's successors. In an alternative version, Elijah said that on May 26, 1933, the police had thrown Fard out of town, and that he had gone to Chicago where he was immediately arrested. But that's only one version of the story, and there is no evidence he was actually arrested in Chicago; all the police records before 1960 were destroyed in a sweep of reform. Perhaps the Detroit police picked up Fard in the middle of the night and just put him on a bus to Chicago. But the Detroit police couldn't track down a case with no information about it. No one knew. Even Elijah, so close to Fard, doesn't seem to know the facts. The general feeling is that Fard simply disappeared.

But what happened when Fard's followers discovered he was gone, just gone? Surely they waited a while, and then they went looking. Some surely wept, keened.

Presumably Elijah Muhammad knew what was happening in Paradise Valley in those days immediately following the disappearance, but he never said. There seems to be no public record of the members of the Nation of Islam showing any public reaction when their revered leader disappeared.

Perhaps that's really what happened: there was no public reaction. Maybe Fard's followers knew he'd been thrown out of town and there was nothing they could do. Or even if they had no idea what had happened to him, as the evidence seems to suggest, perhaps there was no hunt for him. And then no memorial service. Perhaps they believed that God had spirited him off. But that doesn't ring true. It seems more likely that the story I have imagined is closer to the truth. This makes me wonder what strange defect of character or, alternatively, what leap of imagination occurred in Elijah Muhammad when he chose (most of the time) to tell the world that Fard simply took off into the air with no attempt to find him nor any attempt to mourn him by his congregation.

Did Elijah have some notion that a mysterious disappearance would create a splendid spiritual aura around Fard, which would thereby enhance his own position as Fard's Messenger? A little like the aftereffects on the disciples after the Resurrection of Christ? That's not an idea to be quickly dismissed, considering how Elijah deified Fard after he was gone. As Elijah said in *Message to the Blackman*, "THE COMING OF THE SON OF MAN—THE INFIDELS ARE ANGRY. Who is His father if God is not His Father? God is His Father, but the Father is also a man. You have heard of old that God prepared a body, or the expected Son of Man; Jesus is a specially prepared man to do a work of redeeming the lost sheep (the so-called Negro). He had to have a body that would be part of each side (black and white), half and half. Therefore, being born or made from both people, He is able to go among black and white without being discovered or recognized. This He has done in the person of Master W. D. Muhammad [Fard], the man who was made by His Father to go and search for the lost members of the Tribe of Shabazz. Master W. D. Muhammad is that Son of Man whom the world has been expecting to come for 2,000 years, seeking to save that which is lost." And Elijah was Fard's Messenger. "My mission, as the Messenger," he says also in *Message to the Blackman*, "is to bring the truth to the world before the world is destroyed. There will be no other Messenger. I am the last and after me will come God Himself." Since Elijah is dead, Farrakhan often has difficulty deciding whether he is actually God or simply another envoy.

3.

In 1963, thirty years after he supposedly disappeared, it looked like Fard might still be alive, something that Elijah couldn't countenance. He offered a Hearst paper, the *Los Angeles Herald-Examiner*, $100,000 to prove charges made in the paper that a con man named Wallace Dodd was actually Fard.

Then, in the 1990s Warith (Wallace) Deen Muhammad, son of Elijah, long since divorced in hostile fashion from his father's Nation and the leader of an allegedly pure Islamic group, claimed to have found the mysterious Fard, this time as one Muhammad Abdullah. Warith claimed the man had made a clean breast of his earlier heresies against Islam. Despite the fact that this Abdullah made no claim to Fard's identity, Warith was certain of it and happily installed him as an imam in his Oakland, California, temple until he died in 1992. Although Elijah's son had long since rejected his father's theories, he clung to an unworldly faith in this godly creature who had founded his father's religion.

It is not at all far-fetched that Fard's followers viewed his disappearance as a divine act and that my little imaginative version of events merely shows my lack of appreciation for the spirituality of the members of the Nation. Maybe. But I find it nearly impossible to imagine those people, even as romantic and superstitious as they might have been, not reacting at all to the disappearance of their beloved and respected leader. The people Erdmann Beynon describes in the *AJS* as the followers of Fard come across as practical and realistic as well as superstitious and romantic. Elijah's oft-told tale rings with a hidden agenda.

4.

According to Beynon, some members of the Nation readily accepted Elijah as their new leader. Seemingly they knew the Master had gradually been pulling away, giving Elijah more and more responsibility. This group likely understood that without the leadership of Elijah to replace the Master, the Nation would fall apart.

But Beynon implies, and Elijah states openly, that others in the Nation thought he had moved in altogether too quickly, as if he'd just been waiting, as if perhaps he might have had something to do with the Master's disappearance. Malcolm tells in his *Autobiography* of Elijah's descriptions of how "attempts were made on his life, because the other ministers' jealousy had reached such a pitch. . . . These 'hypocrites' forced him to flee to Chicago. Temple Number Two became his headquarters until the 'hypocrites' pursued him there, forcing him to flee again." In the possible case of violence, Elijah was at a disadvantage—a small man at only 150 pounds, just five feet seven, and not known as a street fighter, though he had been a laborer in Sandersville before he emigrated to Detroit.

From Chicago, Elijah went to Washington, D.C., where he organized Temple No. 4, he said. While he was in Washington, Elijah told

Malcolm, he went to the "Congressional Library" where he read books Fard had referred him to. These "contained different pieces of the truth that devil white men had recorded, but which were not in books generally available to the public." The Library of Congress does indeed have a treasure of obscure documents of all kinds, including some that reveal the atrocities of whites against blacks throughout history. Already in 1942 the *World Almanac* describes books, manuscripts, maps and charts, pieces of art and music exceeding twelve million (there were seventy million in 1996), many of them most obscure. But it requires some imagination to see a man with a fourth-grade education from a Georgia school for black sharecroppers' children unearthing the hidden treasures of the Library of Congress. On the other hand, many barely educated people—think of Abraham Lincoln—have accomplished unexpected and extraordinary things, surely among them learning their ways around even such a massive public library.

Soon, Elijah told Malcolm, Washington too became unsafe. He now "fled from city to city, never staying long in any. Whenever able, now and then, he slipped home to see his wife and eight young children, who were fed by other poor Muslims who shared what little they had. Even Mr. Muhammad's original Chicago followers," Malcolm says, "wouldn't know he was at home, for he says the 'hypocrites' made serious efforts to kill him."

Here the story gets a little muddled. Elijah was in Chicago, heading up Temple No. 2, which he had organized earlier with Fard, though Chicago was still not quite safe for him, so he wasn't exactly open. The Nation was yet small, one of several tiny groups trying to bring enlightenment to the rapidly growing black population of Chicago, with sister temples in other cities. Chicago blacks already had a thriving commercial and entertainment district known throughout the country among blacks, with one of the largest black newspapers in the country, the *Chicago Defender*, an active and highly respected public library whose librarian, Vivian G. Harsh, later became well known for her vast collection of black materials, and a great deal of political activity. The way Elijah told the story to Malcolm, he was, on the one hand, in danger from his enemies in the Nation, but, on the other hand, he seemed to be reasonably comfortable in Chicago and was attracting people to the Nation.

Then, his story to Malcolm went, in 1942, the first year of America's involvement in World War II, he was arrested for refusing to be inducted into the army, though he was already forty-five years old, long past the draft age of thirty-eight. All males to age sixty-eight were required to register for the draft, and it is not difficult to imagine Elijah refusing to sign up. He had little respect for the white man's institutions. But he told Malcolm that he was arrested when some "Uncle Tom Negroes had tipped off the devil white man to his teachings." The implication of his story is that he was falsely accused of counseling his followers to refuse to fight in the war; he emphatically denied having done this. Draft-dodging, he insisted, was an individual matter, and in fact the Nation never developed a position on army service during wartime. (The famous case of heavyweight fighter Muhammad Ali's refusal to be drafted was entirely his own decision.) Elijah regularly repeated some version of this story, and others writing and talking about him repeated it: he had been arrested and jailed for resisting the draft.

There is another version, this one documented by the *Chicago Tribune* and the old *Chicago Sun*. It seems that Elijah was arrested in September 1942 along with eighty other blacks on charges of "sedition, conspiracy, and violation of the draft laws," according to the *Tribune*. These were serious charges. Among the others arrested were men considered leaders of the Peace Movement of Ethiopia and the Brotherhood of Liberty for Black People in America. Even though the FBI admitted publicly that no direct connection between the Japanese and the black leaders was ever found, the men were indicted for having "taught Negroes that their interests were in a Japanese victory, and that they were racially akin to the Japanese." The U.S. attorney is quoted in the *Tribune* as having said that "the defendants made statements as vicious as any ever uncovered by a grand jury."

Perhaps the statements made by Elijah and the others were indeed so vicious. Elijah and another Muslim admitted their sympathy for the Japanese, and one can imagine that, given his savage antiwhite speeches and his strong sentiments that all nonwhite people were his brothers, also brutally oppressed by whites, perhaps his statements were pretty ferocious. Most likely those other "race" leaders, as they were called in those days, also made hostile statements about whites and may indeed have made statements supporting the Japanese.

Did the FBI pick them up at their separate meeting halls, going from one to the other all day? Did they all have meeting halls? How many FBI agents were involved in arresting these eighty men, all of whom, according to the *Tribune*, were arrested on September 22, 1942. The *Tribune* fails to say where these arrests were made. It could have happened that the three organizations all happened to have had meetings on the same day, close together, with their leaders all making these scurrilous attacks on the government, and the FBI actually did travel around the South Side making these arrests.

But if one knew anything about the Black Belt in Chicago in the 1940s, it wouldn't take a wild guess to figure that the arrests were likely made in Washington Park, at a famous open-air public debating ground at what was then the edge of the black community in Chicago. There people came from all over to make speeches, often on soapboxes, about every conceivable cause—religious, political, racial, whatever. There was another regular gathering of soapbox orators, mostly white, on the North Side of Chicago, in what was then called Bughouse Square, and other cities had similar spots—for instance, Union Square on 14th Street in New York City. These were just about the only places all these "thinkers" could sound off, but it was not unusual to find well-known politicians and preachers making speeches there.

Anyone who could attract an audience in these parks could speak, and those groups arrested that day in 1942 would probably have attracted good-sized audiences. But as happened at most such public events, there were always in the audience some FBI men. J. Edgar Hoover had little enthusiasm for these soapbox orators or anyone else he could loosely identify as Communist. Blacks who spoke against the white establishment were especially dangerous. So it's not too difficult to imagine Hoover's FBI agents standing watch among the towering elms, the oaks, and the ginkgo trees in Washington Park and deciding that these groups making pro-Japanese statements were a dangerous lot, conspiring together to overturn the U.S. government. That would make them subject to arrest under the newly passed Smith Act.

Perhaps on that day in September, maybe a sunny afternoon when the park was filled with people and the FBI agents had worked up a strong case of outrage about the "seditious" talk they had heard, they arrived with arrest warrants. Or maybe they didn't have arrest warrants; that wouldn't have been so unusual. All we know is that eighty blacks were taken in. Most likely news spread quickly. The black community was tightly knit. Some people in Chicago still remember that event. Perhaps Congressman William Dawson rushed out, but it is unlikely he would have offered much help. He owed his office to the then-powerful Democratic machine and didn't often stick his neck out for people. So those eighty blacks would have been at the mercy of the FBI, which didn't have the best record for fair and equal treatment of blacks. It makes one pause a little before accepting the word of the U.S. attorney. And it makes one shudder a bit that Elijah served three and a half years of a five-year sentence in the federal prison at Milan, Michigan, for preaching a lot of rot.

It appears that Elijah was one of the earliest dissidents sent to jail by the federal government for sedition during World War II. The Chicago arrests in September 1942 don't show up in the *New York Times* Index, but by early 1943 there are long columns in the Index listing "espionage" cases of people either arrested by the FBI or brought to testify and then indicted by the House Committee on Un-American Activity headed by Representative Martin Dies, the notorious forerunner to the House Un-American Activities Committee. Some of those arrested and later jailed were alleged German "aliens," accused of a variety of crimes against the government; many were simply dissidents who spoke out about some aspect of the war. In Newark, New Jersey, for instance, on February 19, 1943, a thirty-seven-year-old black man named Richard Oliver was arrested on "draft evasion" charges. The *New York Times* reported that day that the FBI "was concerned with another Negro cult believed to be Japanese-inspired." Oliver was a citizen of the British West Indies and claimed exception from the United States draft laws. He was also "'a member of the Temple of Islam, a Mohammadan . . . that maintained national headquarters in Chicago' . . . that was believed to be 'Japanese-inspired propaganda to obstruct the registration of Negroes and the darker-skinned races.'"

The *Times* that day also reported that the New Jersey FBI "was instrumental in obtaining the conviction of six members of the House of Israel, another Negro anti-war cult, for violating draft regulations. This group is linked by the FBI to the Japanese-supported Pacific Movement."

5.

As the war proceeded, the FBI and the Dies Committee spread out far and wide across the United States to ferret out what they viewed as dangerous antiwar elements, a fair share of them black, perhaps the largest share completely innocent of any dangerous activities except refusal to serve in the armed forces out of religious or other principled motives. That they were Japanese-inspired is not likely; as in Elijah's case, no links between the Americans and the Japanese were usually discovered.

6.

Considering the circumstances of mid-1942—the Japanese bombing of a major U.S. military installation in Hawaii, launching the country into World War II; a history of anti-Japanese and anti-Asian sentiment in the United States; an executive order to round up all imagined enemy Japanese Americans and ship them to ten squalid detention camps, mostly in the West; and a massive propaganda effort by the U.S. government to whip up hatred for the "Yellow Peril"—was it courage or craziness that led Elijah Muhammad, already upsetting the government with his volatile antiwhite talk, to preach support for America's enemy and to refuse to register for the draft? Was Elijah unaware of the impact these preachings might have? Was he inspiring other black leaders with his ideas? Was he daring the U.S. government to challenge him? Was he showing his people his extraordinary cleverness and defiance, raising the ante to attract more followers by enhancing his attacks against whites in general by offering sympathy to the Japanese? Or did he truly believe in his ideas and feel he had to make them known whatever the consequences might be? C. Eric Lincoln's comment about Elijahs' ferocious attacks on whites is instructive: " . . . Muhammad is aware of the paradox that the less respectable he is, the more he is respected."

When we look at Elijah's report of these events years later, we miss any strutting or reporting of courageous acts. When he tells his closest confidant, his protégé Malcolm X, about his imprisonment, he claims he was the victim of an "Uncle Tom" informer and that he was charged with "draft-dodging." While this story might impress an acolyte, it certainly doesn't have the same panache as the true story. It sounds more as if Elijah would just as soon that part of his life be forgotten, as if he had come to believe that he'd made a mistake.

7.

Nearly thirty years after Fard disappeared in Detroit, another major leader of the Nation, Elijah's obvious heir and a hero to many inside and outside the Nation, "disappeared" in New York City. On February 21, 1965, Malcolm X took eighteen bullets on the stage of the Audubon Ballroom in Harlem. The police arrested three members of the Nation, who were convicted and sent to jail. The evidence against the men was not substantial, but the anger in the black community and the violent battles between Malcolm's followers and the Nation made speed and expediency in the convictions a high order for the city.

Malcolm had sensed for several weeks that his life was endangered. Several assassination attempts had in fact been made, which Malcolm attributed to members of the Nation, even members of his own former Mosque No. 7 in Harlem. In the last days of his life, however, he began to suspect that the FBI was plotting his death. He told Alex Haley, who was helping him to write his *Autobiography*, "The more I keep thinking about this thing . . . I'm not at all sure it's the Muslims. I know what they can do, and what they can't, and they can't do some of the stuff recently going on." He had, after all, taught them a lot about what was then viewed as self-defense, a lot of what he had learned on the streets of Harlem.

But Malcolm had plenty of reason to suspect the Muslims. A number of influential ministers of the Nation, including most forcefully Louis Farrakhan, then known as Minister Louis X of the Boston Mosque, had made public statements both from the pulpit and in the Nation's newspaper, *Muhammad Speaks*, saying that Malcolm deserved to die. Policy in the Nation was clear and forthright. Everyone understood it. People didn't make statements like that unless they were sanctioned by Elijah.

Malcolm had been "silenced" by Elijah in late 1963, ostensibly only temporarily, because, he was told, he made a public remark that Elijah considered injurious to the Nation. Malcolm had said, when President John F. Kennedy was killed, "Being an old farm boy myself, chickens coming home to roost never did make me sad; they've always made me glad"—a remark far less tactful and far more cunning than many others made at the time, implying that the racist atmosphere in this country had led to that terrible act of violence. It was certainly no more inflammatory than remarks Malcolm had been making for years, with Elijah's blessings.

Malcolm thought he was being pushed out of the Nation by Elijah and a variety of people who resented Malcolm's power, which was not surprising. At the time he was the most powerful figure in the Nation, notwithstanding Elijah's ultimate authority. How Elijah viewed Malcolm's growing power is not clear. Once before a leader had disappeared, and afterward there was suspicion about Elijah that he called jealousy. Now Malcolm had accused the Chicago leadership of the Nation of enough jealousy to plan his assassination.

Certainly the assassination attempts that came later could not have occurred without Elijah's knowledge. As Malcolm read the signs during the three-month "silencing," there seemed to be no alternative to resigning. He left the Nation in March 1964 and formed his own organization, the Organization of Afro-American Unity.

In the months that followed, Malcolm preached a new nonracist Islamic philosophy he had acquired in the Middle East, one that completely contradicted Elijah's teachings, including inviting whites to join his organization. And he charged publicly that Elijah had had a number of children by his young, single secretaries. Malcolm claimed, in his *Autobiography*, that Elijah not only admitted his sexual transgressions to him but claimed holy exemption. Malcolm quoted him as saying, "I'm David. When you read about how David took another man's wife, I'm that David. You read about Noah, who got drunk—that's me. You read about Lot, who went and laid up with his own daughters. I have to fulfill all of those things."

But only Malcolm heard this "confession." After he shared it with some of his colleagues, Farrakhan among them, there followed what might have been, in the Nation, where Elijah was worshiped as a God, a predicted development. The messenger was condemned. The membership of the Nation was told that Malcolm was defaming Elijah's name, a sin worthy of death, according to Farrakhan, whom Malcolm insisted had known of Elijah's peccadillos for even seven months before he told him.

Slightly more than a month after Malcolm was killed, the Nation held its annual Saviour's Day convention in Chicago's Coliseum. As Alex Haley says in his epilogue to Malcolm's *Autobiography*, "The ghost of Malcolm X was in the Coliseum." There was, he said, a spooky procession of people marching to the podium to close ranks with Elijah against Malcolm. Elijah's son Wallace, who had earlier strongly supported Malcolm's ideas and had confirmed his suspicions about his father's infidelities, "begged forgiveness for his defection," Haley reports. Then came Malcolm's brothers, who had recruited him into the Nation when he was in prison. One of them, Minister Philbert X of Lansing, Michigan, told the audience, "Malcolm was my own blood brother. . . . No man wants to see his own brother destroyed. But I knew that he was traveling on a very reckless and dangerous road." And when he finished his speech, it was he who had the honored privilege of introducing Elijah to the crowd.

Standing amid his oversized bodyguards, barely visible to the crowd, Elijah told his followers: "For a long time, Malcolm stood here where I stand. In those days, Malcolm was safe, Malcolm was loved. God, Himself, protected Malcolm. . . . For more than a year, Malcolm was given his freedom. He went everywhere—Asia, Europe, Africa, even to Mecca, trying to make enemies for me. He came back preaching that we should not hate the enemy. . . . He came here a few weeks ago to blast away his hate and mud-slinging; everything he could think of to disgrace me. . . . We didn't want to kill Malcolm and didn't try to kill him. They know I didn't harm Malcolm. They know I loved him. His foolish teaching brought him to his own end. . . . He had no right to reject me! . . . He was a star, who went astray! . . . They knew I didn't harm Malcolm, but he tried to make war against me." Elijah spoke, Haley says, for about an hour and a half, at the end of which the crowd shouted, "Yes, sir! . . . So sweet! . . . All praise to Muhammad!"

Although the organization he had founded quickly disappeared, Malcolm retained a strong hold on the imagination of many blacks, which was anathema to the Nation of Islam. Even six years later, in 1971, *Muhammad Speaks* was in effect cursing his name. In one issue, Elijah's son-in-law Raymond Sharrieff wrote, "In worshipping Malcolm, you are hated before God and His Angels." The next month Sharrieff wrote, "Malcolm saw white people in MECCA and he dined with them and ate out of the same dish with them. Judas Iscariot ate out of the dish with Jesus, but Judas was not a Jesus. Judas was a betrayer."

As for Elijah himself, he refused to discuss Malcolm. He said in *Muhammad Speaks* in February 1972, "I am not going to waste my time with going into Malcolm's history. Malcolm, I do not have any time to waste with him." Elijah died without ever raising the question of the assassination of the man who had been closer to him than anyone in his lifetime.

Except for a short time when he was under the thumb of Elijah's son Wallace, who had become known as Warith Deen, Farrakhan maintained for nearly twenty years after Malcolm's death—first as Malcolm's successor at Elijah's side and then as Elijah's successor—that Malcolm had deserved to die, that however he died, his death had had the blessing of his mentor. Periodically and then publicly in 1996, under sudden heavy pressure, Farrakhan apologized for what he claimed was his only role in the murder—helping to create the atmosphere that led to the killing. He now proclaimed that the Nation would have been better off if Malcolm had been alive and part of it.

8.

What is in a name? This book may seem a little obsessed with that question, but it is one of the vital questions raised in this story. Consciously or otherwise, the Nation from its beginning has viewed the concept of naming almost as a step of rebirth, as if it were returning to the first recorded naming in which Adam called his new wife Eve because "she was the mother of all living." Almost before anything else can happen, members of the Nation of Islam must expressly deal, practically and philosophically, with the issue of their names. They must be prepared to give up their birth names, which represent their heritage, in order to declare their allegiance to the Nation. The reason given by the Nation's leaders for this requirement is that it will enhance the members' sense of themselves.

As an adult, one's name, regardless of how many other people might be called by that name, speaks to oneself *of* oneself, of what one has learned from others about oneself and about what one dreams and fears about oneself. Most of us invest all those impressions in the names we've been given at birth. Men rarely consider a change, even when the accumulated associations are painful. After all, a change might be viewed as an insult to their own father. They understand almost unconsciously that their names reflect their father's own fears, dreams, and ambitions, even when never realized. This deep-seated feeling in women has for centuries been dismissed by many societies, which have demanded that women assume their husband's name in marriage—just one of the callous injustices practiced against women.

Women, of course, weren't the only ones forced to surrender their family names. The denial of individual humanity this represented was probably even more marked among the African-born slaves who were stripped of their names by their owners and assigned the name of the owner. The freed slaves retained these names, most often having no idea of the African names of their ancestors who had been brought to America three hundred years before. For their heirs, for whom historical identity is often troublesome enough, and for whom children can represent hope for the future in ways most American whites cannot conceive, names may have even more resonance than for whites. Thus it happens that so many blacks give their children nontraditional first names, often invented, names that offer some special distinction, such as the name Queen Esta, based most likely on the biblical Queen Esther. Susannah Lloyd, an anthropologist at the University of Wisconsin at LaCrosse, collects odd names. In the birth lists in the local paper in the mid-nineties she has found SkyMarie, Hawk Marie, Deltra Latrice, Ondrianana Shaqerra LaShannette, and Jenezette, all female black babies. In an obituary column in a Memphis, Tennessee, paper in 1995 she found a black Lucious White who had died and whose male heirs were Martavia Gray, Jerarcius Deonata Stevenson, and Lucious Deshawn Stevenson. An interesting 1997 book by Justin Kaplan and Anne Bernays, *The Language of Names*, reports that in one

Chicago all-black school district there was not a single repetition of first names.

Despite pressures from within and without, some people do change their names. Some make such simple changes as discarding a disliked first name in favor of a middle name, or changing a spelling to make a name more chic, perhaps Susanna for a simple Susan. A few invent new surnames for themselves, especially those who are anglicizing long, complex Eastern European or other names—the famous writer Joseph Conrad, whose name had been Józef Teodor Konrad Korzeniowski; or George Eliot, who took a male name instead of her original Mary Ann Evans in order to further her career as a writer when women writers were scorned; or Lauren Bacall, who, like so many entertainers, wanted a more glamorous name than her Betty Joan Perske; or John Wayne, a tough guy whose name, Marion Michael Morrison, hardly fit. Since the 1960s, though, with the development of so-called multiculturalism and a greater emphasis on ethnicity or what is viewed by some as individuality or authenticity, fewer people make such changes. Even people whose grandparents anglicized their names when they came to this country—or had them anglicized by clerks at Ellis Island, as happened to many—returned to the family name, unpronounceable to the American tongue as it might be. Whether they go one way or the other, to or from anglicization, we can be sure that the change represents some conflict for them, some ambivalence. Few people abandon their birth name easily, especially when that name represents a memorable, painful, or proud heritage.

When occasionally we come upon someone who has changed his name regularly, from week to week or month to month, or year to year, or is simultaneously known by a variety of names, sometimes called aliases, we quickly assume that this person is in trouble, escaping from the cops, from fellow gangsters, or perhaps from Nazi-hunters. But this picture can instead be one of a confused person who adopts a series of names not for such an ulterior reason but because he is still trying to figure out just who he is, how he wants to be viewed by others.

We must wonder whether the person who acquires such a series of names is not dreadfully insecure. But we might also consider that this person is fiercely ambitious, seeking the name that will bestow upon him not only security but the greatest glory—remembering the biblical injunction, "A good name is rather to be chosen than great riches," choosing instead, with an early-nineteenth-century English poet,

> "Yet leaving here a name, I trust,
> That will not perish in the dust."

One notorious example is the popular performance singer known for years as Prince, who in 1993 adopted an obscure symbol as his name. Because the symbol could not be used verbally, he became known as "the artist formerly known as Prince." He claimed this altogether notorious act was part of an attempt to get out of his record contract with Warner Brothers. Perhaps, but this wasn't the first time Prince had played around with his name. The man born as Prince Rogers Nelson has also at times been known as Alexander Nevermind, Christopher Tracy, The Kid, Jamie Starr, and Camille. Obviously names have a special meaning and value to this character who shines in his eccentricities.

W. D. Fard was another eccentric person for whom names were important. Few people have been more sensitive to the meaning of names than Master Fard. "The name," he said, "is everything." Not just one, though. He doesn't seem to have stuck to one very long. And we do not know what name he took with him when he left Detroit, if he did indeed leave intact. But such gloriously ambitious names as he gave himself—the Master, Mahdi, and Allah—have survived him as he hoped they would.

We also do not know how much sharing of ideas about names there was between Fard and his main pupil, Elijah. We don't know whether Elijah Poole, who was born in 1897 in a tiny town in rural Georgia, one of thirteen children born to parents who had only escaped slavery when they were children, was already changing his name even before he left the South and later conceived the Islamic naming system of the Nation together with Fard; or whether it was only after he'd learned Fard's theory that he began inventing a variety of names for himself. He was known as Elijah Karriem, Gulam Bogans, Muhammad Rassouli, Elijah Much Muhd, Elijah Black, Muhammad Allah, and other aliases. He was also known as the Messenger, the Prophet, the Spiritual Head of the Muslims of the West, Divine Leader, and the Reformer. As his position became more secure over the years, he was most often known as The Honorable Elijah Muhammad, or on some very formal occasions, The Messenger of Allah to the

Lost-Found Nation of Islam in the Wilderness of North America. Clearly he was an imaginative man, and clearly names had great significance for him. What this significance is, we don't know, but that he was preoccupied with the idea of names is clear in much of his writing.

For instance, in *Message to the Blackman* and in other of his writings, he talks at length about the significance of the names under which God is known, ranging around in the Old and New Testaments and the Koran, using such expressions as "the mighty," "the wise," "the best knower," "the light," "the life giver," and the Mahdi, of whom he says, "This is He, Whom I have met and am missioned by."

Did Elijah's preoccupation with names result in part from an intense early wound made by a name? Unlike most of his fellow laborers, Elijah apparently reached a point at which he could no longer tolerate being called nigger, even by his boss, though he had a job that far surpassed that of the common sharecropper. With reasonably decent jobs for blacks always at a premium, and with job security always in jeopardy, particularly in the Deep South, Elijah one day looked his boss in the eye and threatened to leave his job if he called him nigger again. When the foreman fearlessly and arrogantly repeated the insult, Elijah turned his back and walked away. He packed up his wife Clara and their two children and went north, where he had heard that life was better. Perhaps he would find a niche in Detroit where he could be more respected.

But he was no ordinary man who went to the bustling Northern auto manufacturing city simply to find a job, a place to live, a school for his children, a church in which to worship. That wasn't enough for Elijah. He had to experiment with different jobs, different ministers, and different names until he found what seemed to be a place for a new, dramatic himself with a minister who, among other things, was experimenting with names. He endowed Elijah with a new prophetic name, Karriem, the same name previously held by the great Prophet Muhammad. And later, Elijah claimed, his great mentor, whom he had discovered was Allah, conferred upon him the greatest name of all, Muhammad ("one worthy of praise"), along with the instruction that he was to lead all the black people.

But we don't know how much Fard's philosophy of renaming his followers was influenced by Elijah, who clearly was a quick learner. Elijah said in the *Supreme Wisdom* (which history reveals is his work but which has now been credited in the Nation to Fard), as quoted by C. Eric Lincoln, "As the Bible teaches us that He Will Accept those who are called by His Name. And some of us are so foolish as to say, 'What is in a name?' Everything is in a name. The Bible teaches us that all of these Names of Allah (God) is more valuable than fine gold, because in the Judgment it will save your life from being destroyed.

"All people who do not have a Name of the God of Righteousness and Justice will be destroyed."

So it is clear that in the Nation of Islam names are of utmost importance. Even if you have the same name—yes, there are many, many Muhammads in the Nation—each has its own distinctive meaning. The following poem sent anonymously to C. Eric Lincoln had no doubt about which Muhammad he or she was writing about:

Hail to Elijah Muhammad
1
Who is the One the Scriptures meant?
  Elijah Muhammad!
Who is the One Allah has sent?
  Elijah Muhammad!
Who leads where others fear to tread
Who raised us from the living dead
Who put a crown upon our head?
  Elijah Muhammad!

Although Elijah may have adopted that list of names for himself years before, he may have begun using them only after Fard disappeared, when Elijah was determined to take over the Nation and was on the run from his enemies. Or perhaps he was using aliases to escape from the police. Clearly he was an early object of surveillance. As early as 1934 he was leading the resistance to the Detroit school board and the police when they attempted to prevent the Nation's parents from sending their children to their own school. His alternative names show up in newspaper reports a few years later. In the 1942 *Chicago Tribune* account of the arrests of Elijah and others for sedition, the paper describes him as Elijah Poole "who calls himself Elijah Muhammad . . . also known as Elijah Much Muhd, and is known as 'The Prophet.'" Most likely the FBI supplied that information to the *Tribune* reporter. Elijah may have played with his name in a way not so different from Prince.

9.

We have no clear picture of Elijah's life between the mid-1930s, when he left Detroit, and 1942, when he was arrested for sedition. He has said he traveled around the Midwest and the East Coast, no doubt proselytizing, "fishing" for new members as it was called in the Nation, even organizing groups into small temples. He said he and his family were supported by other Nation members, a generosity that would be hard to believe, given the general poverty of those depression years, if we didn't have the poetic picture of the gentle little preacher Elijah, who was apparently not always so gentle, calling himself the Messenger of Allah, proclaiming that he had been sent by Allah to bring justice and equality to his fellow blacks.

Malcolm X, in the *Autobiography*, says that in the first speech he ever heard Elijah make, the Messenger told his audience, "I have not stopped one day for the past twenty-one years. I have been standing, preaching to you throughout those past twenty-one years, while I was free, and even while I was in bondage. . . . I was also deprived of a father's love for his family for seven long years while I was running from hypocrites and other enemies of this word and revelation of God. . . ." Malcolm said, "I was totally unprepared for the Messenger Elijah Muhammad's physical impact upon my emotions."

C. Eric Lincoln thinks Elijah "apparently was able to direct the movement even while in jail, for it gained strength during those years" until he was released in 1946. We know of many inmates whose influence has reached beyond their cells. From the very start Elijah proselytized among prison inmates, swelling the ranks of the Nation both in the jails (though prison officials were wary of the Nation) and outside, when prisoners were released.

Elijah was the quintessential race man, an expression describing an advocate for blacks that emerged sometime after Reconstruction but has largely disappeared since the 1960s. Elijah learned from and then put in the shade most of his predecessors. His basic blueprint— later adapted by others and called "black power," and, after all, invented by Marcus Garvey—was the first to create not only temples of religion but schools, businesses, farms, a newspaper, and real estate for an estimated 100,000 members at its peak. His scheme for economic development required first that his followers "Acknowledge and recognize that you are a member of the Creator's nation and act accordingly. This action, in the name of Allah, requires you, as a Muslim, to set an example for the lost-found, your brothers in the wilderness in North America. This requires action and deeds, not words and lip service. The following blueprint shows the way:

"1. Recognize the necessity for unity and group operations (activities).

"2. Pool your resources, physically as well as financially.

"3. Stop wanton criticisms of everything that is black-owned and black-operated.

"4. Keep in mind—jealousy destroys from within.

"5. Observe the operations of the white man. He is successful. He makes no excuses for his failures. He works hard in a collective manner. You do the same."

An old adage among minority peoples—repeated over many years among Jews, Irish, Asians, blacks—is that to be successful one has to be twice as good as a white man. Did Elijah actually believe that whites never made excuses for their failures and that cooperation, not competition, characterized white men's endeavors? Or did he believe, more likely, that with these words he had the formula for the successful application of that old adage, by urging blacks to copy what was actually only a grand illusion of white people? The genius of Elijah was that he could make such outrageous demands sound utterly reasonable.

10.

Even given his extraordinary ability to bewitch an audience and to make a deal, Elijah might not have achieved his early success without the help of Malcolm X. Only in the late 1950s, after Malcolm had become Elijah's spokesman, after he had begun to preach around the country and gain a radio and television audience, and then, in 1960, had launched from his basement *Muhammad Speaks*, did the Nation begin its marked growth. Only the greater numbers of members, with their money, made the economic growth possible. Malcolm describes in the *Autobiography* his first visit to Elijah in Chicago, where the Messenger had gone from prison to live with his Muslim brother. It was the Sunday before Labor Day, 1952, Malcolm said, when "our two little temples assembled, perhaps only two hundred Muslims, the Chicagoans welcoming and greeting us Detroiters."

Twelve years later he compared that little ten-car caravan in which he first visited Elijah to the 150, 200, and as many as 300 chartered buses that brought people to a city to hear Elijah speak. "On each bus," he said, "two Fruit of Islam men were in charge. Big three-by-nine-foot painted canvas banners hung on the buses' sides, to be read by the highway traffic and thousands of people at home and on the sidewalks of the towns the buses passed through."

But by 1961 Elijah was already suffering the effects of a disabling asthma. He often sat on the podium while the tall, well-built, bright-haired "Big Red," as Malcolm was often called, with his dramatic ringing voice, replaced the wispy, reedy voice of Elijah. But even when he was sick and able to speak only briefly, Elijah's speeches were filled with charismatic charm.

Just how much of the administration of the Nation was handled by Malcolm is difficult to assess. He claims he was largely responsible for much that happened. While he was alive, Elijah credited him as his right-hand man, but after he left the Nation there was little enough said about him. C. Eric Lincoln places him "foremost" among Elijah's inner circle and quotes Alex Haley in 1960, who at that time might still have been an objective observer, as saying that Malcolm was "the best thing that ever happened to Elijah." The evidence does seem to indicate that it was Malcolm who chiefly organized new temples, raised money, and infused the enthusiastic spirit into the Nation that enabled it to create the network of schools, businesses, farms, and real estate that were developed over the years. Malcolm doesn't claim credit for those deals. Given Elijah's tight hold on the nation, and given the later evidence about who owned what in the Nation, those deals surely had his signature on them.

But the money had to be brought in. While Elijah talked only to the black unlettered, lower-class audience that was the Nation's natural constituency, Malcolm also gained an educated middle-class audience at colleges and universities—including Ivy League locales—and on radio and television, a much more affluent audience able to pay substantially more to hear him speak.

Despite Malcolm's huge influence, however, and according to Malcolm, with his complete support, Elijah was firmly established as the Prophet of the Nation of Islam and enjoyed the loyalty of many of the Nation's leading figures. Even later, with the loss of a good many members after the murder of Malcolm, the pattern was so well established that the Nation's finances appeared to continue to prosper even after Malcolm was gone.

Although he did not gain Malcolm's wide support, Farrakhan, as Malcolm's successor, first in the Harlem Mosque and then as Elijah's National Representative, undoubtedly contributed to the well-being of the Nation. It is almost bewildering to read C. Eric Lincoln's description of Farrakhan as he took over Malcolm's positions. Lincoln seems to overlook the fact that Farrakhan had been the leading voice of opposition to Malcolm and had made a variety of violent threats against him, though Malcolm had helped to recruit him to the Nation and had been a close friend and mentor for years. Farrakhan was, Lincoln says, "soft-spoken, patient, and gentle to the point of self-effacement. Farrakhan's scholarly approach is in stark contrast to the eager polemics of Malcolm X." Not the man we have come to know as the Nation's leader.

Did Farrakhan undergo massive changes over the years, or, did Lincoln simply misread the signs here as he read them wrong in so many other aspects of this organization that he had so obviously come to admire and wanted to present in its best light? There is good reason to suspect that Farrakhan did indeed give the appearance of the man Lincoln describes. It seems reasonable that the man Elijah would choose to replace Malcolm would not greatly resemble Malcolm—the man who had betrayed him. His replacement would much more likely have the appearance of a man less inclined to challenge or question Elijah. In the years preceding Malcolm's death, Farrakhan's main claim to fame, as evidenced by references to him in *Muhammad Speaks*, was his strong, public defense of Elijah against Malcolm. He was a competent enough minister of the Boston Mosque, but not a dramatic presence in the Nation. Here clearly was the man for the job.

11.

In the years that followed Malcolm's death, the Nation appeared to prosper sufficiently so that in 1972 Elijah purchased for $4 million (with a $3 million loan from Libya) a large, ugly building on a major thoroughfare on the South Side of Chicago. It had been a Greek Orthodox church, with some suggestion of an Islamic mosque, giving to Elijah's national mosque a bit of physical Islamic identity. In the highly complex transactions that occurred as Elijah's heirs tried to disentangle his financial affairs after his death, the mosque, listed with the Cook County Clerk's office as Muhammad's Holy Temple, went through a process by which Farrakhan, in 1988, now the head of a new Nation of Islam, was able to buy it for $800,000. He renamed it Mosque Maryam—a bit of an oxymoron, Maryam being the Hebrew or Aramaic word for Mary, the name of the Christians' revered mother of Jesus, who has no role in Islamic tradition or history. In one of Elijah's tirades against Christianity, he says, "The Bible . . . makes God guilty of an adultery by charging Him with being the father of Mary's baby (Jesus). . . . What a poison book." In Elijah's own time the mosque was known as Muhammad's Holy Temple.

12.

Malcolm describes the first stores owned by the Nation in the 1950s, a few grocery stores in Chicago. He said of those early days when Elijah was still his God, "In the Muslim-owned combination grocery-drug store on Wentworth and 31st Street, Mr. Muhammad would sweep the floor or something like that. He would do such work himself as an example to his followers whom he taught that idleness and laziness were among the black man's greatest sins against himself. I would want to snatch the broom from Mr. Muhammad's hand, because I thought he was too valuable to be sweeping a floor. But he wouldn't let me do anything but stay with him, and listen while he advised me on the best ways to spread his message."

By 1972, not quite twenty years later, the Nation had fourteen "universities," or K-12 schools, operating in the country and a large network of businesses of all kinds. An exaggerated report by Elijah Muhammad, Jr., then the Nation's farm inspector, in *Muhammad Speaks* in November 1971, claimed ownership of 10,000 acres of farmland in Michigan, Alabama, and Georgia, and the annual sale of 35,000 pounds of beef, 12,000 dozen eggs, 2,200 gallons of milk, 25,000 three-pound bags of apples, 30 truckloads containing about 40,000 pounds of watermelon, and large amounts of beans, lamb, and fish.

In addition to this farm production, the Nation during Elijah's era owned restaurants, groceries, bakeries, barbershops, clothing stores, and extensive real estate, and employed lawyers, doctors, and dentists. C. Eric Lincoln called the Nation "the most potent organized economic force in the black community," though the events surrounding this "economic force" after Elijah's death make this claim suspect.

Before we look closely at the structure of the Nation's "economic force," we need to get a feel of how it works. We are accustomed to businesses starting out with a bit of capital, either acquired from savings or from borrowings, sometimes from families and friends, sometimes from banks. We know there was no substantial wealth among Nation members and no substantial property that could serve as collateral for bank loans, and that banks were not eager to lend money to blacks despite their collateral. So we know that the businesses and farms started by the Nation in the mid-fifties were bought with the pennies, dimes, and quarters that members were able to save and pool together. Eventually, we know, the leaders of the Nation could accumulate enough goodwill and collateral to win bank loans from Chicago's Seaway Bank and the few other black banks in the country. We also know that the members of those businesses worked long and hard hours for very little pay, out of which they gave their tithes to their mosques. We know that Elijah said that if one Muslim has a bowl of soup, all will eat.

One story about Muhammad's business dealings is the tale that he bought a large modern apartment building in Chicago, evicted the white tenants, moved poor blacks from the ghetto into the building, and then lowered the rents. This is one of many stories told by Muslims and sympathetic observers such as C. Eric Lincoln without collaborative evidence. Where was this "large modern apartment building" that Elijah was able to buy and virtually give away to his tenants? When did this happen? Where did the funds come from? Trying to trace much of the property owned by the Nation of Islam reveals that it was held in blind trusts, a practice many real estate owners use in order to protect themselves from tax bills and code violations, and to hide funds. As early as 1972 there were murmurings in the newspapers that the finances of the Nation were in trouble: the businesses, the *New York Times* said, were "in jeopardy of crumbling for lack of cash, and its many small businesses have never really thrived, primarily because the Nation did not possess the financial shrewdness to properly manage them, especially with so many members coming from the streets and the prisons."

C. Eric Lincoln tells another story about a grand act of generosity to help black businessmen get a leg up. Elijah gave them free exhibition space at the Nation's 1960 annual convention at the Coliseum in Chicago, which he had rented. Perhaps Elijah's gift was justified if the businessmen paid the costs of the construction, lighting, and equipment needed to make such a trade fair a success, though Lincoln implies that Elijah paid those costs. Without indicating the source, Lincoln quotes some advance material for the convention. "The three-day convention . . . was designed to 'provide the opportunity for Negro businessmen to promote their businesses in line with Mr. Muhammad's program of Economic Security for the American Negro.'" Apparently this convention, held to coincide with the Nation's Saviour's Day, was expected "to attract some fifteen thousand delegates and visitors" who would provide "an open bid by Muslims for an increasing share of leadership in the black community."

Thinking of Elijah Muhammad, Jr.'s report of farm production for 1971, with his estimate of "truckloads of produce coming and going from places as far away as California, Texas, Georgia, and Alabama, and as near as Michigan, Wisconsin, Indiana, etc.," I was reminded of the seasonal farm workers in all those states who live under terrible conditions, earning less than the minimum wage. Were the members of the Nation living in similar conditions to help create the great economic edifice that Elijah said would save the blacks of this country? After all, Elijah had told them, over and over again, that it was their duty to "Stop wasting your money! . . . go all out to support your own kind." There is no evidence that the Nation's farm workers fared any better, "supporting [their] own kind," than any other farm workers in the country, and there is no evidence that the Nation didn't benefit from their work to the same degree that other farmers did.

13.

After Elijah died, it was a little bewildering to discover that most of the Nation's properties were owned not by the Nation of Islam but by Elijah, willed to his children, an estate variously estimated at $40 million to $100 million. As if that weren't strange enough, the properties were all tied up in trusts, some of them blind trusts, and—the last straw— much of the property was facing bankruptcy. Even though some of the property was susceptible to civil action, the family has so far avoided any charges, but at this writing, in the summer of 1996, they still had not straightened out all the problems of the estate. Farrakhan's lawyers were able to make some arrangements with the Muhammad family that enabled him to buy, at cut-rate prices, not only the massive Chicago mosque but a variety of other Nation businesses and real estate. Farrakhan had another advantage: the Muhammad family and the Farrakhan family have so happily intermarried over the years that the Farrakhans have been able to further benefit from Elijah's large network of financial dealings, though the records of the contemporary Nation of Islam holdings are as complex as many privately held businesses, despite the fact that the Nation is a not-for-profit and therefore public corporation.

14.

Louis Farrakhan came out of a reasonably nurturing, stable, educative, pious background. He had been an acolyte in an Episcopal church, had graduated from the second most prestigious high school in Boston, had spent two years in a reasonably respectable college, and was a highly trained musician. How could it have happened that he was seduced by some of the most hare-brained theories of his or any time, theories that allegedly explain most of the ideas we live with? It is hard to realize that Farrakhan is still seduced by the ideas of his mentor which defy the imagination of all but the looniest.

Of all of Elijah's ideas that have grabbed Farrakhan over the years, perhaps the looniest is his theory of the origin of man.

Wait! Didn't the Victorians call Charles Darwin's and Alfred Russel Wallace's theories of the origin of man loony? Or worse?

Yes, but Darwin advanced an idea that had been floating around for nearly half a century without the empirical evidence to verify it. Darwin provided evidence but was still cautious, like most scientists. Elijah Muhammad was not a scientist and was not the least bit tentative in his ideas. But he did know more than might be expected of someone with a fourth-grade education. What is most interesting about Elijah's theory is not so much its absolute looniness but the extraordinary quality of the imagination involved, and the way he mixes his tiny bits of scientific and historical information with his vast imagination. He manages to ignore completely the actual passage of time in order to create a theory of human origin that makes Genesis look like the work of amateurs. That Farrakhan embraced this theory tells us either that, as Aeschylus said, "Words are the physicians of a mind diseased," or that Farrakhan too is a man of great imagination. For the unlettered to embrace Elijah's ideas is not surprising; they are filled with the kind of race pride and venom against the white race in which the uneducated victim of racism would find a haven. But for the educated these words are either a miracle of invention or simply words to cure a diseased mind.

For all his education, Farrakhan may not have understood all the subtleties involved in his mentor's theory about the origin of man. He may simply have accepted them as the words of the Messenger of God. But Farrakhan certainly knew, as he regularly retold the story of the creation as invented by Elijah, that for his black congregants it was a far better story than the one they'd been told in their Christian churches, a far more intriguing story than he'd grown up with in his own St. Cyprian's Episcopal Church in Boston.

Here is a brief synopsis of that story as told in *Message to the Blackman*:

"It is Allah's (God's) will and purpose that we shall know ourselves. . . . He has declared that we are descendants of the Asian black nation and of the tribe of Shabazz. . . . Originally, they were the tribe that came with the earth (or this part) 66 trillion years ago when a great explosion on our planet divided it into two parts. One we call earth and the other moon. . . . We, the tribe of Shabazz, says Allah (God), were the first to discover the best part of our planet to live on. The rich Nile Valley of Egypt and the present seat of the Holy City, Mecca, Arabia.

"The origin of our kinky hair, says Allah, came from one of our dissatisfied scientists, 50,000 years ago [about fifteen thousand years preceding Cro-Magnon man], who wanted to make all of us tough and hard in order to endure the life of the jungles of East Asia (Africa) and to overcome the beasts there. But he failed to get the others to agree with him.

"He took his family and moved into the jungle to prove to us that we could live there and conquer the wild beasts, and we have. So, being the first and the smartest scientist on the deportation of our moon and the one who suffered most of all, Allah (God) has decided to place us on the top with a thorough knowledge of self and his guidance.

"We are the mighty, the wise, the best, but do not know it. Being without the knowledge, we disgrace ourselves, subjecting ourselves to suffering and shame."

Now, that's one part of Elijah's overall theory, very briefly stated, that accounts in general terms for the origins of man. But to this general theory Elijah has a number of emendations. The most important, most widely told in the Nation, with some variations from the original as it appears in *Message to the Blackman*, follows here:

"Our 66 trillion years from the moon has proven a great and wise show of the original power, to build wonders in the heavens and earth. Six thousand years ago, or to be more exact, 6,600 years ago [shortly before the Egyptians began to build their wonders], as Allah [this Allah is Fard, Elijah's Allah, not the Allah of Islam, though he never troubled to make the distinction] taught me, our nation gave birth to another God whose name was Yakub. He started studying the life germ of man to try making a new creation (new man) whom our twenty-four scientists had foretold 8,400 years before the birth of Mr. Yakub, and the Scientists were aware of his birth and work before he was born, as they are today of the intentions or ideas of the present world.

"According to the word of Allah to me, 'Mr. Yakub was seen by the twenty-three Scientists of the black nation, over 15,000 years ago. They predicted that in the year 8,400 (that was in our calendar year before this world of the white race), this man (Yakub) would be born twenty miles from the present Holy City, Mecca, Arabia. And, that at the time of his birth, the satisfaction and dissatisfaction of the people would be:—70 per cent satisfied, 30 per cent dissatisfied.

"And, that when this man is born, he will change civilization (the world), and produce a new race of people, who would rule the original black nation for 6,000 years (from the nine thousandth year to the fifteenth thousandth year)."

Yakub began his evil process of creating a new race of people that would take over the world when he was only six years old and was sitting happily in the street in Mecca one day, playing with two pieces of steel. Not iron, steel. "He noticed the magnetic power in the steel attracting the other. He looked up at his uncle and said, 'Uncle, when I get to be an old man, I am going to make a people who shall rule you.' The uncle said, 'What will you make; something to make mischief and cause bloodshed in the land?' Yakub said: 'Nevertheless, Uncle, I know that which you do not.'"

Yakub grew up to be a genius and a divine. "At the age of 18, he had finished all of the colleges and universities of his nation, and was seen preaching on the streets of Mecca, making converts [Elijah doesn't say which religion Yakub is preaching]. He made such impressions on the people, that many began following him." He was also called the "big head scientist" because he had an unusually large head.

From his laboratory studies of "the germ of the black man," Yakub reasoned that if he could successfully separate the black germ from the brown germ he had seen under the microscope, "he could graft the brown germ into its last stage, which would be white. With his wisdom, he could make the white, which he discovered was the weaker of the black germ (which would be unalike) rule the black nation for a time until a greater one than Yakub was born."

After serious political altercations with the king (similar to those of Jesus with Pontius Pilate) that landed him in jail, Yakub managed to convince the king not only to permit him to go into exile but to provide passage and basic necessities for twenty years for him and his 59,999 followers. Yakub and his followers sailed, Elijah said, to an island in the Aegean Sea that he called Pelan. There is no such island recorded anywhere; but Elijah said the name was the equivalent of Patmos, an island where, according to the New Testament, John went to receive the word of God and the testimony of Christ and to write "The Revelation of St. John the Divine."

Three questions arise here: first, the Aegean Sea is quite a distance from Mecca. Elijah doesn't say how those sixty thousand people traveled across twenty-five or so miles of barren land of Saudi Arabia to get to the Red Sea and then up a long stretch of it, across more land, and then across the Mediterranean Sea to the Aegean. He just said they set sail. In fact, he said, "After they were loaded into the ships, Mr. Yakub examined each of them to see if they were 100 per cent with him; and to see if they were all healthy and productive people. If not, he would throw them off. Some were found to be unfit and overboard they went."

Which brings us to question two: the Red Sea is much closer to Mecca than is the Aegean; even in those days it wasn't much of a trek. Did Elijah choose the Aegean for Yakub's destiny because he didn't know his geography, or did he choose it because the Aegean was later, some thousand or so years later, the center of classical Greek culture? Did Elijah choose an island in the Aegean Sea because it was part of the heart of Western civilization, the source of white American government and political thought? Because it was a strangely appropriate place for the evil black scientist to carry out his experiments that resulted in the white race. Imagine that! The blacks created not only the white race but the cradle of Western civilization.

Third question: why did Elijah choose this particular Greek island, which acquired so much Christian holiness, for his devil Yakub's evil deeds? And why did he rename the island with a name that doesn't appear anywhere else? Why indeed? What better place for the evil black scientist to create the white race than on this island that is one of the revered sites of Christianity, where the Eastern Orthodox church has had a shrine for centuries, where some believe Mary may have died, and where St. John is known to have died? And this name of Pelan? Did Elijah get it from Pelion, a mountain in Greece, which, according to *Webster's New World Dictionary*, was a site in Greek mythology where the Titans attempted to "reach and attack the gods in heaven"? Well, that's as good a possibility as any, certainly worthy of Elijah.

Was it pure serendipity that enabled Elijah Muhammad to put all this together? Fat chance! This was the man who created an allegedly not-for-profit multimillion-dollar network of businesses in the name of the Nation of Islam that ended up in his own name. This is the same man who claimed to have read a variety of obscure books in the Library of Congress revealing the early American history of slavery.

In any event, when Yakub and his party arrived on Pelan, he first set about getting himself crowned king. Then he "chose doctors, ministers, nurses and a cremator for his top laborers. He called these laborers together and told them his plan for making a new people, who would rule for 6,000 years." Then he started working on his plan. Hitler would have scoffed at it because it took six hundred years. Slowly he manipulated the marriages and births of his 59,999 people so that eventually all blacks were eliminated. Like breeding peas. "After the first 200 years, Mr. Yakub had done away with the black babies and all were brown. After another 200 years, he had all yellow or red, which was 400 years after being on 'Pelan.' Another 200 years, which brings us to the six hundredth year, Mr. Yakub had an all-pale white race of people on this Isle. . . . The Yakub-made devils were really pale white, with really blue eyes; which we think are the ugliest colors for the human eye. They were call[ed] Caucasian—which means, according to some of the Arab scholars, 'One whose evil effect is not confined to one's self alone, but affects all.' [Arab scholars wrote that?]

"There was no good taught to them while on the Island. By teaching the nurses to kill the black baby and save the brown one, so as to graft the white out of it; by lying to the black mother of the baby [saying it was dead], this lie was born into the very nature of the white baby; and murder for the black people [was] also born in them—or made by nature a liar and a murderer." One of Elijah's—and Farrakhan's—best-known *cris du coeur* is how whites are by nature liars and murderers.

These new white devils (Elijah gives no figures) were now instructed to go back among "the Holy people of Islam (the black people) and cause all kinds of chaos. 'When you go back to the holy black nation,' Yakub taught his devils, 'rent a room in their homes. Teach your wives to go out the next morning around the neighbors of the people, and tell that you heard her talking about them last night.

" 'When you have gotten them fighting and killing each other, then ask them to let you help settle their disputes and restore peace among them. If they agree, then you will be able to rule them both.' " And this is how the whites came to rule the blacks. Except there's a hitch. The king got onto the white devils and told the blacks to " 'Gather every one of the devils up and strip them of our costume. Put an apron on them to hide their nakedness. Take all literature from them and take them by way of the desert. Send a caravan, armed with rifles, to keep the devils going westward. Don't allow one of them to turn back: and if they are lucky enough to get across the Arabian Desert, let them go into the hills of West Asia, the place they now call Europe.' . . . Yakub's race of devils were exiled in the hills and caves of West Asia (now called Europe). They were without anything to start civilization and became savages. They remained in such condition for 2,000 years—no guide or literature."

But Allah wasn't about to abandon those poor people forever. After two thousand years he sent Musa (Moses) to bring the white race "again into civilization: to take their place as rulers, as Yakub had intended for them." Moses taught them all about civilization, but "They were so evil (savage) that Moses had to build a ring of fire around him at night; and he would sleep in the center of the ring to keep the devils from harming him. They were afraid of fire, and are still afraid of fire."

This story goes on and on, with all its convolutions and complexities. The serpent raises his ugly head at some point. History moves along until "The heads and bodies of the so-called Negroes are used to test the clubs and guns of the devils and yet the poor, foolish, so-called Negroes admire the devils regardless to how they are treated." But the future will change all that. Just as Egypt suffered the ten plagues before the Jews finally escaped their torments, so "America is now under Divine Plagues. One will come after the other until she is destroyed. Allah has said it."

This has been a highly abbreviated version of Elijah's story of the origin of man, which has been taken from a written version of that story published in 1992 by a Muslim publisher, United Brothers Communications Systems (recently changed to Brothers and Sisters), edited by "Brother" Khalif Khalifah, from what are clearly a variety of pieces published in the newspapers and magazines of the Nation and first published as a book in 1965. Only occasionally in this text is it clear that Elijah was a very rough, barely literate speaker. Reading it over, suddenly, I feel as if a great ox stands on my tongue.

But no such need for silence confronts Minister Farrakhan, who is a much more literate but much more profane speaker. Elijah spoke like a slightly demented, uneducated Southern saint. While Farrakhan does sometimes speak as if he were only a slightly better-educated son of Elijah, he is, for the most part, smooth and literate—"The Charmer," as he was known as a singer in his youth—but he is rarely saintly; he prefers, in his speeches, to "kick butt." As much as he publicly rejoices in and defers to the memory of Elijah's ideas, he has no visible attachment to the Master's style.

At no less than Princeton University, in one of the many speeches he has given as leader of the Nation and as Elijah's representative, Farrakhan gave his own version of Elijah's theory of the origin of man, sometimes dressed up with what appears to be a little more formal learning, at other times designed for his less literate audiences. For instance, he told the Princeton audience in 1984, "The Honorable Elijah Muhammad said that the Black man is the original people of the earth. There were no other people on the earth before us. Races began from us. We are not a race, we are a nation. We are alpha and omega, you can take it or let it alone. It is a mathematical, biological, genetic impossibility for two whites to produce anything other than themselves, they cannot produce Yellow, they can't produce Brown, and they sure can't produce Black, but the Black man can produce it all. [The crossbreeding among blacks, whites, Indians, and so on for four hundred years has indeed produced a wonderful range of colors, but "all"?] This is why Dr. L. S. B. Leakey, the great anthropologist, when he wanted to find the beginnings of man, he didn't go to Europe, he didn't go to Asia, he didn't go to South America, he went to Africa, and there he found the bones of a man he called 'Zinjanthropus' which means Black man. [No source I know of gives that definition.] He said that those bones were 750 thousand years old [in fact Zinjanthropus is now generally known as *Australopithecus boisei* and is thought to have lived 1.75 million years ago, though much of Leakey's work is controversial] and that man had a daddy, so he went back looking for some more bones.

"He found the bones of a man over three million years old [actually it was Mary Leakey who made this find], and the man was not Caucasian he was Black! [How is such a distinction made from a few bones?] You are the ancient builders of civilization. Before there was civilization, you were there, and when civilization was built, your fathers built it. The early Caucasian people who met your father were too respectful of them to call them 'nigger,' because we were their teachers! We gave the Greek philosophy. We gave Aristotle and Pythagorus mathematics. We gave the world medicine, and history, and biology, and science." Well, that's a little embellishment and a little distortion, perhaps just right for a black Princeton student audience which included a fair number who hadn't studied much anthropology and wanted to believe that blacks were really the early intellectual leaders of the world.

But Farrakhan also left out the best, most imaginative parts of Elijah's theory. He talked about how the blacks gave the Greeks their philosophy, but he didn't talk about Yakub and his 59,999 followers on the island of Pelan.

That was at Princeton, an audience consisting of Muslims come to hear their leaders, and students and assorted people come to hear what Farrakhan had to say. Yakub wasn't for Princeton—too much of a stretch. But back home in Chicago at the mosque and elsewhere around the country when he talks to the down-home crowd, he says, " . . . On the island of Pelan . . . Listen, the Honorable Elijah Muhammad taught us about Yakub and how the devil was made. And when he [Elijah] got him on the island every laborer that worked to form the white race was a liar and a murderer, so that lying and murdering was right in the nature of the child that was produced on the Island of Pelan." But even when he is talking to the uneducated, Farrakhan leaves out some of Elijah's poetry. He doesn't say that blacks were on earth 66 trillion years ago. Is he afraid that today's illiterate audience might not be quite that ignorant, or does he find this claim too patently ridiculous? Or does this claim not fit his own poetry?

15.

The basic message—blacks were the makers of civilization, including the races of humanity—is always there. Farrakhan knows that Elijah created some of the world's great myths and that those myths are at the heart of the Nation of Islam, just as the Resurrection of Christ is at the heart of his Anglican church. He has to keep repeating these myths, though his versions are often cut short and often changed to fit the scene. But just as Elijah continually deferred and referred to Fard as his God, so Farrakhan does the same for Elijah. It seems that religion can thrive only on the myths of the past and the authority of the dead prophets, and the success of a religious group depends on how well those myths are retold and how well the new leaders capture the sacred essence of their gods. It will be interesting to see how the Nation fares as Farrakhan departs from the philosophy of Elijah.

16.

Given the fact that Farrakhan deifies Elijah, just as Elijah before him deified Fard, it is surprising that Farrakhan indeed departs from Elijah in some very important respects. And given the fact that Farrakhan clearly has ambitions for himself far beyond the narrow lines drawn for the Nation by Elijah, it is one of the puzzles about Farrakhan that one continues to find so many of Elijah's wacky ideas still receiving prominent attention and support in the Nation. Take the "Mother Plane," for instance.

Exactly when Elijah first propagated his own explanation of UFOs is not known. Judging from an article reprinted in the *Final Call*, Elijah first wrote on UFOs in one of his columns in one of several black newspapers in which he appeared in the late fifties and early sixties, before the start of *Muhammad Speaks* (he wrote in the *Pittsburgh Courier*, the *New York Amsterdam News*, the *Los Angeles Herald-Dispatch*, which the Nation dominated for a time, and others). His only known preserved explanation of UFOs appears in what seems to have been an earlier article in *The Fall of America*, published first in 1962, fifteen years after the first report of a sighting of what was then often called a Flying Saucer, today generally called an Unidentified Flying Object. No doubt the article has been unearthed (pun intended) plenty of times since, but the July 1996 reprinting was either the mark of the true believer or the mark of a true huckster.

How could the editors of the *Final Call* resist it? There they were surrounded by all the hype surrounding the Hollywood release on July 4, 1996, of *Independence Day*, a movie about an invasion from outer space with all those UFOs—and all those huge audiences, some of whom read the *Final Call*. Could the paper miss such an opportunity to present Elijah's version of the story of UFOs? (And Farrakhan's, but that's another story.) And, in addition, to take the opportunity to point out that the Nation is in the foreground of a great American groundswell that seems to be hopelessly warning that the U.S. government has long been withholding information about UFOs from the American public? Even former president Jimmy Carter, who himself sighted a UFO in 1974, was unsuccessful in his effort to "make every piece of information this country has about UFO sightings available to the public," the *Final Call* complained in its editorial on July 16, during the *Independence Day* hubbub.

Elijah had nothing to say regarding government secrecy about UFOs; that bit of pixilation was still ahead when he was writing. In fact, Elijah didn't expect God ever to give any of this information about UFOs to whites. This was strictly for the benefit of blacks. But in the end what Elijah had in mind was much simpler: he wanted people to embrace Allah and follow his commandments to avoid the use of UFOs, which would bring the end of the world.

It wasn't that Elijah was the first to see the "flying saucer" as God's wrath against a sinful world. He learned about it from the prophet Ezekiel in the Old Testament. Elijah just embellished Ezekiel's ideas a bit, bringing them up to date, so to speak, with what he envisioned as a few twentieth-century scientific additions, plus some racial ideas and some prophetic ideas of his own.

A careful reading of the Old Testament will reveal Ezekiel's astonishment in discovering that God had sent into the sky something that appeared to have wheels and wings, and "the living spirit *was* in the wheels." It had "the appearance of the likeness of the glory of the LORD."

The *Final Call* quotes Ezekiel 1:20 to say, "Wherever the spirit would go, they would go, and the wheels would rise along with them, because the spirit of the living creatures was in the wheels." That's not exactly the King James version, which says, "the wheels were lifted up over against them," more in the spirit of God's awful revenge against the Jews, but the basic idea is there: that flying chariot, as Ezekiel saw it, and those words of Ezekiel that the *Final Call* editorial used for its title: "Oh wheel!"

The purpose of the paper's editorial was to give the Nation's take on UFOs, that the government is withholding information because it may be engineering them itself. More important, the government knows these craft may be "designed for the destruction of this world," as Elijah Muhammad predicted. Following the editorial are two pages devoted to reprinting "The Mother Plane," in which Elijah prophesies that "The Mother Plane was made to destroy this world of evil and to show the wisdom and mighty power of the God Who came to destroy an old world and set up a new world." This new God is, of course, "Allah (God), Who came in the Person of Master Fard Muhammad, to Whom all praises are due forever." This plane is "The same type of plane used by the Original God to put mountains on His planets. . . . [It] was used before the making of this world." Elijah said Fard told him that "The Mother Plane is capable of staying out of the earth's gravity for a whole year. She is capable of producing her own sphere of oxygen and hydrogen, as any other planet is able to do.

"The Mother Plane carries the same type of bomb on her that our Black scientists dropped on the planet earth to bring up the mountains out of the earth after the planet earth was created.

"The knowledge of how to do this has not been given to the world (white race), nor will they ever get this knowledge." While knowledge of this formidable object, about which Elijah writes in great detail, cannot be given to whites because they are evil, Elijah doesn't say that blacks will get this knowledge either. Exactly what the fate of this plane is he doesn't seem to know. He says, at the end, "O wheel, made to rock the earth and to heave up mountains upon the earth. O wheel, destroyer of nations. No wonder the prophet Isaiah prophesied that the 'earth shall reel to and fro like a drunkard. . . .' [Is. 24:20]. Let us seek refuge in Allah (God) from the destructive work to come from this Mother of planes." If you think about it, this isn't much different from the apocalyptic thinking about UFOs among any number of evangelical Christians, including Jimmy Carter.

On the other hand, this version of Elijah's view of UFOs is a rather tepid, wishy-washy version which corresponds to what might be called "mainstream" UFO thinking. In *Message to the Blackman*, where Elijah also expresses his ideas about the Mother Plane, he makes clearer what he thinks this UFO business is all about: "Woe, woe to America!" he says. "Her day is near, and she shall be visited. Your enemies warn you that the third and final World War will be decided in your own country and not in theirs. . . . Your scientists are troubled and at their wits' end to find time to make ready, as it is written [by Ezekiel 21:15]: 'I have set the point of the sword against all their gates; that their heart may faint, and their ruins be multiplied. Ah! it is made bright, it is wrapped up for slaughter.' . . . The non-Muslim world cannot win in a war against Allah the great Mahdi, with outer space weapons or inner space weapons. It does not matter, for He has power over everything—the forces of nature and even our brains. . . . You don't need Navys, ground forces, air forces, standing armies to fight this last war. What America needs to win is to give freedom and equal justice to her slaves (the so-called Negroes). This injustice to her slaves is the real cause of this final war."

There is some question whether Elijah really believed there were such things as UFOs. There is no doubt in my mind, at least, that the Mother Plane was another of his glorious metaphors, and that he would have enjoyed immensely the response of his successor to the hype about *Independence Day*. What an opportunity to poetize about the state of the world!

But he would have been disappointed that his successor, whom he didn't choose, lacks a keen grasp of metaphor. (His son Warith [Wallace] Deen, whom he did choose, doesn't do so well in this area either.) Farrakhan doesn't seem able to invent metaphors, which leaves the Nation poorer than it was. But he also sometimes gets confused about what is reality and what is fantasy. How much of what he does is opportunism has eluded most of those who have tried to figure it out. His response to the hype about *Independence Day* is a typical example.

Farrakhan not only keeps alive the words of Elijah but amplifies them, in the tradition, if not so poetic, in which Elijah amplified the words of Ezekiel (or other biblical figures on other occasions). Farrakhan gave a speech at the Mosque Maryam, for instance, on June 9, 1996, preceding by about a month the release of *Independence Day*, entitled "The Divine Destruction of America: Can She Avert It?" In it he claimed to be quoting never-before-heard words that Elijah told him and others thirty-one years earlier, words of revelation about the coming destruction of America. Perhaps these words are indeed new ones from Elijah, suddenly found, or perhaps Farrakhan thought they were so explosive he shouldn't share them before now. Or maybe they were among the millions of words Elijah published here and there over the years that Farrakhan figured would not be recognized, as indeed they probably wouldn't be. Or maybe these are Farrakhan's own words being passed off as his mentor's. Elijah certainly wouldn't have disowned them. The idea of the destruction of the white world because it is so evil was not exactly new to him.

Then, after his momentous speech, slightly more than a month later, and twelve days after *Independence Day* had been released, on July 16, a large section of the *Final Call* was devoted to the subject. First came the editorial. Then came the edited, shortened version of Elijah's article. Then a reprint of Farrakhan's Mosque Maryam speech. And then an ad for the videotape of this speech, advertised as an opportunity to "Hear words of revelation from The Honorable Elijah Muhammad [the name in boldface type] that were spoken to [all in bold face] The Honorable Minister Farrakhan and others nearly 31 years ago which have never been revealed before." Elijah would have loved it all.

But on that advertising page, prominently displayed in the lower right-hand corner, alongside the ad for the video, we find something that would surprise Elijah, evidence that his successor has at least momentarily joined a different world. Farrakhan is not content for his readers simply to have the God-given words of Elijah. It's all very well to put some of our trust in these saintly words, but the world is changing. Now we must also educate ourselves with more worldly, more scientific information. So, along with the offer of the video for "The Divine Destruction of America" is a recommendation by Farrakhan that "encourages us to read and analyze, 'Above Top Secret—The World Wide U.F.O. Cover Up'" [in bold face] by Timothy Good with a foreword by the former Chief of Defense Staff, Lord Hill-Norton, G.C.B. This book is not about Allah. Nor is it a book about justice for blacks. This book is part of the "mainstream" UFO literature, the part that clearly "renders under Caesar's the things which are Caesar's." For this group the U.S. government has all the options, which it is holding dear.

This is no longer a case of dramatic metaphor, it's a case of the Nation of Islam participating in what is clearly a white scamper—to win readers, because God knows there will always be gullible blacks who fall for the whites' games. Elijah surely would turn in his grave.

(Among the variety of such books, Good's book is fairly popular. While my local suburban library has only one copy of it, it is still circulating. The Chicago Public Library and its multiple branches own ten circulating copies, all of which were out when I checked. One reference copy at the central library circulates for one week at a time while the library holds your library card. A large Barnes & Noble bookstore in Chicago still had, in mid-1996, two copies on the shelf, a rarity for a book published in 1988. All of which tells us that anything written on this subject is bound to find a good audience, even if the author does not grace the pages of any normal biographical source, and if his publisher provides no information about Mr. Good or Lord Hill-Norton, G.B.C., who is obviously a former chief of defense staff in England at some unspecified time.)

The Nation has come a long way in its acceptance of white ideas since Elijah wrote about the Mother Plane.

17.

Elijah believed that blacks could thrive only if they were separated from whites. No matter what benefits might accrue to blacks in association with whites, in the long run they could only be injured by that association, let alone the monstrous integration that was promulgated by Martin Luther King, Jr., and his colleagues in the fifties and sixties. Not only was this integrationist movement founded on the false premise that blacks could benefit from it, but, perhaps even worse, it was founded on the Christian premise that justice could be won by "turning the other cheek" and loving one's enemies. It was precisely Fard's repudiation of these ideas as those of the "slave philosophy" that was the basis of the Nation. Fard's repudiation in turn led Elijah to the conviction that "there is no indication that the white man will—or even desires to—treat the so-called Negroes equally. It is not in his nature to treat you or even his own kind right; it cannot be done."

Martin Luther King's remarks upon accepting the Nobel Prize rejected black supremacy along with white, and was therefore the subject of a scathing comment by Elijah. In *Message to the Blackman*, Elijah said, "Reverend Martin Luther King, Jr., the 1964 Nobel Peace Prize winner, would have honored himself and his people if he had refused the medal." He then went on to quote King, saying, "Too many of our white brothers are only concerned with their economical problems, their social status, their political powers and their so-called way of life." Following this, clearly taking the lines out of context, Elijah then went on to say, "Of his own people he said, 'We must not seek to rise from a position of disadvantage to one of advantage, substituting injustice of one type for that of another.' I have never heard of any such talk coming from a leader's mouth in all my life. If a man is NOT going to rise from a position of disadvantage why is he preaching for the passage of the Civil Rights Bill for his people? No wonder he had the privilege of going into a cathedral where no so-called Negro had ever stood in the pulpit."

When Dr. King spoke, as most Nobel Peace Prize winners do, idealistically and a bit loftily of how humans should love and expect love, should have a desire for justice and an expectation to rise above the mundane, these were sentiments that the always cynical Elijah Muhammad would sneer at. His reply to King was, "Since Allah revealed the very nature of the Caucasian race—that they are devils—there is no way of changing them. . . ."

Elijah never changed his mind. In a 1973 edition of *The Fall of America*, quoted from by Arthur Magida in his book *Prophet of Rage*, Elijah said, "Good man that he was, Rev. Martin Luther King, Jr. was deceived and frightened to his very heart by the enemy. . . . He gets no credit for all of the work that he did for his enemies, and his enemies know that. . . . You must put self first. . . . You cannot serve two masters."

But that philosophy had put Elijah in a bind. By the time Malcolm died in 1965, Malcolm had had a meeting of the minds with King. And when Malcolm was murdered, many members of the Nation, in agreement with him about King, left. Elijah's position on integration and Dr. King meant that he was more widely than ever shunned by black leaders, including many black ministers. Only a handful of nationalists, who gained some attention in the late sixties and later, supported him. He had painted himself and the Nation into a corner. He could only demand of whites or of the government the same demand he'd been making for years: land, onto which blacks could go and live separately. He was cut off from any of the new deals offered by the government in the interests of his people. Nor could he use the political arena, as other blacks were trying to do. Didn't all the changes taking place in the country make a difference to him? Not from what he said. He scorned all such efforts. While opportunities for blacks opened as never before, Elijah's philosophy prevented him from doing anything but watching. But there's no evidence he was bothered, and the practical evidence seemed to indicate he was right, that the Nation wasn't suffering from the isolation he had created for it.

He didn't seem to care that his separatism served as a deterrent to many people who might have joined the Nation and enhanced its stature and wealth—that whole class of young people who were beginning to take advantage of new opportunities. Those who were looking outward from the black community into white universities and colleges, corporations, law firms, and hospitals were not likely to be attracted to an organization committed to a separatist philosophy in which no other ideas were tolerated.

It didn't help that Elijah's attitude toward these young people was to call them dupes of the whites. They might briefly prosper, he told them, but it would turn out to be an illusion.

Generally speaking, these young blacks were also deterred by the autocratic structure of the Nation in a time when individual freedom was having great currency. Many of them had attended meetings at mosques, curious to hear the famous Elijah Muhammad speak. It hadn't endeared them to the Nation to be searched before they could enter and to be, as they sat listening, surrounded by grim-faced, white-gloved guards and to see the podium filled with these guards, more formidable than the Secret Service men who normally surround the President of the United States when he goes out to speak in public.

These potential members were also deterred by the great variety of rules that Elijah adapted and expanded from the early rules set down by Fard—rules about food, dress, and almost every aspect of life. Some of them may have read in Malcolm X's *Autobiography* about the strict religious routines, adapted from the Islamic rituals, performed several times daily in the home of Malcolm's brother, routines that only the most devout could consider living with, which would leave out the majority of Americans (Europeans as well). And they might have been put off by the atmosphere in the mosque, so different from the churches they were used to where there was always a sense of gaiety: singing, often very expert and inspiring singing, and a shared feeling of enthusiasm which some might regard as a certain kind of holiness, something missing from the mosque as it was missing from most white Protestant churches, and quite different from the traditional Islamic mosques that engender intense, if largely silent, religious feelings. What prompted the structure and atmosphere of the Nation of Islam mosques, called temples at first, was the intense desire by Fard and Elijah to escape the atmosphere of what they considered those blue-eyed, devil-inspired black Baptist churches that so evilly misled their people. All that singing and recitative, though they might have been spontaneous enough, were truly "the opiate of the people" and were not to be duplicated in the temples of the black Muslims.

Those visitors to the mosque who came to hear Elijah or some other well-known Nation preacher might also have been put off when the women were ushered to one side of the room and men to the other after they'd been searched. Part of this custom is pure traditional Islam—men and women must never be together in any public place, a custom considered weird and distasteful by most non-Muslims, black or white, around the world. But the body search is strictly Elijah's idea. Whatever justification is offered—fear of assassination being the paramount one—people resist being searched. One wonders, when the searches were initiated, what the real dangers were.

The search and separation, with the Nation's other harsh rules, remain among the strongest deterrents to membership. Many Americans see that kind of control as a form of tyranny. Any number of people I talked with told me that while they were sympathetic to the aims of the Nation, its religious and social structure prevented them from joining. Interestingly, however, while this highly autocratic atmosphere limits membership, it hasn't appeared to deter people by the tens of thousands from going to hear Elijah, Malcolm, and then Farrakhan. Over the years the crowds have grown ever larger. It's part of the often steep price of admission blacks have been willing to pay to hear what these divinely inspired *sansculottes* have had to tell them, what messages from God these prophets have had to deliver.

Elijah, and then Farrakhan, have also continued to attract large numbers to their membership rolls despite—perhaps because of—the

Nation's autocratic structure and demands. No one outside the Nation has any idea of its membership, past or present. No figures have ever been released. Most religious groups provide rough numbers to such semiofficial research sources as encyclopedias. Not the Nation. That would accord with Elijah's wondrous view of the white official world. "Why tell them anything?" Still, people do estimate. C. Eric Lincoln, for instance, in his *Black Muslims*, offered that sometime in the eighties "an estimate of between 70,000 and 100,000 seems consistent with what is known about other aspects of the community." What other aspects he doesn't say, but he is, after all, the historian of record on the black Muslims.

Knowing a little about the history of religion, one wouldn't necessarily expect autocracy and heavy demands on the members to lower membership rolls. But history is changing. On one hand, mainstream churches are trying to become more open, less autocratic, less demanding, to match the burgeoning suburban evangelical "pop Christianity" churches that specialize in openness and individuality. On the other hand, the highly autocratic and demanding Mormon church is the fastest-growing church in the world, with seven million members claimed in the 1995 *World Book Encyclopedia*. So it's pretty hard to choose between Lincoln's figures and those of the most recent, highly respectable *Encyclopedia of American Religions*, which claims that in 1989 the Nation had a membership of only five to ten thousand. That could be downright insulting. But Farrakhan seems immune to such insults, as his mentor was; he too ain't talking about his membership.

18.

Elijah Muhammad probably wrote all his adult life. The earliest recorded published materials seem to have been in the *Messenger*, a magazine started by Malcolm X in 1959 (but which faded quickly), and in the very popular and progressive black newspaper the *Pittsburgh Courier*, which published "Mr. Muhammad Speaks," a regular column by Elijah from 1956 until the paper was sold in 1959 to more conservative owners. The *New York Amsterdam News* published his column for a while, then dropped him. Malcolm X accused the editor of the *Ams-*

terdam News, James Hicks, of canceling Elijah's column because of pressure from advertisers. Nat Hentoff, in 1960 a young progressive reporter writing for the *Reporter* (it folded in 1968), asked Hicks about that. Hicks said, "scornfully," according to Hentoff, that "There was no pressure. We dropped him because he was so out of line with everything we thought. He can't get much more real strength. Two or three years ago he was gobbling up a lot of people around here, but he has almost all of those now who are willing to be blindly led. Most of the other Negroes are just watching him. And we've stopped giving him much publicity."

Hicks and several others who told Hentoff that the Nation, then called the Temples of Islam, didn't have much of a future obviously weren't in close touch with that part of the black community in Harlem and elsewhere that had recently emigrated from the South and were probably not regular readers of the *Amsterdam News*.

Elijah must surely have missed the popular New York paper's publicity, but soon enough *Muhammad Speaks*, the Nation's own newspaper, gained a large audience, and Elijah was writing away about everything. Many of those columns he wrote over the years, plus a variety of other materials, have been put together as several books. Along with nearly seventy audiotapes, they are sold regularly through *Final Call* mail-order ads and in bookstores that specialize in black publications. It appears that even in non-Muslim black bookstores, a fair number of people continue to buy Elijah's books, a very small survey revealed. The Afrocentric Bookstore, for instance, in the heart of Chicago's Loop, keeps a regular stock of several of his titles.

That Elijah has always written mostly in metaphors hasn't seemed to bother great numbers of people. And that his rhetoric is often so overwrought that it's not much more believable than his metaphors seems not to trouble people either. In 1960 Nat Hentoff wrote, "It is difficult to be certain how much of his own inflammable rhetoric he believes." The same remark might as easily have been made at any time in Elijah's adult life. How many other people believed his rhetoric is also hard to figure out. It's impossible even to guess how many people thought about him as Reverend Ralph Abernathy did when he told Hentoff, "I don't think the Negro has time—or needs—to apologize for the crackpots in his community. We have a right to our crackpots as you do to yours."

But there were, in the seventies, possibly a hundred thousand blacks who did not view Elijah as a crackpot, and today a large number still revere him as God's messenger. More than that, an alleged half-million readers of the *Final Call* may still read his writings every week. Farrakhan and his editors clearly believe their readers want to see what Elijah has written. And they believe readers want to see the famous picture of Elijah wearing his embroidered fez. Each week, in columns or ads, Elijah's picture graces the pages of the paper six or seven times, by comparison with the ten or eleven times Farrakhan's picture appears. All of this may seem overdone for a newspaper, but this one makes no claims to provide "All the news that's fit to print." What it says on its masthead is "A Message Dedicated to the Resurrection of the Black Man and Woman of America and the World. Published by Minister Louis Farrakhan, National Representative of the Honorable Elijah Muhammad and the Nation of Islam." Given that announcement, why would anyone be surprised to see so many photos of Farrakhan and Elijah in the paper?

19.

At the risk of overkill, I can't resist the temptation to provide just one more example of Elijah's illustrious image-making which typifies a regular weekly feature of the *Final Call*. It is an excerpt from his book *How to Eat to Live*. It prescribes fasting, which is an important element of Islamic law, all of which Fard first and then Elijah freely adapted for their own theology. Here Elijah says, "Fasting is a great act upon true Believers of the true religion of God (Islam). This also helps prolong our lives." Elijah explains that the Koran prescribes that all Muslims fast during Ramadan, the ninth month of the year. He doesn't bother to explain that Muslims fast during Ramadan because it was the month when the Koran was revealed to Muhammad. But his followers don't need to know that. They only need to know what he tells them.

Now Elijah prescribes that his members fast *not* on Ramadan but in December (this excerpt appears in the July 30 issue of the *Call*). Fast in December? No stuff-yourself Christmas dinner? No turkey? No dressing? No mashed potatoes? No cranberries? No pumpkin pie?

You've figured out that Elijah would say, "This month I prescribe for you to fast . . . for the purpose of getting you away from the false teaching of the Jesus' birth on the 25th of December." But it's not so simple as just avoiding Christ's birthday. Elijah explains, "This day . . . He taught me was the birth date of that demon Nimrod, who was born in the Seventeenth century of Moses' era before the birth of Jesus. . . . He was so wicked that the scholars and scientists of scripture of the prophets do not like to teach you of this history of Nimrod."

Should we fast on the birthday of this evil man? It gets more complicated. Elijah says, "And, if it was the birthdate of that righteous prophet Jesus, you certainly in your celebration of the 25th of December have not been showing a clean and holy celebration of a righteous person with your drunkenness and your gambling. Your everything but right [sic] is committed on the 25th day of December in celebrating the birth of a righteous man. But, you are not doing so for righteousness, you are celebrating the birth date of an evil person and the white Christians will send you all the whiskey and beer and wine and swine that you want to eat and drink on that day." In other words, white Christians are really celebrating Nimrod's birthday, but they are conning the blacks, telling them they are celebrating Jesus' birthday.

Concluding, Elijah says, "The Muslims, as I foresaid, do not eat nor drink from before sunrise until after she (the sun) has set. If you take it (the fast of Ramadan) with them, you are doing the right thing, until this evil world has vanished." The question is, if a devout member of the Nation fasts on Ramadan, must he then also fast in December? Elijah leaves us dangling about that. But since this article is being published in July, many people won't worry about it. The bigger question is, why didn't Elijah explain that Muslims end their Ramadan fast with a huge, joyful three-day feast? All he says is that at dusk one may eat.

20.

These few examples from the heavy plate that Elijah set before his people in the forty or so years that he ruled the Nation of Islam do not begin to tell the story of this extraordinary figure. Whether it was important to Farrakhan to deify him in order to reconstruct the Nation for his own purposes, or whether Farrakhan actually believes in the sanctity of Elijah, is unknowable. But the fact is that Elijah is the central godhead of the Nation. No further proof is necessary than the masthead and back page, since its founding in 1981, of every issue of the *Final Call*, which had been the name of a paper founded and published for a short time by Elijah in 1934.

Within heavy black lines around the back page, and featuring a large picture of Elijah, is "The Muslim Program." On the top half of the page is "What the Muslims Want." On the bottom half is "What the Muslims Believe." At the very bottom is a line that says, "He Lives." Point 4 of the first half of the program begins, "We want our people in America whose parents or grandparents were descendants from slaves, to be allowed to establish a separate state or territory of their own—either on this continent or elsewhere."

This is just one of several points in Elijah's program that Farrakhan never mentions in his speeches. But he continues to publish the program, unedited, to tell the world what the Nation is and what it stands for. Farrakhan didn't know his biological father; we have to wonder whether his awesome devotion to Elijah may not be Farrakhan's massive compensation to himself for that earlier loss, that he may have felt a huge hole in his soul where that father's love should have been. His spiritual father has received far more veneration than any biological father could have hoped for.

21.

Through the last ten or so years of Elijah's life—from the early sixties to 1975—he lived mostly in a house he had built in Phoenix, Arizona. There he nursed a case of severe asthma after he was advised to leave the fiercely cold winters and humid, hot summers of Chicago. But he kept in very close contact with the leadership in Chicago and elsewhere, a large share of whom were his sons and sons-in-law, especially after the death of Malcolm in 1965. There are conflicting reports about how much control he exercised in those years. For instance, Arthur Magida, in *Prophet of Rage*, reports that Elijah failed to control violence in the Nation allegedly described by disgruntled former members and from police and FBI reports.

Reports of disgruntled members may have some basis in fact. Attacks on organizations by former members are not always the result of personal grudges. Sometimes they are based on facts. On the other hand, all too often police reports are not. Much of Magida's book is concerned with the violence of the Nation, for which he offers no reliable documentation. Unfortunately, most of those who write about violence among blacks learn all too quickly not to trust FBI and police reports, and at least to question attacks on organizations by disgruntled former members. Still, all the reports Magida quotes from may be true. Perhaps, without Elijah's firm control, the Nation experienced a lack of discipline, including the use of coercion and violence by the Fruit of Islam. After all, many FOI members had been street thugs and ex-cons, and the Nation was very slowly, almost imperceptibly coming apart at the seams.

Despite what appeared to be a dangerous split in the Nation during Elijah's battle with Malcolm in 1964–1965, Elijah managed to survive intact and to go on to build an even larger organization. Some people were upset by what Malcolm claimed were Elijah's extramarital affairs, and left to join Malcolm's organization. But for most members, Farrakhan and others soon enough straightened out the whole matter: Malcolm was a liar.

Meanwhile Elijah was failing. He could handle fewer and fewer of the Nation's obligations of the organization—a highly autocratic one with few decisions made at lower levels. One of the most crucial of these decisions was the succession. A large contingent, led rather forcefully by Farrakhan, fully expected him to be named heir. After all, he was the national representative, presumably the closest man to the top. He was the head of the most populous mosque outside Chicago—Harlem. Farrakhan seemed to have no competition. None of the sons and sons-in-law had shown anything like his leadership. He had for some time been drawing huge crowds when he spoke. The traditionally most likely heir, the eldest son Wallace, had been excommunicated by his father three times. He had publicly repudiated his father's ideas in favor of those of traditional Islam.

But those close to the Muhammad family knew weeks before Elijah died that the Nation would stay in the family. No one knows exactly how soon the bad financial news began to leak out, but by the time that happened the Nation's members had already been shocked to learn that Elijah's family would inherit a considerable financial empire. Those thousands who had given their nickels and dimes, their dollars, and occasionally much bigger bucks, would never see a return on their investment except the pleasure of knowing they had helped build the largest black-owned business network in the country. Plenty of Elijah's followers may have been disappointed they would not share in the returns, yet they were proud their great leader had ended his life as a rich man.

Many of the twenty thousand or so members who had come from around the country to attend a Saviour's Day celebration, and ended up mourning his death on February 25, 1975, were willing to forgive his transgressions. They were even willing to forgive his throwing them wherever they might land when he gave the Nation to his openly rebellious son. And only a couple of years later, even when they learned of the financial mess he had left behind, many of them quickly showed their reverence for Elijah when Farrakhan told them that Elijah had spoken to him and urged him to take up the mantle and recreate the Nation that Wallace had dismantled. Many of them were just waiting for the word to believe that Elijah was immortal. And now a whole new generation looks to the spiritual and social leadership of Elijah through his messenger, Louis Farrakhan.

Part Four

SEEKING ACCESS

1.

Secrecy as a major mode of operation in organizations goes back to early civilization. Throughout the world, at some time in history, in some local tribe, a man, often a male child, has had to swear an oath of secrecy in order to be inducted into his society. Secrecy has sometimes been close to the sacred, and in some groups to violate it has meant certain death. Even today the fraternal orders of the Masons and the Elks, for instance, consider their secret rituals close to the sacred, though one wouldn't lose his head if he violated their oaths.

Far from sacred, intelligence agencies operate much like ancient secret societies, and evidence has surfaced from the files of the Soviet secret police that violation of its secrets did bring death. For years rumors have circulated about the fates of intelligence officers in other countries as well, including the United States. Whether such executions actually occur in the Western world, John Le Carre, the former English spy turned spy-story writer, tells in his 1995 novel *Our Game* about the addictive power of secrecy in the spy community and about how, when they are forced to give it up, spies feel bereft.

Secrecy plays a strong role not only in intelligence but in all kinds of government activities. "National security" is an expression so widely accepted in the United States for just about any government activity that when it is challenged or violated, it is viewed as a national calamity. All too often, though, there is no justification for the secrecy, as occurred in 1969 when the Supreme Court decided that the government had unjustifiably used the shield of national security to try to prevent the *New York Times* from publishing what became known as the Pentagon Papers. New York Senator Daniel P. Moynihan wrote in his introduction to the 1996 edition of *The Torment of Secrecy*, by Edward A. Shils, that in 1994 the Information Security Oversight Office of the U.S. government reported 4,773,897 official secrets. These are best understood, Moynihan says, as a "form of regulation" by a huge bureaucracy which acts almost outside human reason, but which he nevertheless views as "unfailingly public-spirited," an idea many would disagree with. But the idea of government agencies as secret societies that serve nearly sacred purposes of their own is not far from reality.

Secret societies, including all kinds of official ones, have, in other words, a special cachet that carries universal appeal, from the boys in *Tom Sawyer* to the spies in *The Secret Agent.*

(I do wish to make clear that in this discussion of shared secrecy in an organization, I am not referring to the *privacy* valued by most individuals for themselves, even if that need for privacy is, as with some people, more extreme than we might consider within the realm of common sense. The secrecy I am interested in here has to do with groups, with camaraderie, and with the shared knowledge of a symbol system that is for the privileged members only. This symbol system provides a special status that offers an enhancement, sometimes a very crucial one, of personal identity, not very different today from the secret societies of preliterate peoples. Le Carre's description of the psychological disintegration of the spy deprived of his secrecy is a good example.)

Until fairly recently, women were generally excluded from this tradition, as they were from so many others, though some anthropologists insist that matriarchal societies, which would likely have had their own secret societies, preceded the patriarchy. But women did occasionally form their own secret societies. In 1851, for instance, at Wesleyan Female College in Macon, Georgia, a few courageous Southern "belles" joined to form the first sorority, a secret society for women. Their courage ran out when it was time to name their society, and they called it the Adelphian Society, which, ironically enough, roughly translates from the Greek to mean brothers' society. The ladies were not quite ready to compete with their male brothers by using the Greek letters normally associated with fraternities, their male opposites and the source of their rebellion, after all. It took about fifty years for the Adelphian Society to bring itself to adopt a Greek-letter name, Alpha Delta Phi. In 1913, having discovered that a fraternity already had that name, they dropped the h in phi, and today Alpha Delta Pi has 133 chapters in the United States and Canada with 140,000 members in 1996.

2.

That the Nation of Islam has over the years become more and more of a secret society accounts for part of its fascination, especially because black Christian churches have historically provided to their members identity only as anonymous congregants of the great amorphous open church of God. "Blessed is he that cometh in the name of the Lord." That's it, there isn't much more. True, the black church was separate from the white. But it was nonetheless under that great Christian umbrella that was founded and run by whites and had justified slavery not secretly but quite openly, like everything else in the church. It was white even when it was black. The Nation offered an antidote. To make it more appealing to blacks, the Nation offered a new kind of church, a secret society that, with Louis Farrakhan, took on more secrecy as the years passed.

Like certain other organizations, such as the American Communist party, the Nation has justified its secrecy in part by arguing that its ideas clash with the status quo, therefore its members need to be protected from the government. Throughout much of its history in the United States, the Communist party kept secret its own identity and the identities of its members, who usually took aliases. The group used "front" organizations, like false names, to carry out its activities. Unfortunately for them, the FBI managed to penetrate their secrecy all too often, and many of them went to jail, lost their jobs, or were deported or even electrocuted. There is no evidence that the U.S. government has acted against members of the Nation with anywhere near the same ferocity, but the harassment the Nation has experienced does help to explain its obsession with secrecy. As recently as mid-1996 a controversy between a mosque located in the city of Inglewood, California, which serves as the central Nation headquarters in Los Angeles, and its landlord brought out the Bureau of Alcohol, Tobacco, and Firearms, the FBI, the Los Angeles County Police, including a Special Weapons and Tactics Team (SWAT), and the Inglewood police in response to the landlord's request for help with the eviction of the Nation.

Why the Waco-like response to a landlord's call for help with an eviction notice involving a religious center for a group of black Muslims, about whom there is no prior knowledge that constitutes a danger to the community? Muslims don't use guns. They don't drink. They are admonished not to swear. Small wonder that the Muslims maintain strict secrecy among themselves.

On the other hand, while it is easy to see how such occasions would engender fear, it is also true that the fear about such attacks expressed by the Nation appears to be at least exaggerated. The fear is used to justify the secrecy because, as with most secret societies, the secrecy itself provides the magic. An example is the stone wall of secrecy I encountered when I tried to get a copy of the book *Supreme Wisdom*, strangely attributed to Master Fard, founder of the Nation, instead of to its author, Elijah Muhammad, the founder's successor. No one would sell it to me or tell me anything about it except to say it is a secret book that only members are permitted to read. Why this secrecy? Having seen a bit of the book quoted by C. Eric Lincoln in 1960, before it became a secret, it was pretty clear to me that nothing in this book would vindicate such secrecy. Clearly it became at some point a special, privileged token of membership in the Nation.

3.

Having for years encountered the cloak of secrecy with which the Nation surrounds itself, I had little hope that Farrakhan and his lieutenants would be willing to talk with me. It was mid-1994, when Farrakhan was beginning to reveal what seemed like grandiose plans for a million-man march to be held the following year. It was a full year before he would decide to make a deal with a writer to put together his autobiography and try to sell it for $6 million. But he had opened himself to occasional interviews and had appeared before the editorial boards of several newspapers and occasionally on radio and television. Some white reporters even scoffed at him as a publicity seeker. So I hoped I might gain access to him. Some of the people I had talked with, who knew him well, had assured me he would want to see me.

I wasn't as sure as my friends were. I wasn't sure they were seeing what I was seeing as serious obstacles. This wasn't to be a mere interview for a newspaper or magazine, or a brief appearance on television or radio. This was to be the first full-length biography of him in which he would confront a journalist who would press him to reveal himself. (As it turned out, this was the second biography to appear.) This journalist was also a Jew, against whose people Farrakhan had displayed a good deal of rage; she was a woman, about whose peers Farrakhan had a good deal of ambivalence; and perhaps most important, this journalist was known in Chicago as a liberal integrationist, one of the few whites in town to write regularly and extensively about blacks, about which Farrakhan might feel resistant. While he had long since stopped calling Martin Luther King a traitor, and had in fact changed his line considerably, he still could not be described as an integrationist and would be unlikely to want someone with such ideas writing his biography. Finally, he wouldn't be the first black who thought whites couldn't and shouldn't write about blacks.

Don't be silly, those friends of Farrakhan assured me. He's a bright—some said brilliant—broad-minded man. He'll want to talk with you.

So I wrote him. I laid it all out: a proposed outline of the book, a full resumé, and copies of my most recent book and a much earlier one that I thought might interest him, namely a political biography of the first black Chicago mayor, Harold Washington, who had died in 1987. I also mentioned the names of some people who had offered to supply character references. And I asked some of those who claimed to have his confidence to put in a word for me.

I was hopeful. In his *Black Muslims*, C. Eric Lincoln had warmly praised Farrakhan's cooperation with his research. In fact he credited Elijah, Malcolm X, and Farrakhan (who had been Louis X when he met him) as his major sources since the late fifties. On the other hand, Lincoln was a black man, in the fifties affiliated with a black college, whose sympathies to the Nation are evident in his book. And when I called Lincoln to request an interview, he turned me down, saying he was too busy. That made me nervous. Would Farrakhan turn me down too?

4.

It was time to begin arranging interviews with people who could tell me about Farrakhan. I started with people who were not members of the Nation but who were close enough to Farrakhan to be able to speak keenly about him, either pro or con, some of whom I knew well and who had already agreed to talk with me.

I began in Chicago partly because I was there and partly because Chicago was Farrakhan's home base. His national office and his newspaper offices were there. His major Mosque Maryam was there. I called about two dozen people, most of whom agreed to talk and some of whom referred me to others. Every writer expects to encounter some people who refuse to be interviewed. Every journalist makes certain pro forma calls or writes certain letters with a full expectation of being turned down, merely to have those calls or letters on the record. But I was not prepared to be turned down by some of the people on this project who either refused to speak with me or simply didn't return my phone calls. I had expected some of them to be among my most interesting informants. There was nothing apparent about them that prepared me for their responses.

First was the white radical Roman Catholic priest—short, slight, dour-looking—the Reverend Michael Pfleger, who presided over an all-black South Side parish church in Chicago and was widely respected by whatever was left in the city of a left wing. I had seen him numerous times on the streets for one or another liberal cause. He had been, for instance, one of two or three enthusiastic speakers who stood on a wintry night in early 1991 at a downtown rally to protest George Bush's curious war against Iraq. It didn't seem to trouble Pfleger, as he yelled into a megaphone, that he was speaking to no more than a hundred people and no media. Pfleger is a man of deep conscience and commitment, never an altogether popular type but a rare find in the nineties. He was well known for his antidrug program in his neighbor-hood, and he was one of two whites regularly to be glimpsed at Far-rakhan's side or in his entourage.

I viewed Pfleger's support for Farrakhan as that of a man who saw himself as the lone surviving maverick priest, standing in for all the white priests, ministers, and rabbis who had marched and preached in black churches and in civil rights demonstrations in the sixties. They weren't much in evidence now, though there were still some who sup-ported mainstream black activists. But they rejected Farrakhan. Pfleger stood alone, at the side of this fiercely antiwhite, anti-Christ-ian, anti-Semitic preacher. Here was a strange and not easily under-stood dedication. But over the years I'd met any number of strange, not easily understood white clergy, and some black clergy as well, on Martin Luther King's pro-integration staff. Now a couple of those black clergy, among the strangest in the sixties, were strongly support-ing Farrakhan. Reverend James Bevel was regularly writing in the *Final Call* some of the highly peculiar things he'd been saying in the sixties. I wasn't surprised to read his pronouncements in the Nation's paper or to read that the idea of atonement used by Farrakhan in his Million-Man March originated with Bevel.

But Bevel was black, a Baptist, and had been an obvious zealot for thirty years. Pfleger was a younger man, white, and a Roman Catholic priest, which generally meant that one exercised some caution, some hesitation about offending the church.

So I couldn't wait to talk to Pfleger.

When I called him at his church, St. Sabina's, his secretary took my message. He never returned any of my numerous phone calls to the church office or the rectory.

How can I express my dismay? I was dying to ask him so many questions. Was he a loyal papist who easily supported Farrakhan's op-position to abortion and contraception? Or did he withhold his sup-port from Farrakhan on these issues because he was among the radical Catholic clergy who opposed the pope's positions?

And how did this radical priest handle the tirades against Jews and whites that were such a regular feature of Farrakhan's extravaganzas? Did he counsel Farrakhan against them? Or did he just put his fingers in his ears so he couldn't hear them? Or did he listen hard and then re-peat, for his Sunday morning sermons at St. Sabina's, the same kind of "analysis" he'd heard from Farrakhan, such as the 1987 speech called "How to Give Birth to a God," in which Farrakhan said, "The white man can't help himself. He has wreaked more havoc on this Earth than any people in the annals of history"?

What did Pfleger think about that proclamation in later-twentieth-century America? If it's history Farrakhan is teaching, as he claims, he should teach history. If it's hate he is teaching in order to instill in his followers the will to help themselves, what does Pfleger think about that tactic? Or about teaching hate for any purpose?

And what of Farrakhan's attacks on Jews? I badly wanted to know how this highly respected and progressive priest viewed Farrakhan's ferocious anti-Semitism. How did Pfleger feel about the efforts of his church, with some minor deviations, to atone for the damage it had done to the Jews for nearly a millennium? How did he square that with Farrakhan? Did he accept Farrakhan's claim that his attacks on Jews, like his attacks on whites, were not expressions of bigotry but of mere "truth-telling"? Did Father Pfleger, for instance, agree with Farrakhan's defense of his attack on Israel in an audience at Morgan State University in Baltimore in 1983, when he said, "I did say that, that nation called Israel has not had any peace in forty years. Stop, did I lie? Has Israel had any peace in forty years? I said she will not have any peace, because there can never be any peace structured on injustice, thievery, lying, deceit, and using God's name to shield your dirty religion under his holy and righteous name. . . . This is what I said, not of Judaism, but of the state of Israel and Zionism."

It would have been fascinating to know what Father Pfleger thought about all this. While it would certainly tell me a lot about himself, it was what it would have told me about Farrakhan that I wanted. What was there about Farrakhan that could attract and sustain the loyalty of this radical white Catholic priest? Unfortunately Pfleger wouldn't tell me. It was only months later that I decided he had called Farrakhan when he received my numerous messages and been asked not to talk with me.

Meanwhile I tried to remember ever calling a priest or minister or rabbi to ask for an interview and not even receiving a civil reply. I couldn't remember a single instance. I didn't know then that Pfleger would be just the first of several white clergy who had had various kinds of associations with Farrakhan and who would refuse to talk with me. In fact, of the seven or eight I called, only one agreed to an interview, and he was not the forthcoming rabbi I had expected. Farrakhan was not yet nearly so famous as he would soon become, but his treatment of white clergy apparently was such that these people, civil as they normally were, refused to talk with me about their experiences with him and their impressions of him. Interesting that black clergy had no hesitation about talking with me. They were, it turned out, enthusiastic about Mr. Farrakhan.

Another refusenik whom I finally reached after about three weeks, but only for a minute, was Haki Madhubuti, formerly known as Don Lee, who in his youth had been a highly regarded black poet and a dedicated follower of Malcolm X. Although he had never joined the Nation under Elijah, objecting to Elijah's authoritarianism, Madhubuti had nevertheless strongly supported it as had most Black Nationalists while Malcolm was in control. With Malcolm's assassination, Madhubuti and other Black Nationalists withdrew their support.

For years Madhubuti had run a small publishing house in Chicago, Third World Press, which printed the work of black writers, including his own, and the Institute of Positive Education, a "resource center" for Black Nationalism.

In 1977–1978 Madhubuti helped Farrakhan (then known as Abdul) reestablish the Nation after Elijah's son had disbanded it following his father's death. Madhubuti and a group of Black Nationalists assisted Farrakhan in a variety of ways, including money, after he assured them that the new organization would be more open, more democratic than it had been under Elijah. Madhubuti reports this in "The Farrakhan Factor," a chapter in his 1994 *Claiming Earth*. Ignoring those assurances, Farrakhan proceeded to rebuild the Nation in the authoritarian image of Elijah. When his intentions gradually became clear, Madhubuti withdrew his support and since 1979 had spoken to Farrakhan only once.

Although he had regularly raised questions about Farrakhan's leadership among his colleagues, especially about his role in Malcolm's death, Madhubuti had made no public statements about Farrakhan until 1993. When he did he was excoriated by Farrakhan's spokesman. In his 1994 book Madhubuti described his doubts about Farrakhan, saying, "My final concern is the lack of open and honest criticism of

Minister Farrakhan and the NOI from those of us who helped him to rise again."

Many Black Nationalists who worried among themselves about Farrakhan's influence nevertheless withheld public criticism and in fact often gave him public support. Even as Madhubuti voiced his concerns in *Claiming Earth*, he took care to insist that the white criticisms of Farrakhan were racist and that Farrakhan wasn't entirely wrong in his attacks on Jews. On this latter point, Madhubuti, like so many other Black Nationalists, couldn't resist his own criticism of the Jews, much milder than Farrakhan's but still based on anti-Semitic legend, which made it difficult for him to criticize Farrakhan for his more virulent anti-Semitism.

Madhubuti refused to talk to me; he had said all he cared to say in *Claiming Earth*. I ventured that there were questions that went beyond his cautiously written twenty-seven pages on Farrakhan in the book. "I have nothing more to say," he said, and hung up. The fact that I had been referred to him by one of his Black Nationalist friends cut no ice.

Another who didn't want to talk with me was a well-known and apparently well-loved elderly black Jewish South Side restaurateur, Prince Asrael Ben Israel, who seemed to be a jolly fellow. He agreed to see me almost immediately, even insisted on sending his car for me because he didn't want me to be traveling alone in his neighborhood. Then, two days later, his secretary called to break his appointment. She promised to call again but never did, and he never returned my own persistent phone calls. When I called, his secretary always told me he was out of town. Why did he change his mind? My referrals had made it clear that he had a close relationship with Farrakhan. So, for Farrakhan, apparently black Jews hadn't the same stains on them as had white Jews. Did Prince Asrael believe that white Jews were different from black ones? I wouldn't find out.

Perhaps Father Pfleger and Prince Asrael and the others who would not talk with me hadn't accepted the people who referred me to them as trustworthy. Or, as I suggested earlier, perhaps they had asked Farrakhan and he had advised against seeing me. Or perhaps they were afraid. The Nation had created a tangibly threatening atmosphere against those who dared to question Farrakhan. Madhubuti quotes a rabid speech by Farrakhan's spokesman, Khalid Abdul Muhammad, in

1993 in New Orleans: "Some of you heard on the news that the skin-heads had put the Honorable Louis Farrakhan as public enemy number one on their hit list. Well, I think we need to pay the skinheads a visit. We should bum rush them. Black boot stomp their doors down and beat the hell out of every skinhead we can find and put our foot in their behinds everywhere we can find one just for the thought of attacking Louis Farrakhan, just for the thought of doing it.

"And these bootlicking Negroes. I understand that Haki Mad-hubuti, as much respect as I have for him, sent a veiled criticism at the Honorable Louis Farrakhan in the *Chicago [Sun] Times*. . . . Well we're tired and sick and tired of all these attacks that are coming against God's messenger and man in our midst today. And we say today that you're either going to start saying something good about Louis Farrakhan or you ain't gonna say nothing about him at all. You'll just keep his name out of your mouth."

Khalid spoke regularly in this vein in Farrakhan's name to black audiences in churches, on college campuses, and in city auditoriums. Even though there had been no physical attacks on Farrakhan's critics, it wouldn't be surprising if some folks figured it was safer not to talk with a Jewish woman journalist (Khalid also vilely attacked Jews).

On the other hand, their refusals may have been more philosophical. Perhaps they recognized the contradictions in their relationship with Farrakhan and didn't want those contradictions to be exposed, especially by a white. I was learning slowly, as I talked to people across the black community and even to some liberal whites, that most blacks, of all types—of all educational levels and professional levels—were intent on maintaining a solid front of support for Farrakhan. In their eyes he was the one leader in the black community who offered any real hope and help to the poor.

5.

As the weeks and then months passed with no response from Farrakhan to my persistent calls and to calls by others, it seemed clear to me that I would write this biography without access to the subject. Oh no, my contacts assured me, he was just a very busy man. Be patient, they insisted, Farrakhan will want to talk with you. If nothing else, he will welcome the publicity that such a book will provide.

Of course, most of these people rarely read Farrakhan's newspaper or his own books; some had never heard his public speeches. They were themselves very busy people. They knew him, and they'd been to his home for dinner. He was, like them, part of the leadership in Chicago's black community, some in the wider American black community as well. They broke bread together. And Farrakhan, like Elijah before him, was eager to share his hospitality with such people. It helped his aura. He seemed to have been so beguiling, so charming, so charismatic that those guests I talked with—all with positions of power in the city—never sensed, or at least did not admit, that they may have been used the way politicians so often use such people. They believed, or appeared to, that they had been invited as equals to break bread. They had felt like honored guests, though Farrakhan did most of the talking, and they didn't always agree with what he said. A guest doesn't criticize his host, does he?

But if they didn't know him intimately, as occurs often among community leaders, they had heard plenty about him. Word gets around fast when someone attracts 25,000 people who pay to hear a speech in Madison Square Garden. Or when about a quarter of all the blacks in Phoenix, Arizona—about 10,000—pay for a seat in Symphony Hall to hear Farrakhan speak. Or when similar outpourings occur regularly in all the major cities and on many college campuses. Farrakhan was drawing larger crowds than any other leader, black or white.

Word also spread of Farrakhan's successes with rescuing and converting prisoners, ex-cons, drug addicts, teenage mothers, and other criminal types. These were like the successes the Nation had long claimed under Elijah, that C. Eric Lincoln had accepted as bona fide claims without hard evidence, just as people today were accepting these claims though the evidence was vague. The strongest evidence the Nation ever supplied for its successful recruiting in the jails was the story of Malcolm X, who had indeed been recruited from a jail by his family with the special encouragement of Elijah.

If Farrakhan's successes were exaggerated, there was no one to contradict him. He issued no demographics, no information of any kind, and there was no way for anyone outside the Nation to know what went on inside. Ex-cons and drug addicts didn't wear badges. They cut their hair short and wore the same dark suits, white shirts, and bow ties that all the other men in the Nation wore. Surely it wasn't only the criminal types whose suits were poorly tailored and of cheaper fabric than others.

Were there really thousands or even hundreds of ex-cons in the Nation who were now going straight? Were there hundreds or thousands of converted drug addicts who had kicked their habits? Were former gangbangers now peacefully if rather aggressively selling the *Final Call* on street corners all over the country? Were converted teenage mothers now taking good care of their children? Had they stopped fornicating as Farrakhan directed them? No one outside the Nation really knew. And no one in the Nation was telling. But despite the absence of evidence, there was a general sense in the black community that the claims were true. Farrakhan had about him an aura of authority and honesty. And when you saw members of the Nation at a mosque gathering or even on the street, some of them showed in their faces and in their demeanors a fierceness—a saintliness, perhaps—that they shared with some members of religious cults; it said, "I've been saved." Others carried about them a dry sullenness that suggested a deep but controlled inner rage which one might associate with a history of criminality. Can one actually move from casual glances at people to a conclusion that many of them are converts from destructive to constructive lives?

It was also widely believed that the unarmed Fruit of Islam who were serving as security guards in some housing projects around the country were more successful than armed private security guards, because the FOI was composed of tough former convicts who could handle the gangs. Some residents declared that the FOI guards had indeed been more successful at preventing crime in the projects than private security guards. But that wasn't proof that the FOI guards were ex-cons. Perhaps they were just well trained. Judging from reports in the *Final Call*, the FOI had a strong training program.

But other project residents were not so enthusiastic about their FOI guards. They complained bitterly that the guards didn't show up for work, sat idly by as the gangs came and went, hassled tenants, even made deals with the gangs. That didn't indicate that the guards were ex-criminals either. It also didn't prove that the FOI hired ex-cons who were not members, as some who have opposed the hiring of the FOI have claimed. It didn't even prove that the guards weren't well trained. It did say that the FOI does not always supervise its workers well enough. As for evidence that the Nation has thousands of members who have been converted from horribly destructive behavior to living pure lives, the FOI guards don't tell us a thing, nor does any other such sign we might try to use. Ideally we should be skeptical of all such unproved claims, but as early as 1960, C. Eric Lincoln was according credence to these claims by quoting Nation leaders about their successes without offering a scintilla of evidence.

As I said earlier, it's easy to be seduced by appearances if you've been inundated by rumors. I soon concluded that the young Muslim who had been assigned by a Nation leader to drive me on some errands and then home from a meeting I'd had on the South Side was an ex-con. He was heavily muscled, looking quite uncomfortable in his ill-fitting cheap black suit. He told me he was twenty-one, a member of the FOI, assigned to the driving pool, and had been in the FOI a few months. The trip took about two hours. The young man sat beside me throughout that time without another word, without a smile. The only communication that passed between us were his grunts in reply to my questions and his unspoken but clearly stated sullenness and discomfort. It wasn't anger or resentment. This was his assignment, and he would carry it out. But he didn't have to like chauffeuring this white woman all over the white North Side, going where she told him to, waiting while she took her sweet time, did he? The last straw came when he had to come to my door to pick up a book for his boss. I invited him to come in while I went to find the book. He preferred to wait outside. When he was ready to leave, I thanked him for his service. He grunted.

When I went back into my house, I went with the firm conviction that he was an ex-con. This hadn't been a casual glance. I had watched his demeanor, his looks, his unspoken but clear attitudes for close to two hours. Was I so well acquainted with ex-cons that I'd know one when I saw one? Let's face the truth. The main reason I viewed him as I did was because of all the claims made by the leaders of the Nation, and by how much my driver resembled other of the Nation's members whose looks and demeanor my casual glances suggested could be ex-criminal types.

But suppose I was wrong. Suppose this boy had grown up in a devout Nation family. Or, with no criminality in his background, had been attracted to it just as Louis Farrakhan first was, by fiery speeches that said just what he'd been waiting to hear. Perhaps he was so muscle-bound because he was a health fanatic, lifting weights for instance, as Muslims are encouraged to be and as FOI members are trained to be.

Does it help Farrakhan and the Nation's image to encourage among its members the kind of secrecy about themselves that left me speculating so wildly about this young man? The kind of secrecy that leaves the Nation open to all kinds of rumors? If the goal is to maintain a closed society in which its members believe they benefit from their secrecy, then the answer is, of course, yes. And if the goal of the secrecy is have outsiders believe what the Nation chooses only to tell them, then the answer is again yes.

6.

While waiting to hear from Farrakhan I decided to visit Mosque Maryam, a huge former Greek Orthodox church on a main drag through Chicago's South Side, Stony Island Avenue. Elijah Muhammad bought it in 1972, just three years before his death and the subsequent dissolution of the Nation, after the neighborhood had become largely black. Elijah no doubt chose it because it looked vaguely like an original Eastern mosque. Vaguely, that is. It is an incredibly mongrelized building, with a slight suggestion of the traditional Byzantine style of both the Eastern Orthodox church and the Eastern mosque. It has arches and a central dome but is completely bereft of the colorful, elaborate ornamentation that characterizes the Byzantine style. The lone adornment, originally a double cross of the Eastern church above the dome, now is the Islamic star and crescent. The mosque is built on a rise with a great broad expanse of steps leading up from the sidewalks, and seats about two thousand people (my estimate). Next door to the mosque is the "university," the K-12 school, with its massive gymnasium where Farrakhan's speeches are broadcast to overflow crowds.

Upon Elijah's death, more than fifty of the Nation's properties in Chicago, and properties elsewhere, were left largely to his son Wallace, as if they were a family business. They carried an estimated $10 million debt. Sales for taxes, bankruptcy, and other redresses followed. With the cooperation of the executor of the estate, Chicago attorney Rufus Cook, Farrakhan was able to lay claim to some of the property, including the mosque. Finally, in 1988, Farrakhan was able to acquire the mosque for $800,000 and refurbish it as part of his plan to revive the Nation in Elijah's image, and to create an image of himself as the messenger of Elijah.

The occasion for my visit to the mosque came on an evening in the winter of 1995 when Farrakhan held a "press conference" there. He aimed to comment on charges brought by the U.S. attorney for Minneapolis that Malcolm X's daughter, Qubilah Shabazz, had hired a hit man to assassinate Farrakhan in revenge for his having murdered her father. Malcolm's wife Betty had long held Farrakhan responsible for her husband's death. It was incumbent on Farrakhan to respond: his life had ostensibly been threatened. He withheld comment on the charges for several days, though his lawyer had spoken, and then he announced this press conference.

I had somehow missed the time for the press conference. When I called the mosque to ask, I was told the doors would open at 7 p.m. Doors open? Sounded strange. It wasn't the kind of remark you'd expect from someone holding a press conference; it was what churches and other organizations say when they expect a big crowd for some public event.

When I arrived at seven, the steps leading up to the mosque, and the sidewalks and streets surrounding it, were filled with people. In just a few days Farrakhan had brought out a large crowd, obviously not your usual press conference, more like a political rally. Inquiring at the front door about entry for the press, I was referred to a line down the middle of the steps, a long line. Every major media plus a great many black community papers were there for this story.

It was slightly after eight before we were installed in the press gallery, a section of the balcony at the rear of the mosque. Some there were clearly not media; they were Nation members, silent, unfriendly, sullen-looking. Were they FOI guards? They wouldn't say. Farrakhan did have an uneasy relationship with the media, but what did he expect to happen in the press gallery that would require guards? Or perhaps these were simply young men curious about the press, like so many young people are. After all, this was their mosque.

In another thirty minutes or so, all the people outside were seated in the rest of the balconies and on the first floor of the mosque, and guards were stationed in the aisles every dozen or so rows apart. I learned later that while the people in the mosque were being seated, the overflow crowd was being seated in the school's gymnasium.

It had been quite an orderly process. People lined up, women on one side, men on the other, the media off to one side. The FOI guards stationed to search the crowd and guide it into the hall had been very efficient; in about an hour and a half they had thoroughly searched with metal detectors every person who was admitted, about 2,500. All cameras or tape recorders except those owned by the media had to be checked outside the hall. The media's equipment had to be checked before it was admitted.

Down in the heart of the mosque, in the very first row below the stage, were a group of recognizable Farrakhan supporters—Father Pfleger, a number of well-known Black Nationalists, a couple of Baptist ministers, and others, all standing around and greeting one another as they would at a festive or political gathering. On the stage of the mosque stood twenty-five or thirty people, including the ninety-six-year-old wheelchair-bound matriarch of the Nation, Queen Mother Moore, who had been flown into Chicago from New York with her aide for the event. When the program got under way, about six of Farrakhan's lieutenants and other dignitaries, including the aide who spoke for Queen Mother Moore, and a flock of guards prepared for Farrakhan's entrance.

At last, at about 9 p.m., amid wild cheering, Farrakhan, in a peach-colored suit and a handsome bow tie, with his well-oiled curly hair and wire-rimmed glasses, surrounded by his bodyguards and wearing a rapt expression of what seemed to be love and goodwill, took the podium. Alongside were his beautiful wife Khadijah and their five daughters, all arrayed in elegant, obviously handmade street-length long-sleeved dresses and headwear, the female uniform of the black Muslims. While his women stood severely at attention, with the other dignitaries and guards surrounding him, Farrakhan emoted for about an hour, describing the U.S. government's plot to frame Qubilah with the final intent of destroying him and the Nation and, by implication, the entire black people. He went on to explain all the plots that over the years the government had hatched against the Nation and other black organizations.

After this long introduction, he spoke personally and emotionally about the specifics of the case of the thirty-four-year-old Qubilah Shabazz. "Think of Qubilah," he intoned. "Qubilah is a child I knew and held in my arms as a baby. [Malcolm helped recruit Farrakhan into the Nation and remained close to him for years.] I do not believe that Qubilah is an evil woman—and in the numerous reports I have read, most people who know her do not believe it either. Qubilah is a child who loves her father, a child who grieves over the loss of her father's life; a life cut short *not* by Louis Farrakhan but by the same evil forces who throw stones and hide their hands, and who, like Pontius Pilate, wash their hands and allow just men to go to an undeserved destruction.

"I want my wife, Sister Khadijah Farrakhan, and my five daughters to come forward. . . . My wife is a righteous woman, my daughters are righteous young women. They do not engage in unlawful acts. However, I assure you that if anyone were to do harm to me, they would not hesitate to avenge me. And they would not hire someone to do it for them, they would do it themselves! I believe in my heart that no power but Allah (God) could stop them."

So, said Farrakhan, even if Qubilah conspired to kill him, she had to be understood and forgiven. More important, we had to understand that even if she had these terrible thoughts in her head, she was really innocent. She had been tricked and seduced by the government, which did this sort of thing regularly.

"The same government of the United States that did all of these things," he said, "created division within the Nation of Islam and exploited it, made the Nation of Islam and its leadership the number one organization targeted for destruction."

Farrakhan demanded loudly that the government's records of this case and other documents—those related to the trial of Marcus Garvey in the twenties, the assaults on the Black Panther party in the sixties, the deaths of President John F. Kennedy and Robert Kennedy and Martin Luther King, Jr.—be opened so that its role in these events could finally be revealed.

Now Farrakhan reached the high point in his speech, his explanation for the real purpose of the FBI in setting up Qubilah: the U.S. attorney needed to invent "the perfect situation" in which it could indict and convict Farrakhan for the killing of Malcolm. The crowd agreed. There was much shouting and stomping. "The government, even as we speak, is working feverishly to provide a basis to prosecute me, by gathering false witnesses, wicked demons and hypocrites, whose envy of my success and the success of the Nation of Islam is causing them to yield to the temptation to seek my death and destruction."

Farrakhan went on, "In view of all this . . . since all of the leaders throughout our history in this country have been subjected to government harassment and interference, I propose that we, as a people, file a class action suit, charging the U.S. government with the denial of our civil rights, the denial of our human rights, and open all files, with respect to the Honorable Marcus Garvey . . ." and a long list of people and organizations that stretched from the spectacular black singer/actor Paul Robeson, who was hounded out of the country by the FBI and the House Un-American Activities Committee in the fifties for his Communist beliefs, to Lyndon LaRouche, a highly eccentric fascist-tending white political leader who had an alliance with Farrakhan, as Garvey had an alliance with the Ku Klux Klan. LaRouche was convicted and jailed in 1989 for mail fraud and tax evasion. Last on Farrakhan's long FBI victim list was "their number one target, the Nation of Islam."

The opening of the FBI files on those people would indeed reveal what became some famous efforts to deny their civil and human rights by a variety of means. The audience was loud in support of Farrakhan. They were, after all, affirming their leader's life in the face of overwhelming danger.

According to the *Final Call*, the rally was "beamed live via satellite and carried live by 20 television stations and viewed live at 20 colleges around the country and heard on numerous radio stations." While the newspaper often exaggerates the news of the Nation, Farrakhan does have, as of mid-1996, about 135 hookups with radio and television stations (mostly cable) in major markets around the country and in Canada. The Nation either buys or is donated regular time, often several times a week, for his speeches, to advertise the *Final Call*, and to make fund-raising appeals. The listing appears weekly in the *Call*.

Sifting through Farrakhan's rhetoric, I found myself with an awful sense of *déjà vu*. How many times had I been in situations where considerable evidence had indicated infiltration, provocation, and frame-ups by the FBI? How many times had I read of such FBI actions against black and white dissidents, among them some that Farrakhan had listed, since the 1920s? Under all the paranoia and arrogance, wasn't there some truth in Farrakhan's charges against the FBI and the U.S. attorney? The charges against Qubilah didn't ring true, even if Farrakhan's conclusion that the plot was ultimately directed against him resembled all too many other of his delusions.

The problem was, who was Qubilah Shabazz? The thirty-four-year-old daughter of a long-dead black leader? Had the FBI actually targeted her as a public danger?

It didn't help my comfort level when I discovered that the famous radical civil rights lawyer, William Kunstler, and his New York-based Center for Constitutional Rights was handling Qubilah's defense. Kunstler's appearance on a case automatically raised questions about the government's role, though there had certainly been cases in which Kunstler had had to do a little defensive manufacturing of his own.

The evidence the government presented was, from the start, fishy. It had been supplied by the same FBI paid informer who just happened to be the very hit man Qubilah had allegedly hired. A coincidence? He just happened to be available to do this job for her and then went immediately to the FBI to tell them about it? Or did he make himself "available" for the job at the request of the FBI?

According to the *Final Call* of February 8, 1995, the Nation immediately responded to the U.S. attorney's notice that Qubilah was to be indicted with a *real* press conference at which Farrakhan's attorney, an Atlanta-based Nation minister and lawyer, Ava Muhammad, described a meeting she'd had with the FBI several months earlier at which the agency had warned her of a plot against Farrakhan's life by members of a Muslim extremist group. After that warning, the Nation had heard no more from the FBI, Ava told the press. "We were not aware of any ongoing threat [against Farrakhan] until yesterday, just prior to the indictment," she said. The FBI waited until the day before it indicted this would-be assassin before informing the intended victim?

Kunstler's cocounsel, Minneapolis-based Larry Leventhal (Kunstler died in late 1995, several months after the case was in effect settled), supported Ava. He said, "We have no evidence that the government had warned Farrakhan of this plot." He reiterated Ava's remark at the press conference that no evidence had been presented that Qubilah had been a member of any Muslim extremist group. In fact, he said, she tended to avoid politics because she felt too much was expected of her merely because she was Malcolm's daughter. Oh yes, she was having a romance with this proposed hit man, a friend from high school.

So what was this all about? If the informant had been feeding his bosses "evidence" that his girlfriend, Qubilah, was planning an assassination in which he would be the hit man, which is what the FBI claimed, why didn't the government (1) immediately arrest Qubilah, and (2) immediately warn Farrakhan? Could anyone take this thing seriously?

Apparently the FBI did. It seems that this informer, named Michael Fitzpatrick, went to the FBI with a story that Qubilah was talking about hiring a hit man to kill Farrakhan to avenge her father's death, a task he had agreed to do. She paid him $180, he said, a down payment for the hit. That's all she could afford at that point. The FBI, according to Fitzpatrick, paid him $45,000, in two payments, to tape-record his phone conversations with Qubilah about the potential assassination.

Now $45,000 is a small piece of change to the FBI when you compare it with the $5 billion *Newsweek* reported the FBI spent hunting down the Unabomber. Still, $45,000 for the tapes of a few staged phone calls about a murder the FBI already knew about seems pretty steep. And then you have to wonder about the government's indictment of Qubilah on the basis of Fitzpatrick's evidence. And on this heavy-duty murder-for-hire charge, Qubilah was released on an extraordinarily low $10,000 bond. It does make you think about Farrakhan's charges.

Four months later the U.S. attorney agreed to hold the charges against Qubilah in abeyance for two years. He promised to drop them at that time if no further evidence of wrongdoing was uncovered and with a promise from Qubilah to undergo two years of substance-abuse treatment. Oh yes, it emerged that Qubilah had a drinking problem.

This was certainly a graceful exit for Minneapolis U.S. attorney David Lillehaug, who had conducted this whole charade. As all informers do, Fitzpatrick disappeared.

To make this story even nuttier was to read a headline in the issue of the *Call* following Farrakhan's "press conference." "Government, Jewish militant target Farrakhan." Jewish militant? Qubilah's lawyers had exposed Fitzpatrick as a onetime member of the militant Jewish Defense League who had participated in a JDL bomb plot. Larry Leventhal speculated that Fitzpatrick had actually been an agent provocateur who had claimed to be Jewish in order to gain access for the FBI to the potentially violent JDL, and had proposed the bomb plot as provocateurs so often do.

But Farrakhan read the story differently. As suspicious of the FBI as he was, this was one story he didn't question. It worked well for him. The *Call*'s story opened with, "A Jewish militant with a history of violence is the key witness for the U.S. government. . . ." Adding this little fillip of alleged Jewish violence made the story much more exciting and dangerous, lending more credence to Farrakhan's paranoid delusion that the indictment of Qubilah was really a front for a government plot to kill him. And who better to kill him than a militant Jew with a history of violence named Fitzpatrick?

In the end, it seems improbable that this scheme was hatched by a highly ambitious U.S. attorney in combination with an equally ambitious FBI agent and a greedy FBI informer. It's just too silly. Unless Farrakhan's suspicions skirt close to the truth.

Try this scenario: If Qubilah were tried for an attempted assassination of Farrakhan, it would create a sensational case, lots of publicity, in which Qubilah's reason for having Farrakhan killed, namely to avenge her father's death, was at the center of the news. Farrakhan had long been suspected of killing Malcolm; it was old news. But now there was a new Malcolm X admiration society out there; perhaps lots of people would sympathize with his grief-stricken daughter. Maybe their sympathy would translate into rejection of this man who was attracting huge crowds, was in fact fast approaching the influence that Malcolm had had thirty years ago.

Pretty far-fetched? Sounds more like some of Farrakhan's rhetoric? Surely the FBI wasn't so stupid today; J. Edgar Hoover was long since dead. And thirty years after Malcolm's death? Unfortunately the story is not at all inconceivable. The FBI has gotten along quite well without Hoover. Consider the three-month personal surveillance—on the basis of the shoddiest of evidence—of the security guard Richard Jewell after the bombing in Atlanta's Centennial Park during the 1996 Olympics, when the FBI was forced to reveal to the nation that it had no real evidence against the man, not even a reasonable basis for suspicion. Or consider the FBI's role in the Waco, Texas, burnout. Or the totally unjustified killing of the mother and son of an admittedly crazy militia man at Ruby Ridge, Montana. As is so often said in law enforcement circles, a smoking gun is surefire evidence of criminal activity. Should we see these few blazing guns of the FBI as a few isolated incidents?

But you have to give U.S. attorney Lillehaug credit for the intelligence to get himself out of the mess with due haste.

The story was all over for the FBI, for Fitzpatrick, and for Lillehaug, but it wasn't over for Farrakhan. This government foul-up had given Farrakhan a golden opportunity. Almost as unbelievable as the FBI's shenanigans were the extraordinary unforeseen consequences of these events—scarcely a scene the FBI and Lillehaug would have imagined.

"A very meaningful and, indeed, historic moment," Mike Wallace of "60 Minutes" intoned during the event, as he was filming it for a segment of his program that aired on April 14, 1996. The event? A very public, very warm rapprochement between Farrakhan and Betty Shabazz, Qubilah's martyred mother, after thirty years of open and public enmity and separation. An event hardly to be equaled in enhancing Farrakhan's position among those who had scorned him all these years—many in the general black community, Black Nationalists, and large numbers of black Muslims who had been admirers of Malcolm—because Betty had accused Farrakhan of killing her husband.

On May 6, 1995, a few days after the U.S. attorney made his deal with Qubilah, her mother and Farrakhan appeared together at a rally at the historic Apollo Theatre on 125th Street in Harlem under a banner that said, "All praise is due to Allah, Celebrating Unity, the Hon. Minister Louis Farrakhan and Dr. Betty Shabazz." There they embraced each other and raised money to help Qubilah. And who arranged this grand and glorious reunion? The well-known Black Nationalist poet, publisher, and leader who hadn't spoken to Farrakhan for nearly twenty years, Haki Madhubuti. He told the *Call*, "It seems to me that one generation and a decade is enough time for us—outside the Shabazz family—to learn from the mistakes of history."

"There is a Chinese proverb that says, 'The journey of a thousand miles begins with one step,'" Farrakhan told the crowd. "The loss of the sacred life of Malcolm X is comparable to a thousand-mile journey that we pray Allah (God) will bless to end with total reconciliation of us as members of one family"—a 360-degree turn from what Farrakhan had been saying for thirty years, namely that Malcolm deserved to die for defaming Elijah's name. Malcolm's family and followers surely turned Day-Glo colors when Farrakhan referred to Malcolm's "sacred life."

Betty Shabazz replied: "I never expected whatever I experienced here today. . . . I would like to thank Minister Louis Farrakhan for his original, gentle words of assurance for my daughter and myself and her sisters. And for the suggestion of support, as he said, 'We will help brother Malcolm's family.' I like the way he said that. And I hope he continues to see my husband as brother Malcolm."

The government's foolish attack on Qubilah had created for Farrakhan a long overdue opportunity. Over the years Malcolm had become a sacred hero to black youth. Even white youth wore the X. It was time for Farrakhan to join them. The *Call* reported in its issue following the reunion, "The Apollo meeting between Dr. Shabazz and Min. Farrakhan is a first step toward healing deep wounds felt in the Black community and personal pain shared by the Shabazz and Farrakhan families. The 1965 assassination of Malcolm X left a stain on the entire Nation of Islam, created confusion over who ordered and took part in the assassination and left Blacks choosing sides." Now blacks would no longer have to choose sides.

Once again Farrakhan had displayed his uncannily clever ability to figure out how to use the white power structure to reinforce and broaden his position in the black community. What crowing must have occurred at the Farrakhan dinner table when he returned to Chicago!

7.

After three months I was ready to give up trying to gain access to Far-rakhan. All my phone calls to the Farrakhan headquarters had gone unanswered. Then, two days after I had made what I viewed as a final appeal, to Reverend Herbert Martin, a well-known and highly re-garded nondenominational black minister who had also served in Mayor Washington's administration, and who had refused to denounce a fierce black anti-Semite, I received a brusque phone call from Claudette Muhammad, Farrakhan's chief of protocol. With no expla-nation, she told me I was to come at 10 a.m. two days hence to the din-ing room of the Ramada Inn, a popular meeting place on the lakefront in the Hyde Park–Kenwood neighborhood. It was clear that Claudette was used to giving orders and not being questioned.

The Ramada Inn is miles away from the mosque and other Na-tion buildings. It is located in one of Chicago's upscale neighborhoods, not far from the University of Chicago. Many of the city's black elite live there, including Farrakhan, who bought from Elijah's estate the ugly, heavily secured, television-monitored, nineteen-room yellow brick mansion that Elijah had built for himself in the late sixties. At the time he had also built several smaller matching houses along the same street for his adult sons, plus one that he sold to Muhammad Ali, the beloved boxer who was a revered member of the Nation, partly be-cause he helped so generously to fill its coffers. Elijah's son Herbert earned millions of dollars after he took over Ali's management when Ali joined the Nation.

This meeting at the Ramada Inn was, I supposed, to be an initial meeting with Farrakhan in a neutral place. Why a neutral place? Why a public restaurant? Why not at least one of the private meeting rooms at the inn? Wouldn't it have been just ordinary business procedure to see me in his office? Or did he know something about me that pre-vented him from inviting me into that inner sanctum? Was this casual brunch with me just to get Reverend Martin off his back? I was pretty nervous. Little did I suspect how nervous I should be.

Claudette was there when I arrived. She was a large handsome woman arrayed in a colorful, carefully tailored African outfit she had had made recently, she told me, on a trip to Ghana with Farrakhan.

She traveled with him regularly. She also wore a great variety of hand-made bone and wood jewelry that she had bought in Ghana. She car-ried a stuffed leather briefcase plus some smaller leather carriers, as if she had come to have a portentous meeting with me or had several more ahead of her, or perhaps just because stuffed leather briefcases are believed to make people look important.

Soon after, not Farrakhan but the chief of history for the Nation, Jabril Muhammad, a small, slight, balding man wearing a handsomely tailored light brown double-breasted suit, a printed bow tie on a white shirt, and maroon boots, came along. No briefcase. I did a double take. This wasn't Farrakhan. On the other hand, I'd never been this close to Farrakhan. Maybe he looked different across the table. No, it wasn't Farrakhan. Jabril introduced himself as Farrakhan's closest ally for forty years. He lived in Phoenix, Arizona, where I knew that Mosque No. 32 had been Elijah's last stand. Jabril came to Chicago regularly to confer with Farrakhan, who had asked him to meet with me, presum-ably to advise him about whether he should give me a hearing. He was to take my measure.

I was to get to know Jabril Muhammad much better in the months to come by reading his regular columns in the *Final Call*. At this point I hadn't learned to distinguish one Muhammad from an-other among the profusion of them who edited and wrote for the paper. But I picked out his byline quickly after that meeting and gave careful attention to what he wrote, though this was a mighty chore. He contributed a regular column, a page or longer, called "Farrakhan the Traveler," in which he sought to prove that Farrakhan was divine. Nu-merology played a large role in this, as it so often does in prophecy, as it does in the Nation, and as it has in several ancient religions. So did history, if sometimes very distorted and sometimes highly original. Jabril was, after all, the Nation's "historian."

As an example, for no apparent topical reason Jabril took upon himself, in the March 6, 1996, issue, the task of examining history to answer charges that Elijah Muhammad was an immoral man because he had a horde of "wives." Jabril began with a reference to a "writing titled 'Truth Is Stranger than Fiction,'" which he said offered "a view of the domestic life of the Honorable Elijah Muhammad which is in sharp contrast to that which has been given to the public for years." (Actually, hardly anyone outside the Nation has given any thought to

Elijah Muhammad and his many infidelities and illegitimate children for years, but that would have been irrelevant to Jabril. His "public" is the Nation and its sympathizers, and to the members of the Nation, Elijah is still alive.)

One of the great lies, wrote Jabril, was that "since the Honorable Elijah Muhammad was married to more than one wife [he never married these women] it follows that he was an immoral man. Therefore, as their wicked reasoning goes, he was unworthy to be followed and his teachings were false." This is precisely what Malcolm had charged in 1964. But according to Jabril, this moral philosophy was all wrong: adultery doesn't make a man immoral. More important was that "Minister Farrakhan states that the Honorable Elijah Muhammad was and is very moral and very alive." Morality was not determined by social mores or even by God. The Third Commandment was irrelevant. What was relevant was the word of the Honorable Louis Farrakhan.

Jabril repeated this sentiment several times. True believers, he said, "are well aware of the stupendous life-giving values in the stand of the Honorable Louis Farrakhan about the identity and the state of health of the Honorable Elijah Muhammad—that he is the Messiah, that he is alive, that he is doing and will yet do what is written of him." That's the story.

How does Farrakhan know all this? Because he is the living messenger of Elijah, and his authority is supreme. And how does Jabril know *that*? Farrakhan told him so.

In the following issue of April 16, Jabril wrote, "That which is paradoxical to us is never paradoxical to God Almighty. That which is puzzling or confusing to us is never that to God. An unidentified flying object is never that to its pilot; nor to those who built it.

"The above continues comments from the last issue pertaining to the domestic life of the Honorable Elijah Muhammad to be continued next issue, Allah willing."

Perhaps I lack the imagination to figure this out. Perhaps what is confusing to me is not confusing to Jabril's readers. In any event, had I read Jabril's columns before I met him, the morning I spent with him would have been a little different. I would have been dumbstruck that the man I was talking to, the man whose words I've just quoted, was a longtime close adviser to Farrakhan—according to him, Farrakhan's *closest* adviser. I would have wondered what was in store for me in a way

I hadn't even considered. But I hadn't read those columns of Jabril's, so I innocently went along with his program.

With an occasional word from Claudette, Jabril grilled me persistently, though in a friendly, soft-spoken way, showing no enmity, for two hours. He asked about my history—work and family—my politics, my religion, my writing, my personal life, but mostly my "values." He was also concerned with my publisher's values and said he would need to talk with him too. Presumably he had to determine what my values were in order to decide what to recommend to his boss.

It was difficult to associate the Jabril I met that day with the one I met later in his columns. The most articulate people in conversation sometimes make surprisingly bad writers. The least aggressive in conversation can be the most aggressive in print. The most secretive in conversation can be the most outspoken in print. Although I finally realized that morning that Jabril was no ordinary zealot, it took me a quite a while to see that words just didn't mean the same things to us.

Jabril seemed most interested in what I thought of Farrakhan as Allah's messenger. This was touchy. I soon enough realized that my answer could put me out into the cold. But I didn't want to lie; it's not my style. I told him I would report what Farrakhan and others told me about it. I knew that wasn't the answer he would have preferred, but I didn't feel I had a choice. I had decided before this meeting that I should play it straight. "Okay," he said, "but what do you think about it?" He was sure I had an opinion. People have opinions, they just don't always share them. He wanted to hear my opinion. More important, it was impossible that my opinion could be irrelevant to my telling Farrakhan's story.

Perhaps he was right. Perhaps it wasn't irrelevant that I thought the idea of Farrakhan being Allah's messenger was a splendidly imaginative invention of Farrakhan's. After all, Farrakhan had rebuilt the Nation on the basis of that myth; that myth ruled the Nation. Could I write an honest book about a man whose overriding idea I believe is a colorful, self-invented myth? But if I couldn't, how could any journalist ever write decently about things he or she didn't agree with? I tried to explain to Jabril about objective reportage and how it would work in this case, but as he listened and smiled impassively, I felt myself falling. We were in different realms, I knew. But we went on.

I told him I would place Farrakhan in a continuum of black "saviors," whom I then named. He didn't get angry, but he was emphatic: there were only three saviors—Marcus Garvey, Elijah, and Farrakhan. Martin Luther King, Jr., was no savior. Nor was Malcolm X. He was a fraud because he defamed Elijah, made him "appear like a wimp." A wimp? Did Jabril have any idea of the meaning of the word *wimp*? How did accusations of immorality and debauchery make a man look like a wimp?

Jabril then wanted to know about my religion. Another tough question in this anti-Semitic scene. I was a nonpracticing Jew, I said. My religious values could best be described as liberal humanist. He looked blank. What was a liberal humanist? I had said I was a Jew. What was this liberal humanist talk? Jew is a Jew is a Jew. This man who had spent the past forty years as a worker in the Nation's vineyards clearly had not the slightest idea what I was talking about.

So, disregarding what I had said, he went on to ask about Jewish religious practice. I told him I had been raised as a secular Jew and couldn't answer his detailed questions. He looked bewildered. I kept hoping that during these exchanges I had not betrayed my annoyance.

Hoping to help matters without betraying my beliefs, I told Jabril that I believed, as I did, that the Anti-Defamation League had been a little hysterical in its reactions to Farrakhan (as Rabbi Arnold Wolf remarked to me, "Farrakhan has given the ADL the first real shot in the arm it's had for years") but that Farrakhan had strongly provoked them. Jabril once again smiled affably, as he had through all the conversation, but this time it was clearer that I had riled him. Farrakhan, he replied, had never provoked anyone, would never say anything to provoke anyone. He was just telling the truth. It's a good thing to tell the truth. It shouldn't make anyone angry. He himself was certainly not an anti-Semite, Jabril insisted. As did many of Farrakhan's admirers. I had heard it numerous times before. Farrakhan often said and wrote precisely that: "I am not an anti-Semite; I am just telling the truth."

I would have liked to back off, but I couldn't, so I told Jabril that I thought the story told by Farrakhan's spokesman, presumably with his boss's approval, that Jewish doctors had injected the AIDS virus into black babies, was a monstrous absurdity, a tale invented by a virulent anti-Semite simply to incite hatred for Jews among blacks. Jabril and Claudette both smiled wisely. I also told them I thought, whatever his reason, that Farrakhan had been wise to demote Khalid Muhammad, the spokesman, after the ADL and the media had raised strong objections. They nodded again, and Jabril offered to give me the transcript of the press conference Farrakhan had held to discuss the media's and the ADL's responses to Khalid's speech and his own response. I thanked him and said I looked forward to reading it. With that I decided I had to change the subject. It could only get worse because I knew that while Farrakhan had removed Khalid Muhammad's title as the Nation's spokesman, he had also defended the "truth" of his remarks. I had read the reports of that press conference.

Against the clearest odds, I foolishly felt encouraged when I left Claudette and Jabril. During brunch they seemed to have moved from a barely concealed coldness to a warmer cordiality. Perhaps, even though they didn't agree with me about much, they liked the way I presented myself, which they might view as portending well for the book. That's what I dared to hope. Jabril promised to give me a response to my request in a few days. To facilitate his getting a copy of my biography of Mayor Washington, in which he was interested, he suggested sending his driver to my house at the other end of town to pick up one of my copies. He had so little time in Chicago, and I had indicated it might be difficult to find in a bookstore ten years after publication. Well, I had already sent Farrakhan a copy. He could get that one fastest. Claudette looked at me with contempt. "He wants his own copy," she said. So I promised him my only remaining copy in exchange for his promise to return it by mail the next week.

Weeks went by. I didn't hear from Claudette Muhammad or Jabril Muhammad. When I called National House to ask for one of them, I was told they weren't there. They didn't return my calls. Three months later I wrote to Jabril. I was curt, requesting the book and commenting on his failure to follow up on our conversation. I received no reply.

I told Reverend Martin what had happened. He was shocked. It was not the kind of behavior he would have expected from Farrakhan or his lieutenants. To him I was a bright, interesting woman who had written sympathetically about blacks for years. What went wrong? Or was he wrong about Farrakhan and his lieutenants? Was it my liberalness, my Jewishness, my femaleness, or was it what I had not been able to conceal very well—my skepticism about the divinity of the great leader or about his "truth-telling"? There's a big difference between sitting around and sharing ideas and giving someone your cooperation in writing your biography.

My dear aunt Emma, who is spending her later years reading books and having long conversations with anyone who will talk to her, relished this story. She stretched out her still long arms and wrapped them around her knees, and looked up at me. I expected that these long moments she was keeping me waiting would provide a profound analysis of this story. Finally she said, very quietly, with a wave of her hand, "They have no manners, my dear. If they really do live in this isolated world you describe so well, why would you expect them to know how to behave like civilized people?" Could it be so simple? I supposed that if I accepted that explanation, and thus expected a whole lot less, I might get more. Was it Mies who said, "Less is more"?

8.

One of the people whom I had expected would be happy to talk with me was Imam Warith Deen Muhammad, the son of Elijah who had inherited the Nation when his father died. Wallace, as he had been called, had been an uncertain warrior in his father's camp and had for some time been close to Malcolm. He had also been close to Farrakhan off and on through all the years of his father's leadership and especially after Malcolm died, when he had been forced to renounce him. When his father died, Wallace brought Farrakhan to Chicago from New York where he had been heading up Mosque No. 7 since Malcolm's death. He knew that Farrakhan, who fully expected to be the heir, could be a source of trouble for him. Warith hoped to coopt him: he named him "national ambassador" and allegedly gave him $50,000 as a stake. Farrakhan did seem at first to be coopted; he went along with Warith's plan to disassemble the Nation, rejecting the racist secret society of Elijah to create the American Muslim Mission, an integrated, traditional Islamic society. Farrakhan suffered through this process for three years and then resigned. There had been no love lost between the two men, though they have in recent years agreed to speak to each other.

I expected that Warith would welcome an opportunity to review that long history that had been so vital to him. After I left many phone messages with his assistant, Warith finally returned my call and, in a cordial manner, agreed to see me—at the Ramada Inn for lunch. He was another of those South Siders who used the Ramada for business lunches. Why was I filled with foreboding? But of course I went at the appointed time. I drank a tall Bloody Mary and read the morning paper while I waited, over an hour, at which point the hostess called me to the phone. Warith's assistant apologized profusely. The imam had had to rush his little daughter to the hospital. He would call me in a couple of days.

The imam never returned my follow-up phone calls. He had obviously thought it over and decided he didn't wish to talk, even off the record, as I had offered him, about his complicated, highly competitive relationship with Farrakhan. He claimed to have many more members than Farrakhan, though both kept their records secret, and he claimed to be closer to true Islam and to the later teachings of Malcolm X than Farrakhan, which wouldn't be difficult to achieve.

Was Warith afraid of Farrakhan? Or did he retain some secret but intense loyalty to this man who had for so long been such an important figure in his life? Or did he have some strange twisted guilty feeling toward his father that talking about Farrakhan might reveal? It might open old wounds made by his wholesale trashing of his father's organization and in effect his reputation—the organization and reputation that Farrakhan had revived and rebuilt. It took a while for the light to go on, to ask myself why I had expected Warith to talk with me about the man who had made a god of the father whom he had rejected. Why had I expected this man to reveal his feelings about Farrakhan, a man who, having been denied what he felt was his rightful inheritance, went on to claim that Elijah had changed his mind and, after all, had made him his heir? Farrakhan had, in effect, slain his brother. Just as Elijah had, in effect, slain first his father and then his son. Well, at least the Nation hasn't yet been matricidal.

9.

Fast-forward from mid-1994 to July 1996. Basic Books publishes *Prophet of Rage* by Arthur Magida, who tells his readers, in a prologue, of how in 1993, following a concert in North Carolina in which Farrakhan had played a Mendelssohn violin concerto, he had implied this was an overture to the Jews whom he had been so horrifically offending. Deciding that Farrakhan was serious about this gesture, Magida faxed him a note. He explained he was the senior editor of a Jewish newspaper, the *Baltimore Jewish Times*, and that Farrakhan could reach thousands of Jews with his message if he would grant him an interview. "I believed that if Farrakhan's motives were pure and his words of conciliation were genuine, there might be hope yet for black-Jewish relations," Magida writes.

Farrakhan invited Magida to his home in Chicago and talked with him in a way that Magida accepted as sincere. Farrakhan's attacks on Jews continued long after his meetings with Magida, and long after Magida had given Farrakhan a white yarmulke with a request that he wear it at the Million-Man March. This request raises the hair on the back of the neck of a Jew trying to imagine what was going on in the head of this professional Jew when he did that. The yarmulke (or skullcap) is the centuries-old head covering that Jewish men wear as a form of respect and love for their God. Orthodox Jews wear them all the time, others only at religious services and events. Non-Jews often put them on in respect for their Jewish associates when they attend a religious service such as a funeral, as when President Bill Clinton wore a yarmulke at the funeral of Israel's Prime Minister Itzak Rabin.

Magida, however, suggested that this viciously anti-Semitic gentile wear his "sparkling white" yarmulke at a public, nonreligious gathering of blacks, presumably to show all those black men that he is a good friend to the Jews. Is there a Jew in the United States who can take this idea seriously?

On August 21, 1996, Farrakhan again forgot the manners his mother taught him. At the opening session in Nashville, Tennessee, of the annual convention of the National Association of Black Journalists, Farrakhan delivered the keynote speech and once more displayed his contempt, wrath, and jealousy toward those blacks who have been successful in mainstream society. Once again he claimed the right to speak for the unlettered, uneducated members of his world who have no knowledge of the lives and problems of those who, despite good salaries and reputations, continue to suffer indignities at the hands of the whites who employ them. Once again he insulted his hosts, berating them for working for white-owned media and for doing their bosses' bidding and misrepresenting the truth. "A scared-to-death Negro is a slave, you slave writers, slave media people. White folks did not hire you to really tell them what you think because you are too afraid."

A member of the audience told him she had tried to tell the truth about his organization and had called the local mosque, but no one would talk with her. He replied, "That's because we don't trust journalists." Munroe Anderson, a longtime black journalist in Chicago, director of station services and community affairs at WBBM-TV, a CBS-owned affiliate, was one of the founders of the association which was organized in 1975 to help the still small number of black journalists deal with widespread discrimination in newsrooms across the country. About Farrakhan the sweet-tempered, generous Anderson said, "I didn't take him seriously. He was playing to his followers. That's all he cares about." Anderson dismissed him. He knows that Farrakhan doesn't trust, nor is he concerned with, any journalists who might see through his rhetoric, who might find a means to penetrate his secret society.

Clarence Page wasn't so kind. In his syndicated column that week, Page asked: "What do you call someone whom you invite to your house as a guest only to see him trash the carpet and wet all over your walls?" He went on to say, "Many of us were annoyed that Farrakhan would stand there and stereotype black journalists as broadly, ignorantly and destructively as any white editor ever has." Page pointed out that "Farrakhan's standards for fairness are about as suspect as the white editors who, before assigning black reporters to cover Jesse Jackson's presidential campaigns, asked if the reporters would be 'objective' or 'unbiased' about covering a black candidate."

It wouldn't be unlike Farrakhan to turn the journalists' invitation into an opportunity to lecture them. But neither Page nor Anderson would touch the question of why their organization invited Farrakhan to speak. Did they assume he would give them an uplifting, supportive speech? Or had they done what almost every other black organization has done since Farrakhan captured world attention with his Million-Man March? Did they simply invite him, without thought for what he might say, because he was the world's most desired black speaker?

10.

Meanwhile, in my search for access to the Nation, I reached an independent member, Munir Muhammad, a fierce defender and close associate of Farrakhan but a man who keeps his own counsel. Munir founded in 1986 and now manages what are described as the archives of Elijah—The Coalition for the Remembrance of Elijah Muhammad—and he is a frequent television spokesman for the Nation. Munir agreed to talk with me after badgering me about my motives through several phone calls—not always polite but friendly enough. He seemed not to know of my meeting with Jabril and Claudette, though that was improbable. I had been referred to him by a former member of the Nation who remained a Muslim and friendly to the Nation. Munir told me that Farrakhan wasn't "jumping up and down with joy over this one," but he obviously hadn't let that stop him from at least talking with me on the phone in a way that encouraged me not to give up hope of trying to see him and use his archives, whatever they might contain.

He chastised me and the "rest of the press" for deliberately mispronouncing Farrakhan's name, using a short "a" as in *can* at the end instead of the proper sound of *on*. We did this, Munir said, "just out of bigotry. You know what I mean. Just to belittle him." I wondered. Many blacks also used the short "a," but then, after all, most of them know Farrakhan only from television reports. It is true that mispronouncing a name reflects a certain lack of concern with that person's feelings about his name; most people don't like to hear their names mispronounced. Aware of that, television reporters and commentators make a concerted effort to pronounce hard-to-say names correctly. Why not Farrakhan too? It wouldn't be shocking to discover that no effort had been made to get Farrakhan's name right. It can't be said that he has made an effort to befriend the media.

Munir's main concern seemed to be what his payoff would be in talking with me. He told me that people usually paid to use his archives—a donation, of course—though he never told me exactly what was in them ("films, videotapes, and other things"), and never again mentioned money. He wanted a more ephemeral payoff. I couldn't offer him anything. Finally he said, "I like to talk face-to-face," and agreed to see me.

When I arrived at the Coalition office, a large double storefront on West 71st Street on the South Side of Chicago, in an integrated working-class neighborhood (usually that formulation in Chicago would be an oxymoron), Munir wasn't there. But he had left word that I would be arriving, and the video machine was set up with a tape about the history of black oppression to occupy me until he arrived. I saw no space that would have housed voluminous records. Behind a large meeting hall with about twenty rows of folding chairs were a couple of small rooms, a large television set, a video machine, and a camera.

I was relieved when Munir walked in. So was his young assistant, who clearly wasn't used to entertaining older white women. At a glance I knew that Munir was clearly his own man, a short, round, balding fiftyish man with an ear-to-ear grin, a pencil-thin mustache that did nothing to diminish his smile, and thick eyebrows. He wore a perfectly silly, obviously hand-tailored navy blue Nehru-style suit, the jacket trimmed with a double row of large shiny brass buttons and brass tabs at the collar, one of many variations of the gussied-up Nehru-style suits that he usually wears but that otherwise have not been seen in years. He is an independent insurance agent with his business/Coalition office at the rear of the hall.

Munir graciously took me into his little office with his insurance licenses plainly mounted on the wall. He launched into an hour-long monologue on the history of black oppression, the history of the Nation, an attack on Malcolm X—"he set our people back sixty years"—and an attack on Jesse Jackson. He had only contempt for Farrakhan for having become involved in Jackson's 1984 presidential race. Elijah had always opposed electoral politics, and no one had ever improved on Elijah's ideas, despite all these new ideas of Farrakhan's.

Should I have been surprised to hear him stress that he admired my "people," that he had been to Israel, and that he didn't understand why my "people are so interested in the Minister"? When he said, "you," he clearly meant Jew, but I sensed no malice. It was just that all Jews were alike. Most blacks confront such insults all the time—"What do you people want?" One would expect that a black who claims to feel no bigotry toward anyone, as Munir had claimed to me, would be highly sensitive to this habit of denying someone's personhood by talking as if he or she existed only as a member of a given group, as in "you people" or "you blacks" or "you Jews" or "you Hispanics" or "you whites." The worst is just plain "you," as if you weren't even worthy of group identification.

The late philosopher Emmanuel Levinas held that one had a moral duty to acknowledge another as an irreducible person. Certainly Levinas was referring to a good deal more than simply a matter of address, but it seems to me that such a duty has to begin there. Munir Muhammad had not an inkling of his moral duty to acknowledge me as an individual, though he obviously had a strong sense of his own brand of morality and of his own individuality. My aunt Emma would simply say he had no manners.

Suddenly Munir switched gears. Now he would question me. Why was I writing this book? Was I rich? Had I made a million dollars? Why not? Didn't all Jews make millions? Did I have children? What were they doing now? What did I feel about Israel? The Arabs? Was I religious? It didn't bother him at all that he received quick, superficial answers to some questions and none to others. If he didn't already know my answers, he didn't care. It was purely pro forma.

Finally we got down to business. How could he help me? First, he said, he could do some obvious things for me, like sell me videotapes of the history of the Nation. Well, sure, but what I really wanted from him, I explained again, was permission to go through back issues of *Muhammad Speaks* and any other historical materials, old tapes, and so on, Munir sat quietly at his desk, twisting his chubby fingers, obviously considering the matter. Then he said he'd need to find the time for me to do that. I took this to mean he would have to be there while I went through the materials—guard them, as it were. Gently I suggested that might not be necessary. I'd be very careful, and I certainly wouldn't remove anything. He shrugged. He thought a little longer, and then he happily had a new idea. Why didn't I put my request on videotape? I stared. Put my request on videotape in his office? So he could study my request as if I were still sitting before him? It sounded nuts to me, but what could I lose? It had emerged plainly, as we talked, that while Munir was certainly not the isolated religious that Jabril was, he did have his own eccentricities. Didn't we all? He called some instructions to his assistant, and soon enough we were ready to tape.

Munir began by playing the host. He introduced me. Then I made my spiel: I wanted to examine the archives of Elijah Muhammad in order to tell about him and the Nation in my book about Farrakhan. I gave the publisher's name and location and finished by saying that it would be a privilege to read these historic materials and to write this book about Minister Farrakhan.

Munir returned to the camera. He thanked me and said how much he had enjoyed talking with me. "She's not shy," he said. And then he made *his* spiel: to Nation members to follow my example and come to the Coalition to "do their own research." Well, his purpose in this videotape was clear. It had nothing to do with my own request.

As I moved to leave, he seemed perturbed. Why was I leaving so quickly? I smiled, acknowledged his warmth, sat down again, and then, with no prelude, asked Munir how he would have felt if I had addressed him as "you" or "you people," as he had addressed me throughout our conversation. He thought about it a minute and said softly, "Maybe I was wrong." After a short pause, he asked my plan for this book and some explanation of why I was doing it. His tone had changed. He was no longer the smart-ass he had been. He was no longer baiting me. He was chastened. For how long?

I explained that I would trace Farrakhan's history to his antecedents in the early-nineteenth-century back-to-Africa movements and Black Nationalism. "But we're not Black Nationalists," he insisted. What did he think they were? "Surely you agree that the early sources of the Nation go back to the back-to-Africa movements," I said.

"Well, perhaps," Munir replied, "but Elijah got his mission from the prophet Fard. I hope you are going to say that the Minister's mission is based in religion, in the teachings of the honorable Elijah Muhammad." Clearly Munir was a loyal member of the Nation, but his loyalties were still reserved for Elijah. Farrakhan was merely his servant. Unfortunately he shared with his fellow black Muslims their dedication to the secrecy of their religious group. Despite any amount of respect, even admiration, he might come to feel for me, he would not break the sacred bonds to let me in. If he did, he would lose the trust of the Minister, without which his mission in life would be ended. After all, his Coalition depended on Farrakhan's cooperation. And when the media invited him to speak for the Nation, he realized that he had been invited because he held this prestigious and professional job—he was head of the organization's archives. But he couldn't speak for the Nation without Farrakhan's approval. Farrakhan might not like Munir's talking with me, but that was innocent enough. Beyond that, forget it.

I smiled. It was time to go. I thanked him. He was affectionate, this smiling, chubby man who had had no intention of offering me any cooperation beyond this conversation, which he had clearly enjoyed. He was a sophisticated man, wasn't he? Farrakhan might not approve of his talking with me, but he was his own man. I said I would call him later about his archives, and we said goodbye, genuinely glad to have met each other, knowing that we would never meet again.

11.

I walked a couple blocks across 71st Street toward the bus I would take to begin my long trip home. At 71st and Ashland there was a bar, not an inviting bar but one in which I figured I could have a calming drink and make some notes. I hadn't used my tape recorder, nor had I taken any notes during our conversation, sure that Munir would not have co-operated if I had.

The door to the bar was locked, but I could see people inside, so I knocked. The bartender, who turned out to be John, the elderly white owner, let me in. He had no seltzer water and no lemon. He had one half-used bottle of tonic water, flat, and a bottle of vodka among half a dozen bottles of cheap liquor on an otherwise empty back bar. His ice consisted of two old trays of cubes in a battered refrigerator. In the refrigerator there were also a dozen bottles of beer.

I had a vodka and tonic, $1.60, the cheapest drink I'd had in years. This was one of those milder early-winter days when people who were short of money turned off the heat. You just put on a heavy sweater. It was so cold in John's place that I had to keep my coat on. When I asked him why he kept the door locked, he shook his head silently. I said, "I thought this was a nice neighborhood." It was, in fact, an old-fashioned working-class Chicago neighborhood with row after row of small bungalows, Chicago's residential trademark. This one, like many others now on the South Side, was racially integrated, but it seemed to be integrated not block by block, as in so many other neighborhoods, but house by house. There were several small shops on the main drags and a minimall at one major intersection, also integrated.

"It was nice," John said sadly, "but it's changed. It's okay during the day, but you wouldn't want to be out there at night." But John kept his door locked all the time.

These were the remnants of a busy saloon, one that had kept the heat on until the weather turned warm, with a full supply of beer, a well-stocked back bar, an ice machine, and a door through which people walked easily all afternoon and evening. The remnants were all there—the old tables and chairs, the long bar with all its stools, the ceiling fans that were now silent, the yellowed jokey signs on the mirror behind the bar. John would rather see his saloon die on its feet than see the blacks who had invaded his neighborhood sitting on his bar stools. That happened to some white people, even younger ones.

The other two customers in the saloon were having a political argument in which Farrakhan's name came up several times. I noted, with interest, that they pronounced the ending of his name with a short "a."

12.

Should I have been surprised when the Muslims and various others associated with Farrakhan in Washington, D.C., Baltimore, New York, and Boston refused to talk with me, failed to return my phone calls, broke dates? I wasn't surprised, but I was disappointed and sometimes angered when I found I had made plane or train trips with all the attendant expenses, only to find myself sitting in a bar somewhere nursing a drink with no hope that the person with whom I'd had an appointment was going to keep it. I was angered with myself finally for expecting cooperation from anyone close to Farrakhan, no matter how far away from Chicago. I was only grateful that there were so many people out there who wouldn't think for a moment of calling Farrakhan before they spoke to me, though of course none of them had the benefit of membership in his secret society, so I couldn't altogether trust anything he had said to them. Still, from this wide array of people—lawyers, clergymen, academicians, politicians, family, childhood friends, journalists, judges, and others—some of whom spoke to me at great length, I would get impressions of Farrakhan that could provide a sensitive and penetrating view of this highly complex man.

So at last, after many months, I gave up seeking access, of hoping that I would have those hours of conversation with Farrakhan I wanted. I gave up the hope of touring the University of Islam, the school where the Nation's children were taught, or the newspaper offices, or the mosques in other cities. I gave up hoping to have anything more than quick or exploitative conversations with anyone connected with the Nation or in some way endangered by revealing information or opinions about the Nation. In Washington, D.C., and nearby Baltimore, both the congressional Black Caucus and the NAACP refused to speak with me. For different reasons and in different ways, these people clearly feared they could be damaged by Farrakhan or his lieutenants if he were angered by what they said to me.

Meanwhile, through the months of trying to gain access, I had received a view of Farrakhan and the Nation that I might have missed, the view of the secret society I have just described. This picture revealed, as perhaps no others would, his personal view and treatment of what he considers the outside world. He has managed to recruit around him a band of loyalists who support and encourage that view, a view that sees the world beyond the Nation as hostile, on the one hand, but on the other hand easily, smoothly manipulated, conned, and insulted without fear of retribution. These followers believe, and are supported by many in this belief, that Farrakhan speaks for and represents the most disfranchised, neglected, isolated section of the black population, a group that no one else has been able to reach in many years, a group, in fact, that many people in this country, black and white, wish would disappear. Farrakhan is awarded his privileges so as to assuage the guilt of those who believe he is doing what they should be doing but can't. That he is doing it by sometimes dangerous and ugly means is overlooked. As their hero Malcolm said, "By any means necessary."

It was clear from Malcolm's words in the last month of his life that he now meant something new by that slogan. In an interview with Gordon Parks reprinted in *The Final Speeches*, Malcolm said, "I did many things as a Muslim that I'm sorry for now. I was a zombie then—like all Muslims—I was hypnotized, pointed in a certain direction and told to march. . . . That was a bad scene, brother. The sickness and madness of those days—I'm glad to be free of them." Those kinds of words led to Farrakhan's call for Malcolm's assassination. It was the Nation of Islam Malcolm described as mad and sick that Louis Farrakhan revived two years after the death of Elijah and after the effort by Elijah's son to destroy the Nation. There is no evidence that the Nation under Farrakhan would not elicit the same rueful words Malcolm spoke in 1965. At the same time there is plenty of evidence that Farrakhan has put into action some of the ideas for which Malcolm was killed and of which Elijah disapproved, in his effort to build his own future.

The rest of this book will describe the early life of Farrakhan and his forty years with the Nation, but most particularly the years since 1977 when he anointed himself Elijah's messenger, the bearer of the word of the spirit of Allah, the years in which he has tried to recreate and surpass the huge organization that Malcolm built at the right hand of Elijah, the organization that can make him the most powerful black man in the United States.

Part Five

THE TRANSFORMATION OF LOUIS EUGENE WALCOTT

1.

I sat in a back pew of little St. Cyprian's Episcopal Church, a church clearly built with little money, an unadorned rectangle but for several colorful stained glass windows and the cross suspended over the altar in the sanctuary, in the tradition of the Anglican church of England. It was the tradition of these worshipers, mostly from Barbados with some people from other former British West Indies colonies, who had built this modest church for themselves in 1923, after they came to Boston early in the century. Although many of them have since moved to more affluent sections of the city from their old tightly knit community in Lower Roxbury, they continue to come back here on Sunday to worship.

I wore my black knit skirt and grey sweater, black stockings and black suede pumps, with a pair of handmade silver earrings in my ears and a Haitian bejeweled silver necklace around my neck, sure that I would feel right at home. Most of the women, as I had expected, were also conservatively dressed, a few younger ones wearing red silk or a dashing print, but this was not a church of women on parade, the common sight on Sunday morning in so many black churches. The men all wore shirts and ties with subdued suits. The children too were quietly dressed in their Sunday school clothes and were very well behaved.

Even the babies were quiet. This was, after all, an Episcopal church, where one expected subdued behavior and appearances.

It was a traditional high Episcopal service, probably not very different from those of a hundred years ago. No guitars, no folksingers, no modern dance, instead the traditional service with incense, sermon, recitative, and hymns, not the blues-tinted hymns of the black church but the classic baroque hymns of the Anglican church. But unlike the more timid traditional white church, the music here soared out over the church, occasionally feeling, despite itself, like a black Baptist congregation, particularly with the clear soprano voice of a woman sitting near me who sang with her whole heart.

As I watched the acolytes and then the priest move down the aisle before communion, I closed my eyes and sat back to conjure a vision of a young sweet-faced, tall, slender, well-built, light-skinned acolyte moving in that procession carrying a large cross, occasionally unable to suppress a proudful grin. And across the aisle sat his mother, Mae Clarke, as dark-skinned as he was light, with his older brother, Alvan, dark like his mother, a family color story endlessly repeated in the black community, where the range of colors is greater than that of a natural rainbow. They sat there proudly watching him, his mother feeling the sense of accomplishment a mother feels when her child rewards her by following her teachings. She had been strict and demanding, feeling compelled to be both mother and father and to follow the teachings of her strict St. Kitts family and church. And here, walking down the church aisle every Sunday in his red robe and white, freshly starched surplice, looking like an angel, was the successful product of those teachings, and she was proud. Gene wasn't one of those altar boys who so willingly performed their religious tasks on Sunday but raised hell the rest of the week. He was, those who knew him said, a good obedient kid, a little too scared of his mother's wrath to be anything else. Even when he was older, hanging around the jazz clubs on Massachusetts Avenue, he didn't even swear, people said.

Be still, my heart. I began to weep. Could I bear this vision of that twelve- or thirteen-year-old boy, the acolyte bearing his heavy cross, walking slowing down the middle aisle in the procession with the acolytes and the ministers dispersing the incense from their swinging pot and chanting? It was almost too suspenseful to imagine that boy growing up to his young manhood with exciting expectations for himself in the world of music that he had come to know and love so well, helped by a Russian Jewish immigrant teacher who introduced him to the world's great music. Already as a very young man he was beginning to fulfill those expectations, and then, so soon into his manhood, he took the easy way out to become a popular singer and, indeed, began to hit it big. And then. And then to be transformed into a new person, a religious zealot, and then finally, I behold with awe this vision of the man I had lately watched and listened to and found so hard to believe, the character who called himself the Honorable Louis Farrakhan.

As I envisioned him there in that church, I watched this new man tower over that young boy. He is still well-built but now he is much sturdier, still handsome but now age and weight have squared off his large, powerfully built face, framed by stern rimless glasses, to give him a look of power and seem to accentuate his male beauty, his perfectly shaped mouth, small ears clipped to his head. He is balding at sixty, and his remaining hair is now oiled down in the style of many high-style blacks instead of the short, near crew cut of his youth, and his lovely reddish golden skin now has a sheen that looks like he has just spent two weeks on a beach in his native islands, or in the patio of his sun-baked home in Phoenix.

And he still has his shy boyish comic smirk. That smirk reminds me, though in all other physical aspects they are worlds apart, of Adolf Hitler's little smirk. Those little smirks when they are speaking to crowds, as if they are sublimely happy and expect their audiences to be too. Arthur Miller's poignant description of a Hitler speech he had seen on film awakened me to this striking similarity between the two men. Miller wrote, "He went up on his toes in ecstasy, hands clasped under his chin, a sublimely self-satisfied grin on his face, his body swiveling rather cutely," and, Miller said, the actors to whom he'd been showing the film all giggled at Hitler's "overacting." They were seeing him more than fifty years later. I wondered if young people would giggle at that same "overacting" of Farrakhan's, those same gestures, fifty years hence. Would a playwright be showing a film about Farrakhan to acquaint actors with his gestures long after his death? What would people remember of him in fifty or sixty years?

I returned to my fantasy. Here Gene Walcott had left his brightly starched surplice in the church vestry and was now bedecked in an elegant hand-tailored, high-hued (sometimes peach, sometimes mauve, or a deep red, or light blue—someone called them "popsicle-colored") silk suit and a bright printed bow tie that probably made his conservative dressmaker-mother squirm, the costume of a fancy circus ring-leader perhaps, not of a traditional religious leader. But the Nation wasn't a traditional religious group, though it did claim all the regular religious tax deductions. And Farrakhan is not a traditional leader. For a group like his, of which he is the self-appointed divine leader, who is to say what he should wear? The dark suit, bow tie, and embroidered fez that the Prophet Elijah always wore? Well yes, but Farrakhan is a new generation and a new star in the firmament. While he retains most of Elijah's ideas, he is not that man. Certainly he wouldn't wear the black robes over the black suit and the vest and reversed collar of his former church clergy. The rags of Jesus? Well, that takes a stretch of imagination. Or the colorful garb God supposedly prescribed for the Temple priests in Exodus 28: a breastplate, ephod, robe, coat, miter, and girdle of gold, blue, purple, and scarlet? That would be equally imaginative, and it might work. Think of Marcus Garvey and his wild military outfits. No, none of that. Farrakhan is a modern invention, a distinct and proud product of the community that brought the concept of hip to the world.

This adornment of Farrakhan's is reminiscent of the young high rollers of the black ghetto of Farrakhan's youth, not quite the zoot suit of the forties but like the powder blue silk suit that the great jazz singer Billy Eckstine wore. Farrakhan's slick outfit bears no relationship to the outfits of earlier American religious zealots, with good cause. Seeing Farrakhan look like America's most elegant hipster reminds me just a little of the showy but elegant clothes of the late Cecil Patrick, a negotiator for the powerful and prestigious black Brotherhood of Sleeping Car Porters, who told me in the forties that he dressed as he did because his members expected him to. "They don't want any slob representing them. They are the cream of their society." So also perhaps does Farrakhan dress like a fancy man because he thinks that's what his followers want. Or it's simply the image he wants to present to his followers: a man of the streets but not in the streets, a man of sophistication but also of achievement. Exactly how this outfit conveys that he is a messenger of God is not so clear, but then God would not necessarily ordain his messenger's sartorial style, would he?

2.

Farrakhan may have taken his cue on how to dress from Billy Eckstine and other black musicians, but he didn't learn from them what became for him one of the major tenets of his leadership of the Nation of Islam: his anger with and hatred of Jews. His mission, as he told an audience at the University of Illinois at Chicago in 1991, is to "rearrange a relationship" that he is convinced "has been detrimental to us," to "convert," as Henry Louis Gates, Jr., wrote, "a relationship of friendship, alliance and uplift into one of enmity, distrust, and hatred." Gates doesn't have the overall relationship between Jews and blacks exactly right. "Friendship, alliance, and uplift" certainly characterized the jazz world of the forties and fifties, but there was a wider black world out there that Richard Wright described in his 1945 autobiography, *Black Boy*, when he said, "To hold an attitude of antagonism or distrust toward Jews was bred in us from childhood; it was not merely racial prejudice, it was part of our cultural heritage." Black musicians happily transcended that part of their culture, as they did the church and a variety of other aspects of black culture. There was a constant mixing of Jews and blacks in the jazz world of the forties and fifties, with some Jewish musicians but mostly with listeners and hangers on, absorbing the atmosphere (which usually smelled of marijuana) and appreciating one of modern America's greatest accomplishments. What drew those young Jews into this black world and what accounted for their acceptance there is part of the story of six decades during which a relatively small group of Jews and blacks formed that alliance of friendship and uplift that Gates referred to, an alliance to change this country that is yet to be truly understood and has been fiercely repudiated by Farrakhan and many other Black Nationalists.

Farrakhan, of course, still remembers fondly those years in which, for him too, music obliterated racial differences between him and Jews, when his greatest hero was the superb Jewish violinist Jascha Heifitz. But he has managed to create in his mind a special compartment, shaped like the violin case he carried through his youth, in which he keeps those memories separate, so that they don't deter him from his crusade against Jews.

3.

How much of Farrakhan's anti-Semitism he learned in his church is difficult to unravel. While the Church of England was still under the control of the papacy, it helped engineer the first great national expulsion of the Jews from England in 1211. Some of the fierce official anti-Semitism of the Roman church survived in the English church after the rupture from Rome in 1527, when, in a bitter dispute between the pope and King Henry VIII, Henry formed the official Church of England under control of the crown. Innumerable wars between the crown and the papacy were fought before the total break in 1662. But in the half-century or so before, England under the highly controversial leadership of the antipapist Oliver Cromwell was much changed, and the exclusion of the Jews from most activities of life was lifted.

It was members of Henry's newly established Church of England, which still banned Jews, who came to America to set down the first church in this country in 1817. It broke from the mother church more than a century later when the colonies rebelled against the authority of the king. Meanwhile the English in 1793 took control of St. Kitts-Nevis in the Caribbean, the island home of Gene Walcott's mother.

Half a century after Jews had been welcomed back to England, that welcome was still highly conditional. Many were still coerced to convert to Christianity in order to gain equal rights. Those equal rights might lead to smashing successes, such as the famous Jewish convert Benjamin Disraeli, who was made prime minister first in 1868 and then again in 1874, after an illustrious political career. But anti-Semitism lingered on for a long time, said by some like Richard Wright to be bred in the bones of Christians.

By the time Gene Walcott arrived at St. Cyprian's, however, there was not a whisper of *official* anti-Semitism left in the church. On the other hand, as the almost exclusive church of the moneyed class in the United States (until those from the West Indies invaded), and in England and its colonies the state church, the Episcopal church could scarcely have been immune to the general anti-Semitism that prevailed almost everywhere until after World War II. This was a crucial part of the atmosphere in which Gene Walcott grew up.

The historic church of most American blacks, the Baptist church, taught a mixed lesson. On one hand, as James Baldwin wrote in 1964, "They are taught by their preachers that the Jews killed Christ, but Jews in this context mean all those who rejected the light. Then as the Jew became the wandering, persecuted figure, the Negro identifies with him." That image was repeated thirty years later by the black writer and scholar bel hooks, who wrote, "Growing up in the segregated South, the fundamental lesson I was taught via the black Baptist church was that Jews all over the world had suffered exploitation and oppression, that we identified with them and took their struggle to be our own because of shared experience. Most importantly, we were taught that anti-Semitism and antiblack racism were fundamentally connected. One could not be raised in hard-core Klan country and not be aware of that connection."

But the situation in the Northern urban ghetto was, as Baldwin himself makes clear, not as simple. Preachers in the North had to contend with many more economic and social forces than those in the South, with the consequence that Baldwin can recall, like Wright writing twenty years earlier, no black who would trust a Jew.

While the Northern black Baptist church was caught in a dilemma over Jews, there was always the knowledge, though mostly given a subtle voice, that the real enemy was white. Even the most conservative black Baptist churches, which resisted openly condemning whites and later hesitated to support the civil rights movement, recognized that while the Jews may have killed Christ, whites were the slavers, traders, and owners. Only with Farrakhan were Jews too given that honor. But in the few black enclaves around the world that had been created by white missionaries, the Anglican church was a white-controlled church in which antiwhite sentiment was rare. In fact, in this church, sometimes called "the frozen chosen," it was difficult to find any strong feeling at all.

Young Gene may have had little or no knowledge of his church's racial history in America, so different from the historic black Baptist churches, not unlike the treatment of the Jews by his church's forebears in England. He may not have been taught that blacks had long been barred from attendance in most American white churches, including the Episcopal church, and had therefore been forced to establish their own. As a friend of mine who attended an Episcopal church in Memphis throughout her childhood and youth said, "There just weren't any blacks in our church." Perhaps Gene thought his own all-black church was perfectly natural, that churches were naturally segregated. In the case of St. Cyprian's, this might have seemed even more natural, since its membership was all West Indian. It had been built by West Indians, who were majority black. American blacks in fact built Episcopal churches almost from the nation's beginning, the first in 1794 being St. Thomas African Episcopal Church in Philadelphia. But young Gene Walcott knew that his church had difficulty finding a black priest because the church wasn't training blacks for the priesthood. He might have been a priest himself. John Beynoe, an old friend from St. Cyprian's, said, "Heck, he was an acolyte, carrying that big cross, but no one ever encouraged him, invited him in. Think what they missed. But they were very paternalistic." Farrakhan has said he wondered, as a youngster, why black people were buried in separate cemeteries. It's not a huge step to wondering why his church was all black.

Perhaps he was also unaware that, while there was from the mid-eighteenth century a small faction of the Episcopal church that was staunchly abolitionist, and that in the nineteenth century a few of the New England churches were heavily involved in the abolitionist movement, the official American Episcopal church, unlike most other Christian churches, remained officially "neutral" on the subject of slavery. As Northern Methodists, Baptists, Lutherans, and others split from their Southern counterparts to express publicly their opposition to slavery, the Episcopal church kept silent, leaving individual members and a few of its churches to do the work of combating slavery. Richard Seidel, a Chicago Episcopal church historian, says wryly, "They were too busy fighting over internal church doctrine." How far or how close should they get to the Catholic practice? Or perhaps it was simply a matter of unity; should mere slavery be permitted to split this historic, prestigious church?

Did these West Indian blacks at St. Cyprian's, who were so loyal to their church, know its racial history in the United States? Or was that history irrelevant to them? After all, they were not American blacks, and theirs was a different history.

Still, Farrakhan would have us believe, "I hate [the terms 'kike,' 'wop,' 'guinea,' or 'spic'] . . . because I grew up being called 'nigger' "—and there is some suggestion that Gene Walcott was a young alert, race-conscious person who could have been expected to consider his church's racial policies. Instead he ignores those who engaged in the slave trade and the slave owners who flourished in his own church while he is consumed with what he views as the decisive role of the Jews in the slave business. He refers regularly to his major source of information, the 1991, 334-page *Secret Relationship between the Jews and the Blacks*, volume one, a book whose only authors are credited as the Historical Research Department of the Nation of Islam. Farrakhan regularly denies having had a hand in this book which has become the bible of black anti-Semitism. Among the hundreds of "documented" figures (1,275 footnotes) the book offers is, for instance, "Probably close to two-fifths of the Jewish families of 1820 owned slaves." Sounds ominous. But the noted historian David Brion Davis, writing in the *New York Review of Books* for December 22, 1994, explains that in the American South in 1830 there were just 120 Jews among the 45,000 slaveholders who owned 20 or more slaves. And among 12,000 slave-holders who owned 50 or more slaves, there were 20 Jews. It's hard to see how that many Jews could have owned enough slaves to justify Far-rakhan's fierce attacks against the Jews as slaveowners. Where are the book's figures for the number of slave-owning families among the remaining 99.5 percent of the American population of 9.6 million people?

Farrakhan's distraction with the Jewish villains is almost a carica-ture of the "distractions" of early-nineteenth-century Episcopal lead-ers who spent their time worrying about whether or not to include incense in the services and which prayer book to use, instead of how to help the victims of slavery. Farrakhan worries less about the current victims of an economic system gone out of control than about the treatment of blacks by the Jews, historical or otherwise.

After World War II there were large changes in at least parts of the Episcopal church. The priest at my friend's church in Memphis warned his parish in the sixties that blacks might be coming there; the parish should begin to think about its response. Some churches began to integrate in the late fifties, and in 1958 some members formed the Episcopal Society for Cultural and Racial Unity, which became one of the leading forces in the civil rights movement. Later, at the end of the sixties, a group of black clergy which included Farrakhan's priest, Nathan Wright, founded the Union of Black Episcopalians, inspired by the ideas of the Black Nationalists of the period. In 1990 the church authorized a book of black church music entitled *Lift Every Voice*, to be used for services in black churches instead of the traditional hymns, many of which go back to the early English church. And young black men began to receive encouragement to join the ministry. But this was all too late for Gene Walcott, who by this time was Louis X, a zealous member of the Nation of Islam.

Interestingly, in 1995 the Union of Black Episcopalians, still a small group representing the radical wing of blacks in the church, invited him to speak at its national convention in Chicago. There he unveiled to his audience tales of his "struggles with racism in the church while he had been a member," according to Reverend Martini Shaw, a Chicago priest who was present. I asked Shaw if Farrakhan's story rang true to him. He assured me it did, that he too had experienced racism in the church and that it still existed, though he had been admitted to the seminary in 1985 and now ministers to the first all-black Episcopal church established in Chicago in 1878. When I told Shaw of Farrakhan's history at St. Cyprian's, that it was an all-black, West Indian church in a community that was largely West Indian, Shaw explained that while Farrakhan may not have experienced direct racism in his own church, the structure of the Episcopal church, with its central control in each city, would have made the difference. But is it usual for children to go to other churches in the diocese, to know the diocese at all, I wondered? Was this story of racism still another of Farrakhan's exaggerations, another tool to strengthen his support among blacks as their defender against racism?

On the other hand, was Nathan Wright, his priest, transformed by the actions of the sixties to become by 1968 a follower of the American Black Nationalists? Or did he quietly nurture such ideas much earlier, while Farrakhan was still in his church, sharing these ideas with one of his young protégés? Perhaps what Farrakhan told those UBE members were stories his priest had told him. John Beynoe says Wright was surely a liberal, "perhaps even a little ahead of his time, but certainly no radical." The only real evidence, Beynoe says, of racism in their church was the fact that they excluded blacks from the ministry.

If it is true that, in addition to the racism he found growing up in Boston, Farrakhan experienced firsthand the struggles against racism in his own church, how is it that, as he said in 1996, he experienced the full impact of racism only when he was refused a seat at the movies in Washington, D.C.?

4.

While Gene probably didn't hear much anti-Semitism in his church, there certainly could have been a fair dose of it among those, including members of his family, who admired Marcus Garvey. As we have seen, Garvey was not only fiercely antiwhite but also anti-Semitic, though Jews were never one of his important targets. We can't be sure that Mae Clarke and her relatives, in their enthusiasm for Garvey, might not have echoed some of his anti-Semitism along with his antiwhite feelings to her sons, though she and many other West Indians obviously ignored Garvey's preaching against the church and his efforts to form a new church.

5.

The woman described to me as Gene Walcott's mother might well have echoed anti-Semitic sentiments. She was a strong, opinionated, very religious woman, with only slight education. None of these characteristics makes her an anti-Semite, but together they put her in an eligible position. And the stories that her son tells of her bitter experiences with Jews in her earliest years in this country, in the depths of the depression, may have prejudiced her and left a strong mark on her son. These stories were apparently told widely in New York and seem to be in part true, if also strongly tinged with anti-Semitism.

When Mae first came to New York from the islands, living in the Bronx, her only source of income for a while was from what came to be known as the "slave markets," in which black women went to local street corners and competed with one another for a day's labor offered by the local middle-class housewives, allegedly Jewish.

The same depression that sent black women to these street corners also sent white middle-class housewives there. These housewives had not been reduced to the same conditions as the black women, but they had only a little money to pay for the housecleaning tasks that were such a vital part of their middle-class lives. They had enough to buy groceries and then, with the few pennies left over, they could splurge occasionally and treat themselves to a maid for the day.

The black women, by contrast, were so desperate that they would work for practically nothing—a few pennies, maybe thirty cents an hour, or half that much if they had to. Perhaps they might also get a few cents for carfare or for extra-heavy work such as washing windows. If they weren't hired in the morning they would set out boxes to sit and wait. Eventually someone would give them some work, though the wage in the afternoon was only half of what it had been in the early morning, when the youngest, strongest girls were hired.

Once hired "on the 'slave market,'" the *Daily Worker* said on May 5, 1940, "women often find after a day's backbreaking toil, that they worked longer than was arranged, got less than was promised, were forced to accept clothing instead of cash and were exploited beyond human endurance. Only the urgent need for money makes them submit to this routine daily."

The newspaper pointed out that this "slave trade" was not a new institution. As early as 1834, New York statutes provided for places to be set aside on city streets "where those seeking work could meet with those who wanted workers." According to the *Worker*, these informal, open-air "hiring halls" functioned for men as well as women in middle-class communities in the depression years, in the Bronx and Brooklyn, Greenwich Village, Richmond and Queens. While there seems to be evidence for these slave markets existing only in New York, they may simply have gone undocumented in other cities and in time formed the foundations of the current version of the slave market that exists in most big cities today. One popular contemporary variety, such as Manpower, hires the homeless as well as others more or less permanently unemployed. A small entrepreneur advertising as a supplier of day labor for unskilled jobs in construction, horticulture, or other mainly rough menial jobs collects, in a storefront, a crew of mostly men. They are then driven in buses to work sites at the beginning of the day and brought back at the end, at which time they are paid, with a percentage of their wages deducted. Another variety describes itself with such names as Mighty Maids and supplies housecleaning services, hiring black, Hispanic, and illegal immigrant women by the day, though these services are usually contracted a day or so in advance, and the hours are strictly limited. Although the working conditions of these contemporary day laborers are better than those that prevailed in the early New York slave markets, an average maid takes home only about a third of what the agency is paid—not a far stretch from the New York housewives who allegedly regularly cheated their day maids.

In the *Worker* article the ethnic backgrounds of the housewife-buyers in this slave trade are not mentioned. Several different geographical areas are, though all within New York City, suggesting that numerous kinds of people participated in these markets. The writer gives no indication that this was a Jewish slave market, as Farrakhan maintained his mother worked in. But an article in the *Nation*, shortly after the one in the *Worker*, concentrates only on the Bronx, in fact only on certain street corners in the Bronx. There, the writer implies, because the streets were primarily lived in by Jews, the buyers were all Jewish.

To introduce us to this story, the writer says, "The slave market in the Bronx is different. You don't see the husky auctioneer; you don't see the whip. You don't see a line of half-naked Negroes with chains about their wrists and ankles. But you see hundreds of Negro women, thin, tattered, haggard, sitting on soap boxes or leaning against lamp posts, begging some white woman to buy their services for as little as fifteen cents an hour." Having set the scene, the writer describes with the same dramatic flair the abuses of this slave market. He identifies the culprits: these slavers are "almost invariably Jews," which, he says, has ugly repercussions. "These practices create an undercurrent of bitter hatred for the Bronx housewives. The Negro women return to Harlem, and whenever they get together swap stories of oppression. . . . The bitter feelings of the workers are easily steered into the broad channel of anti-Semitism. Political charlatans of every stripe, from the outright professional Hitlerite to the Blackmanite [one who advocates the annihilation of all whites, beginning with the Jewish businessmen of Harlem], capitalize upon 'the Jewish oppression in the Bronx.'"

Apparently Mae Clarke was one of those women who went to Burnside and Davidson Avenues, or Simpson Street and Westchester Avenue, or the hundred or so other street corners in the Bronx where one of the Jewish slavers would buy her services.

The *Nation's* writer, Carl Offord, who may have been a much better reporter than Louise Mitchell at the *Worker* (and was also black), told much more graphic stories than she did about the treatment of these workers by the Jewish housewives, perhaps based on interviews with the workers, though he doesn't say so. Even if Mae told only the milder stories that Louise Mitchell told, and even if her feelings about these housewives weren't "steered into the broad channel of anti-Semitism," it isn't difficult to imagine that Mae Clarke might have imparted feelings to her sons that would make them pretty angry at those Jewish housewives, might even have helped sow the seeds of anti-Semitism that were beginning to sprout in Gene—or perhaps this was only the first planting.

Later, though under better circumstances in the Roxbury area of Boston, Mae continued to work as a domestic, and it was still Jewish housewives for whom she worked and whom Farrakhan describes as having mistreated her. As the depression eased, Jewish housewives no longer had to resort to street-corner markets but could use word of mouth and ads in the paper to find their victims.

Left out of these reports is that, in those depression years, all too many white women were also in search of work, any kind of work. They were the preferred workers among the housewives of New York City—and every other city. That the practice of the "slave markets" preceded the depression by about a hundred years is made clear in the *Worker* story, if ignored in the other, but the *Worker* doesn't indicate whether these slave markets were always limited to black workers. By 1860 there were already 49,000 blacks living in the state of New York, most of them in New York City, and it is possible that, given the nature of race relations in the United States, all too many blacks were reduced to obtaining work in these slave markets.

That these depression-era slave markets around the city may been run by Jews alone, however, seems far-fetched. More likely the Jews were scapegoated as guilty when in fact they were simply part of the group. But if only Jewish women indeed formed these markets, some possible reasons occur. First, while a sizable number of Jews had attained a measure of prosperity in the 1920s, it was only a prosperity relative to whites. A *Fortune* magazine survey in 1936 showed Jews scarcely present in most high-income businesses. Even in the professions, Jews were represented in the lower-income ranks. Whatever affluence Jews had attained was usually quite marginal, often based on risky occupations, many of which were heavily impaired by the depression, so that while many Jews managed to survive the economic crisis, they had less money than whites. And blacks, much more devastated and desperate for work, would work for less money (would in fact later scab for striking workers). The implication that Jewish housewives who took advantage of this situation were more greedy than their white counterparts, or more nasty to their workers, is based on one of the longtime assumptions about Jews, not any comparative information about other white housewives.

Another, more subtle factor was at work in this story as told by the *Nation*: it seems that people in the Bronx became troubled by the anti-Jewish feelings that were developing as a consequence of these markets. They organized an ecumenical Bronx Committee for Improvement of Domestic Employees, led by a local rabbi. The committee planned to create shelters for "the domestic workers in bad weather and to see that prospective employers pay a fair wage." This so-called education effort by the clergy led to a union organizing effort that failed. "The housewife," the *Nation* said, "clung to her position—that she was going to get as much as possible for the least possible amount of money." Implication: no amount of education or union pressure can budge these Jewish housewives from their greedy ways. On the other hand, the article makes clear, there were plenty of Jews in the Bronx who tried to convince their neighbors to be more generous. These Jews are certainly a complex lot.

What was someone like Mae Clarke supposed to think of all this? Did she hear about that Bronx committee? If so, did it affect her attitudes? Did she simply believe, as her son tells the story, that all Jews are greedy and mean? Did she and her family, in fact, ever hear anything to change that impression? Where? From whom? Would anyone in Gene's school or his church have suggested that Jews shared with blacks a scourge of hatred and persecution and that, for that reason, Jews are often more tolerant toward others than Christians? Since they have gained financial prosperity themselves, some Jews have been more likely than whites generally to give blacks and other minorities jobs, rent to them, serve them in restaurants, and so on. A 1944 book, *Negro-Jewish Relationships*, reports that a study made that year in Detroit, following a race riot in the city, found that "seventy percent of the Jews interviewed believed that they had an obligation to treat Negroes well, since they, too, had known persecution. Only fifty percent . . . thought they actually treated the Negro better, however."

I well remember the young black men who worked at various unskilled jobs in my Jewish father's modest bakery in Chicago in the forties, in an all-white neighborhood where blacks rarely ventured. Why had he hired them? I asked him. "They came to the back door asking for work and they seemed to be clean and honest, so why not?" he told me. Variations on that story have been told to me by numerous blacks who found jobs with small Jewish entrepreneurs when they had all but given up finding a job. Young black men who grew up during the depression often swap stories about learning Yiddish and all kinds of other things working for first-generation Jewish store owners in their neighborhoods in Chicago. The idea that Mae Clarke and her family, along with most other urban blacks, believed, as her son implies, that all Jews are mean and nasty is contradicted by a 1944 Detroit study. There half the blacks interviewed "believed that Jews treat Negroes better than do non-Jewish whites" and, even more important, they expected better treatment "since Jews know what it is to be persecuted." Did Farrakhan, in 1944, as a youngster, know that some blacks held this attitude? Did he even perhaps share it? Or is this an attitude created by a lie, as happens with so many surveys? Did the people interviewed simply tell their questioners what they thought they wanted to hear? And does the result of this survey necessarily contradict the impressions of Richard Wright and James Baldwin? Isn't it possible that blacks might expect more from Jews, understanding that they too had suffered persecution, while at the same time believing they were mean and nasty?

In fact, that survey result showing higher expectations of Jews by blacks has been, in one form or another, discussed for many years. It was this ambivalent mixture of higher black expectations of Jews and a long-standing anti-Semitism inherited from the white world that made the scapegoating of the Jews by some blacks almost natural. "They suffered as much as we did, and now they are getting ahead, so they should help us out, but what do they do instead, they exploit us worse than the whites do." Black writer Joe Wood, writing in an essay in *Blacks and Jews*, conducts an imaginary dialogue with an anti-Semitic black whom he is trying to convert. His imagined friend says, "My theory is they [Jews] produced the civil rights movement and they pumped up King and all them preachers as a public relations diversion so no one would notice them buying mortgages." How's that for ambivalence? "Sure, the Jews helped the civil rights movement. Won't deny that. But did they do it to help us, as they claim? Once again, we expected their help, and, sure they gave it to us, but for us? Hell, no!"

Which is not to say that Jews do not include among them plenty of bigots. A survey done at the University of Chicago in 1960, not twenty years after that earlier Detroit survey, arrived at a very different conclusion. It said "the Jewish respondents . . . display a level of [racial] prejudice that very nearly matches that of the native non-white European population." The study indicated that Jews viewed blacks pretty much as do most white Americans, "as outsiders and inferiors." Observations by two social scientists writing in *Essays on Jewish Life in America* in 1969 offer many examples of a range of Jewish attitudes toward blacks, from indifference to outright hostility. Was there really such a change from 1944 to 1960, or did the surveys ask different kinds of questions and hence come to different conclusions?

What this 1960 survey doesn't consider, which would make its results more nearly in tune with the 1944 survey, is that a Jewish bigot is quite often a different animal from other white bigots. He reflects an ambivalence that matches the black anti-Semite's ambivalence. The Jew, with exceptions, was too long himself the object of bigotry to be a strong *advocate* of it. My father, for instance, regularly spoke disparagingly behind their backs of the *shvartzers*, but he treated them fairly, even kindly, in his shop. More important, he saw to it they were taught skills to advance into better jobs in the shop. The word *shvartzer*, Yiddish for black man, or *shvartzeh* for black woman, apparently developed as Jews could afford to hire black servants or employees. It was not a flattering term, though it never carried the weight of the word *nigger* as used by whites. But in his 1968 edition of *The Joys of Yiddish*, an annotated dictionary, Leo Rosten comments, "Since the growth of the civil rights movement, these uses [of *shvartzer* and *shvartzeh*] have declined. Many Jews would not, for instance, approve of the retelling now of the following true, well-known, and (to me, at least) disarming story:

"A Jewish matron dialed a number and asked, 'Hello, Mrs. Weiss?'

" 'No, ma'am,' came a melodious voice. 'This is the *shvartzeh.'* "

That little tale was published in 1968, the year Martin Luther King was killed. It is doubtful, even in the interest of illustrating his words, as Rosten does with most words in his dictionary, that he would have told this rather harmless story in 1996. It would have no resonance for most younger Jews today, who, though they may have *shvartzehs* working for them, and may even have strong antipathies toward blacks, have nevertheless dropped such words from their vocabularies. A study conducted by the National Opinion Research Center in 1988 for the American Jewish Committee shows yet another view: "The overall movement of Jewish attitudes toward racial tolerance is abundantly evident." Still, in Mae Clarke's day there were plenty of Jewish housewives for whom that story would resonate clearly and for their black maids like Mae Clarke would arouse sharp resentment— even, as reported in the *Nation*, considerable anti-Semitism. The word, like *nigger*, sticks in the craw. No less so today. As Joe Wood writes about Jewish bigotry, "It's like nothing is more pathetic to me than a Jewish person—with all the Jews the Germans killed—calling somebody a *schwartze*. But I still have to keep telling myself it's not *only* them. Because it's not." (Yiddish spelling is phonetic; no two people agree on it.)

While we know that some blacks did understand the peculiarity of the Jew like my father, we also know that those Jewish housewives were viewed as guiltier in their treatment of blacks than the immensely greater number of Episcopalian, Congregationalist, Methodist, or Catholic white housewives in New York who were going out to the corners of Greenwich Village, Richmond, Queens, and Brooklyn to buy day maids during the depression. Of course, it's possible that only Jewish housewives used those slave markets, but not probable. That the Jews should have been singled out as objects of rage and revenge could occur only in the confused minds of those who had to make sense of the dreadful state in which they themselves had lived for generations. Their tortured vision made them grasp for blame at those so well known in history as the arch-villains. Pain can cause emotional and intellectual blindness as well as provide great insight. Unfortunately human nature tends to favor the former. That Farrakhan is still repeating those evils done to his mother by those Jewish housewives tells us something about his pain.

This impression is intensified when we read, in a November 18, 1996, *New Yorker* piece by Hilton Als, another black man's reminiscences about his mother. From her wide range of jobs over the years, he chooses to tell about only two, one in a black beauty salon, the other as a member of that hated slave trade. "'We called ourselves Daily Woikers,' my mother said, in a Yiddish-American accent, laughing," he recounts. Als then goes on to tell about his family's relationship to their landlord, the Schwartzes, of whom he says, "I loved them." He tells about how his mother told Mrs. Schwartze that her son wanted to be a writer, and, "Shortly afterward, Mrs. Schwartze gave me a gift. It was a typewriter that had belonged to her son, the Doctor."

Farrakhan's version of his mother's participation in the slave trade is quite different from Als's. Als goes the whole distance to say how he loved his elderly Jewish landlords and wanted to be a Jew himself as a child. But that story his mother told of how she went to a street corner in Flatbush, in Brooklyn, standing there while "people—mostly Jews . . . drive by in their big cars, from which they would look out to see which of the women seemed healthy and clean enough to do day work in their homes," was one of the only two anecdotes he chose to tell about his mother's lifelong employment history, which is only a very brief part of his story.

Does that slave market story still carry the weight in his life that it does in Farrakhan's? Als would deny that. Yet this black writer, whose work is sophisticated enough to appear regularly in a major highbrow American magazine, has chosen to give such prominence to a story that is also one of Louis Farrakhan's landmark stories about anti-Semitism but is otherwise almost completely forgotten in this country. (I found only one published mention of it since the forties, in a 1988 book on women's labor history. This is not to say there aren't still a few women who privately remember their own slave market days.)

The intangible, almost abstract, bottom line here is not whether Jews might feel justifiably or unjustifiably maligned, or whether blacks may feel once again a horror at recalling an ugly discrimination against innocent young black women. What is important is that despite the phenomenal changes that have occurred in the last half of this century in the lives of so many Jews and so many blacks, this slave market story keeps making its way into the world.

Many of the changes in American life over the last fifty years have been due to the activities of Jews and blacks, cooperative or otherwise. Now, at the end of the century, history and culture have found terrible ways of working that leave us with the scars of all those years before, years we hoped we had eclipsed. Here we are with so little actual entwinement of blacks or Jews in each other's lives, yet still unable to separate. We are still attached to each other at the hip, so to speak. Of all of us, Farrakhan may need the most awful surgery, should he decide to sever those ties. He has built an entire intellectual, social, economic, and religious career—a small empire—based on his love-hate relationship with Jews. One doesn't break such ties easily. Black writers like Hilton Als and Jewish writers like, well, why exempt myself, also find themselves occasionally writing critically of the other group, sometimes trapped quite inadvertently in our own myths. We can't avoid it. Let's be honest, it's easy. Didn't W. E. B. Du Bois say that the crucial issue before Americans was race? Has anyone suggested that his prophetic statement no longer holds? Besides, it sometimes helps to sell books.

6.

While some of those "slave market" stories were partly exaggerated and partly falsely assigned to Jewish women alone, we know that many blacks in Northern cities had true stories of exploitation to tell about landlords, shopkeepers, and other kinds of Jewish entrepreneurs in the ghettos. In many cities blacks took over neighborhoods that Jews abandoned as they became more prosperous and could penetrate housing that had previously been closed to them—just as blacks were moving into neighborhoods previously closed to them. Plenty of those Jews also moved simply because blacks were beginning to move into their neighborhood, and they didn't want to live alongside blacks. Some "liberal" Jews proudly describe their martyrdom when they stayed in their homes until they were the only whites left in the neighborhood, "hoping we wouldn't have to leave," they say.

It didn't occur to them to wonder how the blacks, whom their liberal organizations were urging to "break the barriers" in white neighborhoods, might feel about being the only blacks. All too many horror stories tell of those blacks who were the first to move into all-white neighborhoods, or children who were the first to attend an all-white school, the most famous of whom was Linda Brown of Topeka, Kansas. Her father lent their name to the suit *Brown v. Board of Education of Topeka, Kansas*, which decided finally that children would be breaking the color barriers in schools all over the country, often to the sound of rocks and stones and "Nigger, go home."

Of course it was not only Jews who, beginning in the forties, engaged in what was once called "white flight." Now it is dignified with different motives. Those who fled the encroaching blacks in their neighborhoods, it is now said, were looking for wider spaces, better schools, that glorious life offered by the burgeoning suburban tracts. It is also said that panic-peddling by greedy real estate brokers is what drove people out. Yet the facts continue to show that whole neighborhoods, not slums but ordinary middle-class neighborhoods with well-kept homes, tree-lined streets, and swings in the backyards, were without any but a few whites within a few short months after the first few blacks moved in. It would appear that the fear of living among blacks was deep and widespread among all whites, Jews included, because the panic peddlers were able to buy houses at low prices by threatening that real estate values would fall with the "invasion" of blacks. Those brokers were then able to resell the properties to blacks at much higher prices. While over time real estate values did drop in some white-flight neighborhoods, they rose in others. The evidence seems to indicate that, had whites stayed while blacks bought houses or rented apartments slowly, as they were naturally vacated, real estate values would have followed the general market. But that happened only in a few neighborhoods in the 1980s.

The difference between Jews and other whites was a crucial one in the short term, but not in the long term: there were no burning crosses or bombs thrown at the first blacks who moved into Jewish neighborhoods. People just moved out. As one Jew in a community outside Boston told an interviewer for a B'nai B'rith Women's Local Area Study in the sixties, "As far as citizens rights go, the Negro as anybody else should be equal. They have a right to live anywhere, but of course I can move."

White flight in fact began with the Jews before World War II.

Jews were gaining some prosperity; they could afford to move. At the same time blacks were fleeing the poverty-stricken South, coming to the industrial North in search of jobs. The ghettos to which they'd been confined were overflowing. One by one, they began moving into the one place in the city where people would rent to them: what had earlier been called the Jewish ghetto. A few Jews had become prosperous enough to move out and rented their apartments to blacks. Did they rent to blacks because they could extort high rents from people who had so few choices, as so many blacks claim? Perhaps. Or perhaps they simply responded to the pressure of black needs. Whichever was true, as landlords rented or sold to blacks, other Jews fled until none remained.

But while they moved their families and their synagogues, they didn't move their neighborhood businesses. And where they had bought property, they retained ownership and rented to blacks. Why did they move their synagogues, some blacks ask? "When the Irish and the Italians flee blacks, they leave their churches behind and provide some continuity in the neighborhood." Jews were not interested in converting blacks—or any non-Jew, for that matter—to their religion. Said simply, Jews view themselves as God's chosen people, not to be contaminated by outsiders. It was some years before this phenomenon was noted by blacks, only after white flight had taken on wider proportions. But by 1966 blacks were beginning to take note, according to a highly self-critical article in an American Jewish Congress publication.

Much earlier, blacks began to complain that the Jewish grocers who kept their businesses in their former neighborhoods sold them rotten meat. They also insisted they were overcharged. And not only had Jewish landlords rented to them in order to charge higher rents than they could get from whites, but they continued to charge excessive rents and withdrew services from the buildings. Unfortunately some of these charges were all too true.

In Chicago, for instance, in the 1970s the housing courts were filled with Jewish landlords of ghetto property who were charged with all kinds of violations of the law—broken plaster, broken plumbing, broken windows, rats, roaches, broken locks, to name just a few. The buildings were among the oldest in the city and had accumulated some of the natural results of age—broken heating and plumbing, for instance—but they had also been badly abused and allowed to disintegrate. Poor blacks, some of them new immigrants from the South, who had little money and were barred from living outside what had become a new ghetto, went on paying rent and pleading for service, often appealing to Legal Aid lawyers for help. In court, landlords claimed the building had become too expensive to maintain properly; in fact the costs, after so much neglect, would have been enormous. So landlords went on collecting rents where they could, occasionally paid the small fines judges laid on them when they were brought into court, finally stopped paying taxes, and then just abandoned the buildings, leaving them for the city to tear down or for some ghetto inhabitants to burn down. Some of these landlords soon enough became known as slumlords and didn't enhance the general reputation of the Jewish community, especially when they had hidden their ownership of these buildings in blind trusts for years and meanwhile become well-known solid citizens.

As blacks moved into other city neighborhoods that were also abandoned in the process of white flight and suburbanization, slumlords other than Jews also emerged—Greeks, Italians, Irish. But as had happened with the New York slave markets, it was the Jewish slumlords who were most strongly attacked. It didn't help the reputation of the Jews in Chicago when one of the late Mayor Richard J. Daley's favorite henchmen, to whom he entrusted the Chicago Housing Authority for many years, turned out to be one of Chicago's worst slumlords. It wasn't viewed among many blacks as a coincidence that the Jewish Charles Swibel mismanaged the CHA and enriched himself and his friends on CHA contracts for twenty years so that the buildings were finally almost unlivable, years before that fate beset so many other public housing projects.

Over the years, partly because their owners had died or retired, or because Jewish businesses were burned down in the riots after the murder of Martin Luther King, Jr., in 1968, Jews gradually abandoned their business properties in the ghettos, and others moved in to take them over. But the complaints continued. Now it was not Jews selling rotten meat and overcharging but Koreans, Arabs, Vietnamese, and others. In the sixties, blacks had burned and looted Jewish businesses. In the nineties, in South Central Los Angeles, blacks and Latinos combined to burn down Korean businesses. In St. Petersburg, Florida, blacks burned Vietnamese businesses along with others. Were these fires the result of anger at the local businessmen, or was the cause much more complex, the anger rooted in the social conditions of the ghetto that appear to be intractable? The economics and social conditions of small business in poor minority neighborhoods can encourage business practices that anywhere else would force the owner out of business. But city inspectors tend to ignore them, and poor people have few other resources and usually lack the strength and ability to change even the quality of food they are sold, let alone the place they can live. Burn, baby, burn sometimes seems the only solution, often when the burnings themselves have little relation to the act that ignited the fire.

The memories of those long-since departed Jewish businessmen and landlords who gave their fellow honest merchants and landlords a bad name in the black communities continues to nourish anti-Semitism among blacks and to provide ammunition for Farrakhan. His need to maintain the image of the scapegoat helps sustain the victim role among blacks, a role that Farrakhan famously rejects all the time he is carefully nurturing it. These two statements from a 1994 speech in Chicago at the mosque illustrate. "The suffering of the human family is directly related to our rejection of the way of God," he says, not exactly a new sentiment in the pulpit. But black people, Farrakhan implies, are not quite of the *human* family. They are a race apart, a distinction one doesn't hear often. "The suffering of *black* people specifically in America," Farrakhan says, "is directly related to the lifestyle that we have chosen or that has been forced upon us by the slavemasters and their children." A bit of martyrdom mixed with a dose of self-criticism. Enough on one hand to justify the use of a scapegoat to explain suffering, and right alongside, enough of the condemnation of the "sufferer's" own evil choices to lead to self-improvement.

7.

Mae Manning Clarke *may* have been just a bit of a free spirit as a young woman. She took a lover with whom she had a child, Alvan, after her husband briefly disappeared, then found herself pregnant again by her husband during one of his "visits." According to Farrakhan, this mix-up was particularly troubling because his father, Mae's husband, was light-skinned or perhaps all white, while Mae's lover was dark-skinned. So, Farrakhan says, Mae believed she was in danger of having a light-skinned baby, thus revealing to her lover, with whom she was apparently more involved than with her husband, that she had been with another man. So she tried, he says, three times "to kill me when I was a child, her baby in her womb." She just couldn't bear the shame.

This is a perplexing story, with a hollow ring to it. It sounds as if Farrakhan might be inventing this story as a strangely poignant one to use against one of his favorite targets, abortion and birth control. "Birth control" he told an audience at Princeton University, "is aimed at you, Black women, Asian and Hispanic women. They want to kill the fruit of your womb, because they know that the fruit of your womb is the answer to your prayers." We are being asked to believe that Farrakhan's mother told him this story about her abortion attempts and her reasons. Was she an extraordinarily cruel woman, or a stupid woman, or did she simply confide everything to her younger son?

Whatever the story says about his mother, what it says about Farrakhan's attitude toward his mother is much more significant. Although the theory that a child can only be as light as the lightest parent and as dark as the darkest, an idea attributed to geneticists, has long since been discredited, Farrakhan obviously is certain that his own skin color reflects his allegedly light-skinned father (he sometimes claims the man was white) with whom his mother had had an "affair" while her lover was away. A major scientist, Amrin Scheinfeld, in a seminal book, *Your Heredity and Environment*, as early as 1965 provided clear evidence that genetic inheritance works far differently and more intricately than simple early theory suggested.

But Farrakhan seems not at all concerned with facts or the truth. What seems to be his concern here is to condemn his mother's alleged promiscuity and attempts at abortion. Perhaps he doesn't know himself that all the crossbreeding that has gone on since the beginning of slavery has produced huge variations in the skin color of the progeny of even the most monogamous parents with some black blood. There are literally millions of black families with various children ranging from white to—as Mae was described by her cousin Elma—"black as ink" from the same two parents, regardless of their own color. Did his mother, in fact, tell Farrakhan this story? Since she is dead, we cannot know.

8.

As a mother, Mae Clarke was puritanical and a strong disciplinarian, her cousin, Gwen Williams, said. "A good mother, but very strict." Most people who knew her remember her as a mother who gave her children no quarter, who was harsher than was considered necessary.

But Mae was also kind and generous, Williams said. She had worked hard all her life, first as a domestic and then as a seamstress who sewed wedding dresses for the local affluent folk to provide her sons with every opportunity she could, particularly the music lessons that meant so much to her. These included lessons and a piano for Alvan and a violin for Gene, beginning when he was six. "They had a gift, those boys," says John Beynoe, who was older than the Walcott boys. Their musical gift may have been only part of the cause of Mae Clarke's generosity; musical careers were beginning to provide an occasional road to fame and fortune for talented blacks. Gene Walcott already had a taste of what might lie ahead when he was only sixteen and won an opportunity to perform on a very early (1949) popular national television amateur show, Ted Mack's Original Amateur Hour. One of the best known of these talent showcases in that era, unlike most others it was open to blacks. Within a short time Gene began to fulfill his mother's hopes, gaining success as a singer-performer who called himself the Charmer. Not a classical violinist, it's true, but it *was* music, and the path was much easier and more open than that of a violinist. He was not only gifted on the violin but was said to have the best voice in the church choir, the voice that rescued him from a frustrated college career. Mae's other son, Alvan, had a successful career as a jazz musician, though there haven't been many jazz musicians who have earned substantial money. Gene Walcott, on the other hand, has probably become much richer as Louis Farrakhan than he ever would have as the Charmer. But who knows? He was considered a second Harry Belafonte, who has become a whole lot richer than Louis Farrakhan.

Although Farrakhan was forced to give up his music for the Nation, he always made sure people knew of this sacrifice of his budding career in music. Before Elijah Muhammad banned music from the Nation, the young Louis X performed regularly for his fellow Muslims, sometimes at public rallies, though the lyrics he sang for the Muslims were not the calypso tunes he had sung earlier. Louis X's songs of the fifties, before they were banned by Elijah, can most accurately be called didactic race tunes. He wrote them to propagate the Nation's ideas, and the most famous of them was "A White Man's Heaven Is a Black Man's Hell," which is considered the anthem of the Nation. One of the several verses of the long song is:

" . . . The Black man everywhere
is on the rise.
He has kicked the white man
out of Asia
And he's going fast out of Africa.
With every ounce of strength and breadth
His cry is 'Give us liberty or
give us death.'
The whole black world has
their eyes on you.
To see what the so-called Negro
is going to do.
So, my friend, it's easy to tell
Our unity will give the white man hell."

To complete his saga of the death and destruction of whites and the emergence of blacks as rich and powerful leaders of the world, Louis X used the theme of Genesis:

"God made a promise to Abraham.
His seed would be a stranger
in a strange land.
They would suffer and be
afflicted for 400 years.
But He would come and wipe
away their tears.
Our God and Savior Allah has come

He has declared the white
man's day as done."

That was the early fifties, when Farrakhan had forsaken his former life, the gay life of the calypso singer and occasional serious turns with the violin. For him it was a means to continue his musical life, but it was a mystery to his former friends in music, who didn't see much relationship between his songs for the Nation of Islam and what he had done before.

But then even that music was foreclosed. Did Elijah fear that those musicians who had joined him would not be serious enough at their religious calling? Or did he wish to break all manner of their ties, all similarities to the churches of their past, of the past of all his followers? Would such a break offer one more piece of evidence that here, with Elijah in the Nation of Islam, was the only salvation for blacks? "You may get music to soothe your souls and make you feel better in those Christian churches, but it is all a fraud designed to make you a slave," Elijah may have been saying. Or this sacrifice required by Elijah may simply have made those young men more dependent on him.

Ah, then, forty years later, in 1993, in one more of his totally unexpected moves, Farrakhan took up his violin again. This was to be the first time Minister Farrakhan would once again savor the music of his own past. Now that he was so secure in his position, it was time to show the world that there was more to this man than people knew or imagined, more than the fierce speaker, more than the religious leader, more than the savior of the poor and deprived, and more than what was believed to be the clever manipulator of people. It was time to show the world that this man had an immense, if long-buried, aesthetic talent as well. It was time to give a new and brilliant cast to his image.

With the same assurance he brought to everything else he did, Farrakhan organized a classical concert to celebrate his sixtieth birthday. He would play his violin with a group of professional musicians he hired and called the New World Orchestra. He described it as composed of Christians, Jews, and Muslims, though a representative of the Civic Orchestra of Chicago, Juan Carlos Siviero, recalls it being mostly Jews, among them a number of Chicago Symphony Orchestra players, with a few blacks, including the conductor, Michael Morgan, a black who was then the assistant director of the CSO.

Farrakhan sought out a teacher to refresh his talent—his secretary called Roosevelt University, a commuter school in downtown Chicago which has a highly diverse student body and caters to the local popula- tion, but which has a highly regarded music school, and asked to be re- ferred to a teacher. For eighteen months Farrakhan took lessons with Elaine Skorodin Fohrman, a Jewish part-time member of Roosevelt's music faculty who has been in the music business for fifty years. As an observant Jew who knew of Farrakhan's reputation as an anti-Semite, she hesitated a moment before agreeing to take him on. It was a chal- lenge, she said. His earlier Jewish teacher in Boston, a Russian immi- grant, would no doubt be surprised that his successor would have to make a political judgment about whether to teach his very talented stu- dent.

But Farrakhan turned out to be a splendid student. He was, Fohrman says, "a very accomplished musician and worked hard." They rarely talked about anything but music. "He was very cordial and very respectful. I was a music teacher and he was the student."

Then, on May 17, 1993, a few days after his actual birthday, Far- rakhan astounded the world by playing, for an audience described by the *Chicago Tribune* as three thousand Muslims, what critics deemed a highly creditable performance. He played not at Orchestra Hall or in any other music venue but at a well-known nondenominational black Christian church in the farthest southern reaches of Chicago, the Christ Universal Temple. After all, Farrakhan was a religious leader. What would be more appropriate as a setting for his birthday celebra- tion concert than this famous church? That the audience consisted mostly of his own followers was not exactly according to plan, but that was okay. His teacher, who sat in the first row beside Farrakhan's wife and family, suggested that perhaps his listeners might not have at- tended such a concert were it not that Farrakhan was the star per- former. He repeated the concert a month later in Winston-Salem, North Carolina.

Meanwhile Farrakhan expressed his pleasure to be playing music again. He told an interviewer on National Public Radio, "Music, as it expands my breadth, it expands my breadth to include the beauty of human beings—all human beings." And it appears that slowly he is permitting music in the Nation, not as part of the religious ritual but to be appreciated personally.

Rumors had spread that the music Farrakhan planned to play, the very beautiful crowd-pleaser called by Fohrman "a dazzler," the Mendelssohn Violin Concerto in E Minor, was selected because Mendelssohn had been a Jew. Here was to be an olive branch extended to the Jews. The concert and the selection were to be "a departure from the doctrine of separation," understood by most to be in this case a euphemism for anti-Semitism. Only the most cynical would not be moved. His teacher described it as a "nice gesture."

Unfortunately for Farrakhan, all those Jews he was extending his arm to, with violin in hand, were not at the concert to hear him. Anyway, Louis Farrakhan a highly talented violinist? Ridiculous! One of the variety of ways in which Farrakhan is not only unknown to the public but completely unanticipated.

The story would have ended there—Farrakhan disappointed at not being taken seriously before the concert, but deeply gratified afterward when he was described as an excellent musician by the critics, who probably expected something quite different. But there's another piece of this story, as there usually is in stories about Farrakhan.

Ironically, he was misinformed. When Farrakhan told her he wanted to play the Mendelssohn violin concerto, his music teacher told him that Mendelssohn was a Jew. It seemed a strange choice to her, knowing of his anti-Semitism. But Farrakhan told her he hadn't known Mendelssohn was Jewish, that he had chosen the piece because he had partly learned it as a teenager, had enjoyed it, and now wanted to play the whole thing. She was surprised, she said, but after all, "music transcends such differences."

Although Fohrman knew that Mendelssohn had converted to Catholicism, many others continued to count him as a Jew. Even in classical musical circles it is not well-known that Felix Mendelssohn, the German composer, was not a Jew except by the most humiliating standards. He was indeed the grandson of the famous Jewish philosopher Moses Mendelssohn, a major figure in the fight against the persecution of the Jews, but his son, Felix's father, probably caused Moses' greatest pain. He became a wealthy Berlin banker, and to gain the wider favors of the Christian world, like so many other Jews in nineteenth-century Europe, he converted his family to Christianity and had his children baptized into the church. Felix Mendelssohn was a Christian from the time he was seven years old, and there is no record he ever renounced his conversion or revealed his Jewish roots, unlike his fellow German artist, the poet Heinrich Heine, who had also converted and said, near the end of his life, "I make no secret of my Judaism, to which I have not returned because I have never left it."

What Forhman claimed not to know was that Jewish musicians and their followers in nineteenth-century Europe had claimed Mendelssohn as a Jew to counter the criticism that Jews couldn't write music. While Jews could certainly perform well, the bigots said, they could not *compose* music. But there was the Jew Mendelssohn to prove them wrong.

On the other hand, anti-Semites went along with the idea of Mendelssohn's Jewishness because it helped their argument. True, Mendelssohn was a Jewish composer, but could he be compared to Mozart, Haydn, Beethoven, Brahms? Not by a long shot. This simply proved that even when the Jews produced a composer, he could not be counted among the greats.

The argument about the merit of Jewish composers becomes pretty silly when one realizes that Gustav Mahler, hardly a third-rate composer, an Austrian Jew, never made a secret of the fact that he was forced to convert to Catholicism in 1897 in order to win an appointment as director of the illustrious Vienna Court Orchestra, more than eighty years after Mendelssohn had been baptized.

Anti-Semitism and racism have, in their madness, led to all kinds of incomprehensible and reprehensible ideas and acts, among the victims as well as the victimizers. Not a few of those ideas have made Farrakhan a hero or a villain to many people, black and white. It might be said that in the Western world, since Hitler, there has been no battle with the Jews to match Farrakhan's since he opened up that can of worms again. Which is not to say that Farrakhan is alone in the gentile "battle" against Jews. The woods are full of them, but no one else has managed to corral a substantial sympathetic audience.

Should we criticize Farrakhan's olive branch—a bit of a lie but nevertheless an olive branch—because it was based on a racist lie? How can we do that when his Jewish teacher assured me that Farrakhan had no knowledge of that lie, that he told her he knew nothing of Mendelssohn's religious background?

Perhaps Farrakhan had not known that Mendelssohn was viewed as Jewish, and it was only a small fib he told when he said he had selected the Mendelssohn piece as an olive branch to the Jews. He hadn't at first selected it for that reason, but once he found out that Mendelssohn was a Jew, what a great gesture he could make! That's reasonable. But he also told Fohrman he hadn't known that most of the great performers of his era—Rubenstein, Milstein, Heifetz, Serkin, Stern, Menuhin—were Jews. How did one manage to study a major classical instrument, even as a teenager, with a Russian Jewish teacher, without knowing that those enormously famous and feted performers of his era, many of them from Russia, were Jews? Maybe in the same way a black could discover the impact of racism only when he was refused a ticket to a movie.

Whether Farrakhan knew the truth about Mendelssohn or not, whether it was only a small, harmless lie he concocted long after he had chosen the Mendelssohn to play because it would be easiest for him to learn quickly, his alleged olive branch to the Jews is nonetheless one of those frauds he periodically presents as his good intentions. One could say that this harmless lie might have had some positive effects, so why worry about it? But one always worries about lies. And their purposes. Without even hinting at any serious parallels, one can't help recall Hitler's lies. Or that harmless, little lie Lyndon Baines Johnson told Congress about the Gulf of Tonkin incident that led to the escalation of the Vietnam War and 58,000 American deaths. There's no real comparison, of course, but lies are lies. And one has difficulty figuring out the purpose of this little lie in the context of the Nazi-like lies about the Jews that Farrakhan has been telling for years. Did he truly mean to offer an olive branch? Did his music enable him to transcend his mad bigotry? While he had to tell a little lie to make this gesture to the Jews, wasn't it important that he made the gesture?

After all, his teacher was perfectly willing to overlook the little lie and call Farrakhan's fraud "a nice gesture." She and her husband had been to his house a few times for dinner, and he had always been "cordial and respectful" of her. So he lied a little. Even if he didn't tell the whole truth, she felt sure he really wanted this concert to be a gesture of goodwill toward the Jews.

Now let's think this through. Farrakhan decides to give this concert to enhance his image. He allegedly finds out from his Jewish teacher that the composer whose concerto he had decided to play—because it would be easiest for him to learn quickly and is certainly one of the most popular violin concerti—is a Jew. As long as he's enhancing his image, why not go a little further and make it an olive branch to the Jews? It certainly couldn't hurt him, could it? Who would know his ignorance about Mendelssohn being Jewish except his teacher, and she seemed so intrigued by him that she was unlikely to figure out that this ploy was a fraud.

On the other hand, he may have lied to his teacher. He may have been led to believe years ago that Mendelssohn was a Jew, and chose the concerto to play so that he could make this offer to the Jews. Maybe. In any event, there was no way he could lose. True, he learned later that Mendelssohn really wasn't a Jew, and some people thereby ridiculed his olive branch. But Farrakhan had been ridiculed before by white intellectuals, especially Jews, plenty of times. Who listened to them?

This seems to be a small, insignificant story. So Farrakhan played a concert, was praised, made a gesture to the Jews. So what? Why make so much of this story? Because it tells us so much about Farrakhan and about his role in society. First we have to ask, do we join in the ridicule of him? Given the apparent widespread belief in this myth about Mendelssohn, shouldn't we withhold ridicule and instead feel not a little sad that conditions in the Western world have led to the creation of that and plenty of other such racist myths? Then, shouldn't we be saddened that this man, so much himself the victim of racist myths, is so guilty of spreading so many of them? Perhaps we are entitled to a laugh, or maybe a cry, that Farrakhan was trapped in a racist myth about a Jew by another Jew. Perhaps we should extend our sympathies to the Jews who fell for Farrakhan's ploy and were also trapped in their own mythology.

And shouldn't we marvel not only at the cleverness and even wiliness but also the many talents of this strange man? Sure, there are plenty of competent, even excellent violinists, but how many of them would organize an orchestra that includes first-rate talent, beguile a longtime professional music teacher into utterly believing in you and your talent, study seriously for eighteen months to perfect a famous concerto for performance, pronounce to the world that this concert was not only your sixtieth birthday celebration but also your effort to overcome the separatism of this world by playing this beloved concerto of a famous Jewish composer, and then—perform that concert in a black church for a mostly black audience, most of whom are members of your own mosque and have probably never heard a symphonic concert before?

Now add to this an idea that is not often mentioned in polite society: this wasn't just one of the thousands of first-rate violinists out there. This was a sixty-year-old black violinist who, as a young man hoping to learn to excel at his instrument at a first-class music school, was instead given a sports scholarship to a small black college in the South; for many years afterward, had he indeed learned to excel at the violin, he would have been excluded from American symphonic orchestras. This was a sixty-year-old master violinist who was a member of a race that, until not very long ago, was considered incapable of playing such music as the Mendelssohn Concerto in E Minor. This was a sixty-year-old black violinist who, as a young man, may never have seen the inside of Boston's Symphony Hall. This concert was not only an extravagant and spectacular sixtieth birthday party, and perhaps an absurd effort to make a conciliatory gesture to the Jews, it was above all one of the most extraordinary banners of defiance of the white world Minister Louis Farrakhan has ever hung and perhaps ever will again. Elaine Fohrman asked me why I had chosen to write about Farrakhan.

After standing beside him at a music stand for eighteen months and attending that unusual concert and eating dinner with Farrakhan and his family, Elaine Fohrman, like so many other people, obviously didn't have a clue about this man. This is not because she is insensitive or unintelligent but because, she said, music transcended everything else for them. For Forhman, Farrakhan was a musician. He talked, walked, and played like a musician because that was the man he wanted to present to his teacher, the man he wanted to be for those short periods. One would nevertheless expect Forhman to have acquired some other ideas about this man with whom she spent all those hours. But Farrakhan is not a man who gives off what most of us expect as normal clues. He seems to be able to choose his persona. That is no doubt because he believes he is God, which gives him an extraordinary scope, though it depends on whom he is talking to whether he claims actually to be *the* God or to be only "A God," or "A Jesus, walking in the footsteps of THE Jesus." He claims at times to be *the* Messiah, and, at other times, "not THE Messiah . . . [only] a functionary of His." But a man with such delusions about himself is not likely to provide many readable clues about himself, and about what he thinks and feels. One must listen most closely—read between and through the lines—to even begin to guess what he is thinking.

9.

Mae Clarke, along with several members of her family, was a devout churchgoer. It had been the voice of Mae's now seventy-five-year-old cousin, Gwen Williams, that I had heard soaring above the church that Sunday, putting the choir to shame. I learned this later over lunch with her at Rebecca's Restaurant, right off the Boston Common. Gwen Williams was a traditional West Indian lady who had rarely missed a Sunday at church in her life, like most of the family, which had always been close, she said. She had always been fond of her Walcott cousins. Her father had once remarked about the five-year-old Gene, "That boy will do anything he wants in life. He'll go anyplace he wants to go." Gwen hoped to get to Chicago to see the Salaam, the fancy new restaurant that the Nation had just opened, but she had never had much use for Gene's preachings and hadn't been altogether sympathetic when he managed to convert his mother and brother to the Nation. It had been a loss to the church when Gene, and then later Alvan and his mother, had left the church. Mae and her sons had made a big contribution to the church. She had instilled in them a real love for the church, Gwen believed. But of course most of the West Indian kids went to church even if their parents didn't. It was a center of all kinds of activities and a haven of comfort and safety in a world that didn't offer a lot of those qualities. When Mae and the boys became Muslims, that put some strains on the family ties, but they had remained part of the family even if, after they left Roxbury, they didn't see each other very often. That's the way it is with so many families. Alvan went to New York where work was better for him, and Mae went to Chicago. Gwen's son was still in Boston, on the police force; she was proud of him. She stopped a cop on the street as we were walking along the Common to ask if he knew her son. Everybody knew him, she said.

10.

That Mae Clarke was a staunch Episcopalian (Anglican, as it is called in the islands) throughout most of her life, and that she was generous and kind and loved music and was strongly devoted to her children, is not evidence to prove that Gene Walcott did not learn at his mother's knee some of the bigotry he later revealed. After all, many Germans shared Mae Clarke's personal traits.

That she had a hard life is evident from her cousin's description and those of others who knew the family. She had either left her allegedly philandering fair-skinned, handsome husband (Farrakhan once suggested his father was partly Jewish, but he generally admits he didn't know him) or been abandoned by him shortly after she came to the Bronx from the West Indies. A few years later, after she arrived in Boston with her two sons, she apparently refused to tell relatives and friends what had happened in her life before she got there.

She was, however, determined that her sons have a fair chance in the world and be prepared to take opportunities as they appeared. This is clear from stories about her. The boys apparently didn't get away with much. She was old-fashioned, perhaps even harsh. She is not described as a bitter woman, one who would be likely to fill her sons full of bigoted talk; but it is quite clear from some of Farrakhan's public descriptions of her that she was not the tenderest of mothers. In families similar to the one he describes as his own, bigotry and hatred are often bred. But history makes clear that out of such families also come a great range of personalities with an equally wide range of ideas. It is sheer foolishness to suggest that one kind of family environment produces just one type of personality with one set of ideas.

All such disclaimers stated, it is nevertheless interesting to compare the similarities and differences in the homes and careers of Adolf Hitler and Louis Farrakhan, without giving any credence at all to those who accuse Farrakhan of being a Hitler. That being said, it can also be said that Farrakhan shows just enough resemblance to Hitler to make it worthwhile to compare their early histories. He displays a mild version of Hitler's almost violent need to control his environment, his ability to display an immensely variable persona, his paranoia, his egotistical hours-long public speeches, and, of course, his extreme anti-Semitism.

Hitler's father was such a petty tyrant that his nagging drove his older son out of the house in his adolescence. Hitler wrote in *Mein Kampf* that, after being the compliant and cooperative child—he was an altar boy—"I was forced . . . into opposition. Hard and determined as my father might be in putting through plans . . . his son was just as determined and recalcitrant in rejecting an idea that appealed to him not at all." Hitler's father was apparently not a cruel man, only a petty despot.

Mae Clarke seems to have had that quality in common with Hitler's father. But she was a woman, and much more vulnerable. While Hitler reserved his attacks on his father until he was long since dead, Farrakhan showed not the least bit of discretion or valor in attacking his mother during her lifetime. He told audiences, as in his 1987 speech, "How to Give Birth to a God," that had his mother had her way, he wouldn't be speaking to them. Instead he would have been a product of her abortion. Farrakhan would have had to be pretty angry at her to tell such a story, true or not.

It gets worse. Listen to the actual words he used to tell a Chicago audience in 1987 about his relationship with his mother: "It is a good thing that God has given us the nature to submit, and the nature to rebel. Because if I did not rebel against the circumstances into which I was born I could never be what I am today. Because my mother tried to kill me when I was a child, her baby in her womb. She did not know what she was carrying. She regrets that to this day and she tells me as she goes into the valley of death. She begs the pardon of God for trying to kill this which was in her womb, but she marked me with her own thinking. . . . I thank Allah that a wise God puts his hand over a mother, who though good and wonderful, in her ignorance set a mark on her child. But Allah said no, I'm going to give him the will to overcome his mother and her thinking when she was forming him in the womb. I'm going to give him the will to say I rebel against that. And so as a young boy no matter what she said, I said I'll show her. As a child I said I'll show you mamma. The world will respect me one day, I'll show you. And because I was determined to overcome the circumstances of my birth, I am where I am by the help of God."

If his mother did in fact tell him she had planned to "kill him," it makes us pause to think about this mother's devotion to her children and about the kind of person she was. It isn't a big stretch from imagining a woman telling her son that she wanted to abort him, to telling him angry stories about, for instance, the Jewish housewives for whom she cleaned. Or other stories that it wasn't hard to come by in the thirties. One could merely turn on one's radio to hear Father Coughlin, a Catholic priest whom the church endorsed in his tirades against Jews, or his colleague, Gerald L. K. Smith, who also filled the airways with support for Hitler and railed against the infamous Protocols of Zion, a writ that supposedly originated in Russia in the early part of the century and described the conspiracies of the Jews to take over the world. Farrakhan unearthed and preached the Protocols after they had been buried for years.

Did Mae Clarke supply her son with a generous earful of this talk, along with urgings to practice the violin, do well in school, attend church, stay clean, and do his chores, as did so many mothers in the Western world? Did she build in him such a reservoir of bitterness and hatred that it would later be the unconscious source of his turning on her and using her so disgustingly?

Or was Mae Clarke quite innocent in her son's outcome, guilty perhaps of trying too hard, as Hitler's father had, to make him a good solid citizen, but without the rancor and bitterness that he implies for her? Hitler's lifelong civil servant father was no more than a commonplace Austrian anti-Semite, less intense in his feelings than many of his countrymen. After all, when Hitler returned to Vienna in 1938 at the head of the occupying German army, the Austrians cheered and happily led the extermination of the Jews. But Hitler did not learn his political and racial lessons from his father; he learned them from his favorite history teacher, Leopold Poetsch, of whom he wrote, "Perhaps it affected my whole later life that good fortune sent me a history teacher who was one of the few who knew how to make . . . this approach [Nazism] the dominant one."

Mae Clarke was probably also just a run-of-the-mill anti-Semite, a sentiment learned in the British-owned St. Kitts, where she grew up. Perhaps she was more than usually bitter and angry at whites, though I didn't encounter the same bitterness among the West Indians who were part of her community that one encounters among American blacks. We simply don't know whether it was Mae Clarke or some other early source in Farrakhan's life that prepared him to reject the church in which he'd grown up and join the Nation of Islam to release the anger and bitterness he obviously had nurtured all those years. Perhaps those feelings had been entirely random until he was already in his twenties, when he heard Elijah Muhammad speak.

We do know that in his adolescence he was having trouble in his relationships with whites. After just one year he rejected the prized place he had won as one of only a handful of black boys, most of whom were West Indian, to attend the most prestigious high school in Boston, Boston Latin School. Instead he transferred to Boston English School, the second most highly regarded high school in Boston, where there were more black (also West Indian) students.

One of Gene's early churchmates, Leonard de Cordova, who is still an active member of St. Cyprian's, entered Boston Latin a year before Gene. He suggested that while Gene's decision to change schools after only one year may have resulted from the much more intense academic competition at Latin, along with less emphasis on athletic activities, at which Gene excelled, he had the strong feeling that Gene was simply not comfortable in a school that was so heavily white and not without discrimination. "I have to admit it wasn't always easy to stay in that atmosphere," de Cordova says, "but graduation from Boston Latin was a certificate to go anywhere, and I wasn't going to pass it up just because I was sometimes unhappy. I suspect Gene felt more strongly than I did, maybe was just more sensitive about the way blacks got handled, and just couldn't take it."

11.

In 1996 Farrakhan told Henry Louis Gates, a black professor at Harvard who writes regularly about black issues, that "he experienced the full impact of racism" on a trip to Washington, D.C., in 1950, on his way to college in the South. He was refused a ticket to a movie house. "A very close friend of mine had just been killed in Korea, and I walked down the street with a twenty-dollar bill in one hand, my wallet in the other, and at that point I was very, very angry with America. . . . I started writing a calypso song called, 'Why America Is No Democracy,'" he told Gates. This was the moment when he experienced, he said, the full impact of racism. It would seem that Farrakhan had managed to suppress his earlier experiences of racism that no black in the thirties and forties in Boston could have escaped, making it more likely that, when the moment was right, the lancing of the wound was far more explosive.

There is also the possibility that Farrakhan rearranged his life story a bit for Gates, who was writing for a special issue of the *New Yorker* on blacks (largely read by whites), of which Farrakhan was quite aware. The story that he told Gates paints him as a basically simple-minded young man who occasionally expressed black distress in a calypso song, but who chose the Nation of Islam as a more forthright and honest religious offering. He was not, in other words, an angry, bitter young man who grasped at the "blue-eyed white devil" message he heard at the Nation of Islam to help rid him of his demons. He was growing disillusioned with his church. "I couldn't understand why Jesus would preach so much love and why there was so much hate demonstrated by white Christians against black Christians." Although he was having such feelings, somehow it happened that the first full impact of racism came when he was refused a ticket to a movie.

He knew that he would create a softer, gentler impression of himself with that story about the incident at the movie theater in Washington. This is not the man his followers see, the man who one senses has seen a good deal of racism, when he tells his audiences characteristically: "You could not do the things that you do if you were not animal in human form. You don't steal from another human being. You don't beat an old man, and an old woman in the head. This is not white people doing this; this is you Black man, doing this to yourself. You don't take a young girl and throw her down in the alley and rape her. She is not offering herself to you; that is the act of an animal, a sick depraved man. You are a sick people and you need a doctor." That ferociously angry, deeply feeling, haunted man does not often make an appearance for whites or their surrogates. It is a much milder Farrakhan whom most whites know.

The mild-mannered story that Farrakhan presented to Gates is, of course, one side of the man, but it has a hollowness to it that makes one wonder whether it wasn't invented for a *New Yorker* audience. As a youngster in the forties, living in the segregated section of Boston, a city that was largely off-limits to blacks until the seventies, did Farrakhan have to go to Washington, D.C., and be excluded from a movie theater to experience the full impact of racism? Then, only a few years after he made that fateful trip, he was suddenly transformed from an innocent boy into the stormy Muslim who wrote such songs as "A White Man's Heaven Is a Black Man's Hell," or the play he wrote, directed, and acted in, *Orgena*, in which he portrays whites as evil criminals to be sentenced to death by their black jurors.

If youth is a time of swift and dramatic transformation, why should we doubt that Gene Walcott had such a transformation, beginning in Washington, D.C., on that day? Only because we have to doubt whether a highly intelligent, sensitive youth could have grown up in a segregated environment, and gone to a mixed school where he likely faced discrimination, and still escaped racism. Boston is the city where the struggle over court-mandated school desegregation took its most violent form in the North, where one of the opening shots of the whites against the desegregation order by a federal judge was the near lynching of a black man who happened to be driving through a white neighborhood. The white Boston School Committee led a three-year battle to block desegregation. The head of the Save Boston Committee, when he resented the television coverage of one black reporter, described him as "one generation out of the trees—I bet he loves bananas." In 1967, with David Duke at its head, the Ku Klux Klan was able to rally five hundred whites in two neighborhoods in Boston where blacks had been assigned to attend formerly all-white schools. To Duke's shout to the crowd, "We don't believe Negroes fit into modern society," the Bostonians roared back, "They're not Negroes: in Southie, we call them *niggers*." To which Duke responded, "The real issue isn't education. The real issue isn't a school here or a school there . . . the real issue is *niggers*," as reported by Jon Hillson in *The Battle of Boston*. In April 1965 Martin Luther King, Jr., went to Boston, where he had been a student at Boston University, to try to bring peace to a city under siege, and led a march of fifteen thousand to demand an end to segregated schools.

Boston was also the city about which Hillson says, "Administering a system which featured widespread unemployment, deteriorating social services, and perhaps the poorest school system in the North, the Democratic Party needed something more than patronage, nepotism, and the dispensing of small favors to retain its base in the white neighborhoods. Therefore its message to its rank and file was: It is not only what you have, which may not be much, but what you might lose to them—to the Blacks. Fear of the Blacks became the machine's watchwords as Boston's Afro-American population grew, as the civil rights movement campaigned in the South, as the struggle it inspired for school desegregation in Boston began in the 1950s."

Racism in Boston didn't wear a symmetrical face. As in other cities, but even more pronounced in Boston, while the white poor and working class made their racism all too obvious, the city's elite displayed their racism in more subtle ways and were more susceptible to change than their poorer neighbors. Thus in 1966, with the extraordinary impact of the civil rights movement, a Boston black—to be sure, a fair-skinned black, but a black nevertheless—was able to win the first senatorial seat held by a black since Reconstruction. It helped that his opponent was involved in a family scandal. But Edward Brooke won that seat as a Republican, the minority party of Massachusetts, with the help of black voters and what had become a sizable liberal elite, including the Jews of Boston, who played a large role in what was viewed as a protest election campaign against the still racist Democratic party. But for Farrakhan, Edward Brooke and what he came to represent in Boston were still part of the unknown, unimagined future.

Could this bright, sensitive youngster living in this city that is described by his former schoolmate de Cordova as a "thoroughly racist city where no institution, school, business, or any other with rare exception would accept anyone of another color," never have encountered the Boston Southies who routinely beat up blacks for the hell of it? It is simply too difficult to believe that Gene Walcott had to wait until he was past eighteen and being refused a movie ticket in Washington, D.C., to realize the "full impact of racism."

True, in most Northern cities, blacks weren't barred from movies, so this would have been a new unpleasant experience. But they might have encountered trouble going to a movie in an all-white section of town. Had this young black man been so unadventurous, so sheltered, that he never ventured into the places in Boston where, if they didn't outright refuse entry to blacks, they were pretty nasty? Had he never tried to get a job in Boston for which no blacks need have applied? Was he never lucky enough, having made the mistake of walking into a white Boston neighborhood at night, to meet a white cop who only searched him, threatened to arrest him, then chased him out of the neighborhood instead of beating him up and leaving him in the street far from that neighborhood?

Maybe Farrakhan lived a charmed life. Maybe he escaped the fate of so many black youth, not only in Boston but in all Northern cities. Still, a man who in his early twenties turns from a benign, somewhat integrated, success-oriented life in show business to one dedicated to creating a separate black nation, and to a crusade to awaken his fellow blacks to their semislave condition in the white world, probably has some intimate knowledge of racism. De Cordova told me he could well imagine that Farrakhan's embrace of the Nation of Islam was inspired by his experience of growing up in Boston.

If my skepticism is justified, why would Farrakhan want to invent such a low-key incident to describe the turning point in his life? Why would he, in effect, dismiss all his youthful experiences and impressions of racism? Did he think that story would provide him a façade of the peaceful man who, in choosing the Nation, simply chose a higher form of spirituality? Did he feel he would enhance his reputation among whites and among black intellectuals if he acted as if he had no real recognition or recriminations about the racism in his life? A little like Booker T. Washington reassuring all those whites that blacks would work well and productively for and beside them but wouldn't threaten the status quo?

Booker T. Washington never revealed that piece of him that was secretly trying to undo the Jim Crow laws. His position would have been wiped from under him by the white establishment that supported him so strongly, that enabled him to help many blacks but mainly allowed him to appear to the world as a hero. Farrakhan has no such problem. He lives in another era. It's almost as if it were another planet. He can say whatever he likes to whomever he likes. If he presents one picture of himself to one audience and a different one to another audience, well, perhaps the FBI might know, but few others. Farrakhan's various audiences don't much overlap.

So the picture Farrakhan presented to Gates and presents to other writers for the white media is quite different from the one he presents to his followers. For them he has a deep and enduring vision of shaking up the status quo, like the slaves who revolted against their masters and who are among his strongest heroes. It is his young black audiences to whom he reveals this vision. For them he mixes fact with fantasy and says whatever he believes will enhance that vision, a vision that Gates and others have only been given hints of.

To a crowd at Princeton University, for instance, when he was stumping for Jesse Jackson's run for the presidency in 1984, he scolded, "We never backed Nat Turner, Denmark Vecsey, or Gabriel Prosser. We never stood up with David Walker." So far so good, he's got that hero track right, but then he gets confused. "We were not really with Booker T. [Washington, a leader of revolt?] and W. E. B. Du Bois." Ah now, he's on another track. "We weren't with Marcus Garvey [who wanted to build businesses], we weren't with Noble Drew Ali [a true spiritualist], we weren't with Martin [no one was so forcefully against Martin Luther King, Jr., as the Nation], we weren't with Malcolm [Farrakhan admits creating the atmosphere that led to his murder], we weren't with Elijah! [considering Elijah's success, and comparing him to earlier black leaders, and considering that he opposed electoral politics, it doesn't seem fair to accuse young blacks of not being with Elijah]" One wonders about this list, which omits all the black politicians around the country who were elected to office in the years before Jesse Jackson ran, whom the Nation refused to support.

Farrakhan then heightened his harangue. "Every Black leader that God gave you out of the masses, out of your fear of white people's censure, you backed away from your own leaders, allowing them to be killed, and then all you can do is have a jive time stinkin' holiday where you look at their picture and keep off of work, but you don't think enough of the principles that those men lived and died on to carry those principles into practice in your own miserable lives. You won't get away no more. You won't get away no more. You're through, all of you, Black and white! You deserve the chastisement. You should get it if you don't act in a way to avert it."

Farrakhan was conscious of the conflict between this speech and his voting record and the electoral record of the Nation. He admitted to this audience, "I'm fifty years old, I never voted, never registered." But he was justified, he said. He only had a choice between "the fire of the dragon or the deceit of Satan." Never mind all those other black politicians he could have helped. Now he had decided that Jesse Jackson's bandwagon was a good one for him to join. Jesse wasn't running for mayor, or county sheriff, or the board of election. This was the big leagues, the presidency, and there was no way Farrakhan was going to miss this. So he was telling this crowd that now he had a real choice and they should all follow him to exercise that choice.

"Now why would you do that for Farrakhan?" he asks his audience. "So that you won't have anything to say to me if this alternative fails. I got another one in my back pocket." And what is this alternative he's got in his back pocket? "I ain't never read in the book where we got integrated and all that. The book didn't say that." Jackson is running this thing he calls the Rainbow Coalition, an integrated campaign. The next time around, if Jackson fails, Farrakhan makes clear, we'll know better than that.

Before the 1984 campaign was over, Farrakhan had overplayed his hand and Jesse had to disown his support. Threatening to kill a black reporter who had reported an anti-Semitic remark by Jesse was not exactly the way to win the support of the media or the voters, but it was a big hit with many of Farrakhan's followers. In the end, however, after Jesse avoided any contact with Farrakhan for years, he was forced to eat crow. Too many black men were supporting Farrakhan's Million-Man March for him to keep his word that he wouldn't speak at the rally. He was one of dozens of speakers who were followed at the end by the man with the vision. Jesse spoke for ten minutes. Farrakhan spoke for two and a half hours.

But this vision is not the one Farrakhan wishes to convey to whites. That picture, which whites don't usually believe, is of a man under attack by whites, by the media, by the government, most of all by Jews. That picture also shows a man who is the leading light among the most oppressed of blacks, the man who saves drug addicts and gangbangers and criminals who have nowhere else to turn. That picture Farrakhan presents to the white public (by which is meant the white media) is a man of compromise, though he can be oppositional if he is challenged, if he believes he is wrongly accused. He was publicly enraged when he was threatened with congressional investigation into the circumstances of his 1996 travels to Africa and the Middle East.

12.

To compare the presumed parental traits of Mae Clarke with those of Alois Hitler in order to suggest that both their sons had acquired some of the bitterness and hatred of their later lives in their parents' households is not to say that the two men are more than distantly alike. There is no evidence from Hitler's adult life that points to any of the normal familial instincts and compassion toward others that can be clearly seen in Louis Farrakhan, and there is no evidence of the total lawlessness of Hitler in Farrakhan. In looking at these differences—and a few similarities—between them, remember that it is folly to predict a certain kind of behavior from a given upbringing.

Hitler was of course quite unlike Farrakhan, for he was a member of a dominant class and race in his part of the world. His family, unlike Farrakhan's, was economically comfortable. Hitler was free to go and come as he wished without racial or religious barriers. He was forced to attend the local *realschule*, a vocational school, instead of the *gymnasium* that would have prepared him for an academic career, because his father was not sympathetic with his ideals.

Later, like Farrakhan, his artistic academic ambitions were thwarted, though in Hitler's case it was not money or class or race or religion or his father's interference (he was dead by then) but only his lack of artistic talent that kept Hitler out of the most illustrious art school in Austria. He had all those other advantages. The Academy's rejection left him feeling despised and rejected and, at the same time, filled with delusions of grandeur: he was too good for them.

For Gene Walcott, by contrast, his rather exceptional talent didn't help him a bit. It was money, class, but mostly race that destroyed his dream of attending the Juilliard School of Music. If he had, like Hitler, some thoughts that he was too good for Juilliard, it didn't prevent him from accepting the only offer he received, an athletic scholarship at a small, all-black Southern teachers' college.

Farrakhan's mother may indeed have been a petty tyrant like Hitler's father and like many mothers. She may even have been cruel, as he implied. But Mae Clarke was no ordinary tyrannical mother. She was black, and it was not at all unusual for black children to have "tiger" mothers who felt they must protect their children and prepare them to protect themselves from the racist world outside and to attain some means to succeed financially in a world that didn't offer them much opportunity. All too many black mothers were not only tyrannical but filled with fear and anger over their own fate, fear and anger that often reached into their children's psyches as well.

But if Mae Clarke tried too hard to protect and prepare her sons for the career of *her* choice, as Hitler's father did, the similarity bears greater examination. Hitler's father, too, lived in an unfair class system, in which opportunity was not easy to come by, though Mae Clarke might have considered it heaven. And if he believed his sons would be best off if they followed his career in one of the safe, secure, well-paid civil service jobs in Austria, it wasn't so surprising or unusual. Unfortunately his children rejected his choices for them.

Mae Clarke's position was far different. She had no security to offer her sons. She knew that whatever they chose to do with their lives, they could end up poor like her and most of her friends and relatives. And she knew that there were few opportunities open to them. But she decided that if they could become very accomplished musicians, they might find their way. The world of the arts was not nearly as bigoted as were other areas of life, though that was only relative. So it was music she urged on them, perhaps browbeat them into, with perhaps the same rigidity as Hitler's father. Gene Walcott and his brother Alvan, unlike Hitler and his brother, followed their mother's advice and became outstanding musicians. Their mother had sufficiently encouraged them that they became good students. No vocational school for Mae Clarke's son. He was also a highly accomplished athlete. One of his teammates at Boston English, Gerald D'Alfonso, said he was the most competitive member of the track team, that he was willing to practice even on marble floors when he had no alternative. He had all kinds of qualifications that Hitler lacked, qualifications that would have justifiably led him to hope for a scholarship to the famous Juilliard School of Music. Short of that, surely he would get financial help from some other leading music school. With such a record today, the universities and colleges would be swarming all over him. But in 1950 the young West Indian black, whatever talents he may have had, received no such offers. He tells a story about learning early on how his ambitions were simply too lofty for an

American black, a variation on a story that is part of American black history:

Walcott was a contestant on the Ted Mack Original Amateur Hour on television when he was in his teens. "I was very good," he said, "and I will never forget, we were doing rehearsal and you know, you have to talk before you play, so they asked me . . . 'Louis, what do you want to do when you grow up?' and I said, 'Oh, I want to be able to play the violin as great as Yassha Hiefitz [sic].' At that time, Yassha Hiefitz was the world's greatest violinist and to this day, he remains an actual . . . well, I'll just call him monstrous in playing the violin. Now for me to take Yassha Hiefitz and make him my goal, who is the best in the world, that says I had lofty ambitions. Those that heard me say that said, 'We can't let this Negro say that.' They didn't say that to me, but that's what they must have said, because [before we went on the air, while they were preparing us] they changed my innocent truthful expression. . . . I was a track star and they asked again, 'What would you like to do when you grow up?' and the words that they gave me to say were, 'Oh, I'd like to be able to play the violin one day as fast as I can run.' Are you listening to me?"

In some respects Hitler actually had a more difficult time making his way than Farrakhan did, no doubt because he was not nearly as artistically talented as Farrakhan. He had been denied his opportunity for an academic career by a willful father who did not understand him. But with paternal pressure he nevertheless continued his studies at the *realschule* until his father died. Then the pressure to study and behave like a solid citizen was lifted. He drifted, though he did finally graduate. Despite this mediocre record he went to Vienna to apply for entry into the outstanding art school in Austria. After all, there were no real barriers to his acceptance, he was certain. But he got lazy again, and it was a whole year before he applied to the Academy . He had to prepare a formal drawing presentation. His expectation of being accepted seems to have been in large part fantasy. He wrote in *Mein Kampf* that he expected to "romp" through the entrance exams. After all, he was the son of a highly respected civil servant, he'd been a decent student, he was, by his standards, a gifted artist. The drawings he submitted were beautiful, he believed. Why should he expect to be turned down?

Farrakhan's is a different story. One of Hitler's biographers,

Werner Maser, says Hitler was "deeply disappointed and depressed" when he was turned down by the Academy because he did not satisfy the artistic requirements of the school. He showed all kinds of symptoms of mental disturbance.

Later, after first trying to avoid, then being turned down by, the Austrian army, he joined the more powerful German army and was soon promoted and awarded the Iron Cross for his valorous conduct at the front in World War I. His time in the war, he later said, was the best time of his life.

Eventually Hitler returned to his drawing and was able to sell a few of his architectural drawings that could not be described as anything but pedestrian and derivative. Along with occasional housepainting, they temporarily provided him with a scant livelihood until he found a more exciting life in politics.

Farrakhan, on the other hand, studied at that teachers' college for a couple years and then quit to become a singer-performer. His older brother was already getting jobs as a sax player. Farrakhan's old friend, John Beynoe, now a lawyer, recalls saying to a group of his football buddies, "We got to bring that Gerald Clark and his Calypsonians to Boston. It was the first Calypso dance we'd had in Boston. Gene was there that night and he said, 'I can do that,' and the next thing we knew he was the Prince Charmer, singing that calypso stuff, and he was a young Belafonte. He was out of sight." Music clubs abounded in the fifties, and Gene played in clubs all over the Northeast and Midwest. He was on his way to a successful career until he too found a more exciting life as a visionary.

These two early life histories are different in so many ways that they scarcely bear mentioning, except that both men were badly thwarted in their artistic expectations. Eventually both converted their artistic ambitions into visions of themselves as saviors, with racial hatred and bitterness as their leading motif. It didn't happen right away, and it happened differently in each case. Needless to add, though Hitler had his subhuman "successes," he ended up dead at a relatively early age in a bunker under his headquarters in a city that had been bombed to the ground as a result of his sick intransigence. Farrakhan, the more cautious and disciplined youth, has moved from one more than modest success to a greater one, hale and hearty. In one of his rare impulsive, misbegotten moments, Farrakhan famously expressed his admiration for Hitler, saying he was "wickedly great." It was one of his foolish efforts to appear "heroic." But fortunately or unfortunately for him, Farrakhan is neither as wicked nor as "great" as Hitler.

And even if he had Hitler's temperament, he has a huge obstacle in his heroic path that would have prevented him from ever attaining Hitler's "accomplishments": Farrakhan is black in America.

In the highly unlikely event that even a sizable minority of whites in America were to rally to the flag of a racial bigot, that person would have to be white. Even if a racist black in America were able to (indeed has) capture the loyalty of a substantial segment of American blacks, who comprise only 11 percent of the total population, plus a few Hispanics and Native Americans, he could not command enough support in a national election to equal even the minority that voted for Hitler in 1933 and enabled him to take power in what appeared to be a democratic government. The simple mathematics of racism in America today means that a Hitlerite who could command such a takeover in a democratic government would have to be a white racist. (This could change in fifty years, when the white population in the United States is expected to be overwhelmed by the minorities, particularly the Hispanics. Jorge Oclander, editor of the popular Chicago Spanish-language *La Raza* newspaper, remarked to me, "I certainly wish *we* had a strong political figure capable of challenging the status quo, but it wouldn't be Farrakhan. It would be a Hispanic.") In the nature of American racial politics and population figures, Farrakhan's political opportunities are limited.

But he does try. His hours-long speeches, reminiscent of Hitler's (and Fidel Castro's), are one of the favorite techniques of the demagogue. And Farrakhan's audiences respond with the same enthusiasm as did Hitler's. But Farrakhan's audiences are almost entirely black. While he continually reaches out to Hispanics and Native Americans, he has had little success with them, and there is no shortage of anti-black feeling among some Hispanics, especially Mexicans.

The politically correct atmosphere of the nineties will not tolerate the media drawing a comparison of Farrakhan's speeches to Hitler's (assuming they know), but it will tolerate quite comfortably ignoring him. Among those who object to his words, including those in government, with the almost single exception of the Anti-Defamation League, there is some feeling that all but ignoring him is the best possible tactic. For instance, to commemorate the wildly successful Million-Man March of the year before, Farrakhan gave a three-hour oration on October 16, 1996, at his World's Day of Atonement. Hundreds of thousands of people lined the streets of New York City for as many as a dozen blocks on all the approaches to Dag Hammarskjöld Plaza at the United Nations—the largest outpouring ever to appear at the UN and surely one of the largest crowds in New York City in many years. Television and newspaper coverage of this event was almost nonexistent. The national edition of the paper of record in this country and the major paper of the city of New York, the *New York Times*, printed a quarter-page story with one picture on page 10 of the second section of the paper the next day. Television and radio producers provided thirty-second sound bites on the evening news. Even CNN, which had broadcast the entire day's events for the Million-Man March, all but ignored this event. After all, they had given Farrakhan his day only a year earlier, and they had given him numerous sound bites for his trip to Africa and the Middle East. Another exposure of his influence, especially when he was not this time surrounded by a variety of black leaders (Farrakhan was temporarily deserted on this occasion after the bad publicity he received from his trip abroad, when he cozied up to some of the worst dictators of our time), didn't make good sense.

The abbreviated coverage of this event reminded me of how the media for several years all but blacked out the anti–Vietnam War demonstrations of thousands of people in Washington, D.C. While one might be aghast at much of what Farrakhan says, and therefore might be tempted to pull down the curtain on his influence, the fact is that this massive gathering in New York was a signal that American blacks were crying out to the world for help with their problems. Although that cry had been orchestrated by Farrakhan, the near blackout by the media of that demonstration, like those in the sixties, was unconscionable.

It is also unconscionable for the media not to draw a parallel between Farrakhan's harangues and those of the man who drew his admiration and whom he resembles in so many ways. But except for the *Chicago Tribune* columnist Clarence Page, who attacks Farrakhan regularly, and the syndicated columnist Charles Rowan, who sometimes joins him, most reporters don't engage in critical discussions of blacks, whoever they are. It's too likely to stir up problems that everyone wants to avoid. It's politically incorrect. Jesse Jackson might organize a picket line. It's almost as if they had taken to heart at least the first line of AA's "Serenity Prayer," sometimes attributed to the sixth-century Roman philosopher Boethius, who supposedly wrote it while he was awaiting execution: "God, give me courage to accept the things I cannot change." It's as if there is widespread unspoken recognition among the elite that efforts to change the conditions under which so many blacks live came almost to a standstill years ago. Now these efforts have lost so much support at every level of both government and the voters that any reporter might reasonably repeat Boethius's soother.

13.

Add to all these facts the crucial one: Gene Walcott and his family and friends, his fellow congregants at St. Cyprian's Church in Roxbury, weren't ordinary blacks. They weren't American blacks, though many, including Gene and Alvan Walcott, had been born here. The tight little community, called the Village, in which Gene Walcott grew up was West Indian, a community that did not consider itself ordinary American blacks. The early history of blacks in the West Indies differs considerably from that of American blacks and marks them off as different from the start. First, perhaps most important, they were the majority in the Caribbean Islands, not the 11 or so percent blacks were in the United States. Second, almost as important, slavery was abolished in the islands in 1833, about thirty years before it was ended in the States, and in a much more peaceful way. It had taken a long time for the English abolitionists to win their fight, but the end of slavery in the British Empire was finally decreed by law. The battles in the streets and in the courts had sometimes been ugly, but no hideous civil war had been fought over slavery in the islands (though the British backed the American South in the Civil War). Then, because so few whites lived in the islands, and because no war had devastated the white economy, there was not the revolution and terrible counterrevolution that followed Reconstruction in the South. The end of slavery simply meant that many West Indian blacks could begin to prosper.

The consequence of that West Indies history from 1833 until the turn of the century, when island blacks began to come to New York and Boston, was that, as writer Malcolm Gladwell described it in the *New Yorker*'s special issue on blacks, resident American blacks called those from the Caribbean Jewmaicans for their intense emphasis on hard work and education. (One has to ask, when one hears this expression of disdain, does anyone still believe that American black anti-Semitism is a recent development?) The dedication to education and hard work was intense in the Village. John Beynoe's parents, he says, "couldn't afford to send my elder brother to college. It was the early thirties. But they did it, somehow. And he graduated from Northeastern [University] as an engineer in 1937. Couldn't find a job no way. Went back and got a law degree and became very successful. But we never had the attitude that you couldn't do something just because you were black. That just wasn't in our thinking." It wasn't in the way of thinking of many American blacks as well, and many of them became highly accomplished over the years. But they were, unfortunately, overwhelmed in the public eye by those who had suffered more from the damning longtime psychological effects of slavery and Jim Crow—a fact that might not diminish the feelings among West Indians that they were considerably more effective people.

At the suggestion that Farrakhan, despite having grown up in the same atmosphere, now seems to say much the opposite, that blacks can only fare well if they gain separation from whites, Beynoe says, "I think he is just saying those kinds of things because of the audience he has."

"If this is true, isn't there some hypocrisy in Farrakhan's preaching?" I wonder.

"No," says Beynoe, "it's like a coach getting his team ready. He has to alert them about what's going on around them. I don't see him in any way being hateful. I think he just expresses a lot of the feeling that the masses have but may not have the capacity to verbalize." It's a good thing to give expression to people's feeling of hatred? "Well, you can't help what people feel." Nor can Beynoe help his slightly superior feeling that, while it is a good thing for Farrakhan to give aid and comfort to the black American "masses" who can't verbalize their feelings, he certainly would not expect these attitudes among West Indians. In his seventies, having lived in Boston all his life, having somehow been well educated and well cared for in Boston, and being of a kindly and generous personality, Beynoe is the specially endowed islander. Were Farrakhan directing his racist remarks to his fellow islanders, Beynoe would not likely be so tolerant.

Even before slavery ended in the islands, there were signs of high ambition among some nonwhites, as a generation of what were called "coloreds" began to emerge from the mixed marriages of overseers and slave women. While American slaveowners easily hired married white overseers from a large pool of Southern whites, thus avoiding the hated race mixing—though it was common enough between owners and their slaves—the West Indies had no such large white population. The English had colonized the islands—as they did Africa and Asia—for commercial purposes but had never established large settlements. So overseers were often bachelors come from the British Isles to work in the islands. And they married or simply lived with slaves, whose children, in turn, formed a large class of mixed breeds that soon commanded a higher status. They were not, as they were so often in the American South, denied their paternity rights and sold to other plantations. After the end of slavery in the islands, these now freed coloreds soon enough became the middle class of the West Indies, educated, often in England, skilled, ambitious, and, crucially, light-skinned. An amalgam of whites and coloreds began running the society in the name of England. St. Kitts, where Mae Clarke was born, gained its independence only in 1983, when it was economically sensible for England to shed its colonies.

It was generally the lower economic ranks of this middle class that emigrated to America, bringing with them high ambitions, and, Gladwell explains, a special set of expectations. These expectations were quite different and much higher than most American blacks ever dared to have. West Indians, Gladwell, a West Indian himself, says, were "born of a certainty that American blacks did not have—that their values were the same as those of society as a whole [the society, after all, was theirs, unlike the society that surrounded but did not include American blacks], and that hard work and talent could actually be rewarded."

But Gladwell tells only one part of the story of the West Indies. He hardly mentions the part that was made famous by Marcus Garvey. Dark-skinned blacks didn't have the same benefits as the colored middle class, and many of them suffered some of the same indignities at the hands of the coloreds and British whites that American blacks suffered from whites in the States—though the key word in that sentence is *some*. There were no Jim Crow laws, no lynchings. And there was none of the terrible criminality pervasive in the post-Reconstruction South and regularly found in the North as well. But while there was no official segregation of housing and schools, an effective unofficial separation existed. What there was, in the West Indies, was a firm grasp of the economic and governmental reins of power by English whites and coloreds working together, excluding most darker-skinned blacks, and inferior schooling and other services for these blacks in rural areas, of which there were many.

That exclusion and denial produced the bitter and angry Marcus Garvey and his handful of followers. His fellow islanders, however, showed him little sympathy. They had faith that things could work out for them, even if they were dark-skinned. After all, they were the majority. Foolish, naive, stupid, said Garvey. It was that so-called foolishness that sent him to New York, where he expected that most people would feel as he did. He never understood that most blacks in America in the twenties, despite their hardships, like those in the West Indies, believed that if they had enough faith and worked hard enough, their lot would change.

There certainly was, in the States as in the Caribbean, a strong prejudice against a dark skin among lighter-skinned blacks, and many of those lighter-skinned people had more advantage among whites. But in the States, no matter how light-skinned one might be, in the eyes of whites one was still black. The "one-drop-of-black-blood-is-enough" theory, part of the Black Codes that began to emerge to control the behavior of fair-skinned freed blacks—the products of slaves and their masters—in the early eighteenth century and intensified and extended after the Civil War, never died. No matter how fair, a light-skinned American black always, in the end, bore the stigma of being black among whites. If they were "passing," as some did, they lived in constant terror of being exposed. In 1996 Henry Louis Gates, himself a brown-skinned man, published an article which revealed that the literary critic Anatole Broyard had lived his whole life "passing," always fearful of being exposed, unable to tell even his own two white children by his white wife (he had lived in dread fear they might turn out to be dark-skinned) when he was dying of cancer.

(Although many in New York knew that Broyard had that one drop of blood, it seems that Gates found it important, and his *New Yorker* editors agreed, to make Broyard's secret widely known. Perhaps Gates thought it was important to write this piece to show, as he said, what lengths a black writer might go to to avoid being pegged a "black writer." As I read this piece, I felt uncomfortable in the presence of what seemed like simply a personal animus being expressed toward a fellow black who had successfully passed into the white world, as if that were a grave sin, a repudiation of his people.)

In a 1931 short story by the black writer Claude McKay, called "Near White," that Gates quotes, a young girl asks her mother, "But if some people are light enough to live like white, mother, why should there be such a fuss? Why should they live colored when they could be happier living white?" Why indeed?

As Garvey made all too clear, fair-skinned blacks bore the stigma of being resented by their darker-skinned brothers for the privileges they had. At the same time light-skinned blacks were discriminating both socially and economically against their darker-skinned brothers. Barbara Neely, a black writer of mystery tales, makes these themes the stuff of her books. Her dark-skinned heroine, Blanche, says, "Everybody in the country got color on the brain—white folks trying to brown themselves up and hate everything that ain't white at the same time; black folks putting each other down for being too black; brown folks trying to make sure nobody mistakes them for blacks; yellow folks trying to convince themselves they're white." That one-drop rule was observed by all. Gates quotes Broyard's dark-skinned sister as saying, "The hypocrisy that surrounds this issue is so thick you could chew it."

While light-skinned blacks did discriminate against their darker-skinned fellows in the United States, as E. Franklin Frazier so aptly described in *Black Bourgeoisie* in 1962, those barriers were much more fluid and changing than they were in the Caribbean. And this finally undid Garvey. Expecting to find the same situation here that he had left behind in the islands, he didn't understand American history. He didn't see how people might feel as part of a small minority in which one was viewed as black if one revealed even one drop of black blood. He didn't grasp the much more subtle relations among blacks that were the consequence of the use of color by slave masters and events during and after Reconstruction. And he didn't understand that, while all those racial prejudices existed, they were unspoken. They were the dirty laundry that was never revealed to whites and not even much openly discussed among blacks. As Neely's Blanche would say, "It wasn't natural for a picture of black people in a public place to all be the same complexion. . . ." It was natural for dark- and light-skinned blacks in the United States to have strong alliances despite the problems between them. Some of the strongest alliances, in fact, were the marriages between wealthy dark men and their light wives.

Garvey should have seen some of that, but he just didn't figure it out. He proceeded to carry out his crusade as he had in his native Jamaica—loudly, harshly, often wildly, crying out against the light-skinned American blacks, accusing them of discrimination against him and his other dark-skinned brothers. He was unprepared for the reaction, especially from the black leadership, which included several light-skinned men, among them W. E. B. Du Bois. They were outraged, insulted at such accusations. Those alliances of angry men turned the tide of opinion against Garvey and may have sent him to jail and out of the country. (Farrakhan reversed the process, marrying a woman darker than he.)

Despite being rejected by the black leadership and its press, then being harassed, jailed, and later deported by the U.S. government, and finally dead in obscurity, Garvey retained the loyalty of many, especially island immigrants. Mae Clarke and others believed that Garvey had represented them in their frustration over the discrimination they suffered. Gene Walcott grew up hearing praise and honor heaped on the ferocious race man who had been thrown out of the United States.

So the young Gene Walcott was literally blitzed with signs of racial hatred and discrimination. He not only confronted the standard white American racism—"the only good black I ever saw was dead," to borrow an expression from the Civil War general Philip Sheridan, who offered that opinion about Indians in 1869—for which his family was unprepared; he also confronted the fact that American racism extended to *all* blacks, regardless of their lineage or accomplishments. This young West Indian youth, fair-skinned and handsome, well educated, highly skilled and talented, had every expectation that he would be rewarded for his hard work, his talent, and dedication. Instead he had been treated no better than any ordinary "nigger."

Meanwhile there floated about him stories of anger and bitterness over the American treatment of the island martyr, Marcus Garvey, who had tried to build black businesses, to take blacks back to Africa, to create a special black church. In response the American authorities had jailed and then deported him. That American black leaders had turned against him, questioning whether he was just a bad businessman or a thief, only made him more of a martyr for many of his followers, especially his fellow island immigrants. Among the people who remember Mae Clarke well, her reverence for Marcus Garvey is a strong recollection.

14.

To complete the atmosphere of racism that surrounded Gene Walcott were the rumors, in the streets and in black newspapers, many still vague, of resistance to segregation and discrimination. Nothing was well organized or well publicized, but here and there were pockets of people beginning to protest, which raised hope and a small sense of defiance in many blacks. The hope that winning World War II held some promise of freedom and equality for American blacks was everywhere in the air, though most of the time ignored by white governments. On the other hand, black war veterans were going to college with whites and sometimes forming alliances with them.

While the NAACP lawyers had for years tried to win small but important legal victories for blacks in the South, the fifties brought a fight of another nature entirely: now the NAACP began to take on the entire social structure of the South. In seeking to overturn school segregation, it might change the entire racial landscape, not only of the South, which practiced de jure segregation, but in the North, where de facto school segregation ruled.

Earlier, in the forties, an integrated group calling itself the Congress of Racial Equality (CORE), founded in Chicago in 1942, was making courageous attempts to bring change. Together with another group called the Fellowship of Reconciliation, in 1947 CORE made the first of what later became famously known as the "Freedom Rides." Groups of people traveled together on Greyhound and Trailways buses through the South to test a 1946 Supreme Court decision that outlawed segregation aboard buses engaged in interstate commerce. This was one of a handful of legal decisions to tear down segregation that blacks were slowly winning, but that were not being enforced. They came to be enforced only after much blood was spilled.

These Freedom Rides led to the first arrests and extreme violence against what came to be called civil rights workers in the South. It was a rebirth of the violence in the South that had subsided after World War II. Now again there were burnings, this time bus burnings, terrible beatings, and arrests, with some of the riders serving three months on a chain gang.

Another CORE campaign in the forties tried to desegregate Palisades amusement park in New Jersey and White City amusement park in Chicago. (The Chicago park was finally halfheartedly opened to blacks but was then allowed to decay. Just about the time the neighborhood in which it was located turned all black, the white owners tore it down rather than serve an all-black clientele.) A tiny band of black and white CORE members also successfully desegregated a number of downtown Chicago restaurants.

Boston wasn't on the CORE circuit. It couldn't have been described as an activist town. But though Gene Walcott was not personally involved, certainly the news of a rising defiance among blacks, especially young ones, contributed to Farrakhan's reporting to Gates that he had felt the full impact of racism in Washington, D.C., in 1950. There, after his dream of Juilliard had been shattered, visiting the highly segregated capital of the United States and beginning to feel a resistance to racism, he may indeed have felt its full impact—not because of a ticket to a movie, but because all the events of his life, even those not so conscious, conspired at that moment to reveal racism's harsh realities.

For many years Farrakhan has not referred publicly to his origins. He appears to be fully identified with those American blacks who are and have always been the followers of the Nation of Islam—largely dark-skinned people. The Nation surely reflects the same rainbow of colors to be found in any "photograph" of blacks in the country, but the appeal of the Nation is mostly to the young, the under- and uneducated who are often jobless, often involved in criminality and/or drugs, and often in prison, among whom there is a heavy concentration of dark-skinned people. (Many in the Nation's leadership, beginning with its founder, have been and are light-skinned. But the range of color is so great that it is dangerous to draw conclusions. On the other hand, watching the weekly reports in the *Final Call* of its best newspaper salesmen, who represent the membership of the Nation, does tempt one to characterize them as darker than those who lead them.)

Perhaps Farrakhan has not done as well as he would want to escape the effects of the color caste system that created him. His heavy, intolerant, often bitter, and often lofty harangues to his followers about hard work, education, self-control, self-discipline, and so on are in good part the legacy of his West Indian family and community with its strong caste system. While his "sermons" have some resemblance to those of fire-and-brimstone fundamentalist preachers who warn their congregants of the devilish consequences of their immoral acts, it would be a rare fundamentalist who would go as far as Farrakhan goes in his warnings. They reflect the contempt of the light-skinned black for his dark-skinned brother.

Moreover, it is scarcely conceivable that a black preacher would, as do some white fundamentalists, use his religious fervor as a tactic to, in effect, punish his people. It is precisely for their offers of redemption and a promise of a brighter future in heaven that the Nation condemns black Christian preachers. Some modern clergy do preach a sermon that, without the insults and brutal attacks, might be said to resemble Farrakhan's. But it is impossible to imagine a black preacher reaching out to arouse the guilt and pain that are likely to occur in Farrakhan's followers when he shouts to them of how they are lazy, conscienceless, lacking the will to work, violent, sexually promiscuous, drunk, dirty, selfish, and in need of redemption that they can find only under his tutelage. While this general line of self-improvement goes back to the beginning of the Nation—certainly Elijah and Malcolm were good at it—it has taken Farrakhan to make an art of it. He may have learned the art from his mother's West Indian culture which traditionally had little use for American blacks. People in that culture have sometimes, though unintentionally, used that contempt in order to obtain jobs and other benefits often denied their American black competitors, something that Farrakhan would deny about himself. But surely, as John Milton said, "The childhood shows the man, / As morning shows the day."

15.

Sitting there in St. Cyprian's, imagining Farrakhan as a boy acolyte and then as that fierce man shouting from his podium, I envisioned him at the pulpit of this small church, tearfully telling the congregation, "I've come home," as he'd done in 1994. He came to celebrate the dedication of a silver chalice to the church. Elma Lewis, the daughter of Farrakhan's godmother and a longtime arts teacher and leader in the Roxbury community, was honoring her mother. When Farrakhan was a highly regarded Nation minister strongly opposed to any form of racial integration, Elma Lewis had been a leader in the infamous struggle for school integration in Boston. Here he was, twenty years later, come back to his fold to honor Lewis and her mother.

John Beynoe, who preceded Gene Walcott in the church by ten years, recalls Farrakhan's visit. "The church was packed, with the Nation of Islam people all around. There'd been a little bit of controversy about him coming to the church, but the minister was really on the ball. [Modern Episcopalians are, as a rule, opposed to racism. Some had objected to Farrakhan's anti-Semitism, others had objected to his attacks on whites, but the minister convinced them they should overlook these problems. After all, he was one of theirs.]

"He went up in that pulpit," Beynoe says, "and he stood there a couple minutes, looking down, and then he said, 'I've come home,' and the tears were running down my face. You can't explain it, it was just one of those very emotional moments. Then he went on to give a lecture about Christianity, Judaism, and the Muslim religion and . . . I wished to God I had a tape with me. It was the most fantastic testament of religion I've ever heard. I'll never forget it as long as I live.

"I heard him just last week on the TV. I was fooling around with the dial and caught him in Georgia or South Carolina. I caught just the last ten minutes and was amazed to hear what he was talking about. I'm a high-degree Mason, and he was talking about the white Masons and the white Shriners. I was amazed at what he knew. That man must read and read and read. I don't know whether the people who sit there and applaud him even know what he's talking about. But you talk about separatism and nationalism. I don't think he's into that. He's just into blacks building up for themselves." How could this man, who can speak so brilliantly, believe in the nationalism and separatism he preaches? No, Beynoe insists, Farrakhan could certainly not have come to believe the things he preaches; no West Indian would ever think like that. Mr. Beynoe doesn't leave the observer with a lot of choices.

What had Farrakhan been thinking as he stood in that pulpit of St. Cyprian's, where he hadn't been for so many years but where he may have occasionally envisioned himself as he carried that cross down the aisle? What was he thinking there in front of his mother, his cousin Elma, his brother, all those people with whom he'd grown up, and his Roxbury followers who had come to pay him homage in their home-town, where he had once been their minister? What were his recollec-tions of childhood and youth spent in this Christian church? I imagined him saying to himself, "Sure, those years were okay, maybe even good, but this church? What has this church to say to me, to my people? How can this church offer my people salvation? Here there is only hypocrisy. Those people sitting out there in the church are black, but this is a white man's church, this was a church that sanctified slav-ery. It's not a church to nurture us." Not exactly the kinds of words that John Beynoe would have expected him to be thinking.

And, of course, he wouldn't have said that publicly. He had grown up here. These people had been his family and friends. He had loved them. Many of them now admired him, though he had heard there were some who opposed his speaking here. He was sorry about those people, but they hardly counted, did they? This church had nurtured him for a long time. He had loved Father Wright, his minister. He had loved the ritual, deeply ingrained in his soul. He is still quoting that Bible, but he has also learned about the perfidies of this white church. He didn't understand as a youth. And now? Did he understand that, while he had been praying to Jesus and carrying the cross, he was silently, unconsciously, building the great reservoir of bitterness and hatred that would emerge only a few years later? No, it's not bitterness and hatred—he is merely offering true descriptions of whites and Jews. "Oh well," I imagine him saying as he leaves this church with a nostal-gic wave, surrounded by family and his unsmiling Fruit of Islam body-guards and other Boston black Muslim faithful, "that's history, and I have grown far beyond it."

16.

In this church on Tremont Street in Roxbury, Boston, I was the only white person present, feeling like any other guest in the church. I had been welcomed by an usher and led to a pew and given a prayer book. At the end of the service, people shook hands all around in that modern gesture of brotherhood, and those near me seemed eager to include me. As people gathered in the aisles after the service, the tall, gangly, light-skinned West Indian priest, Father Brome, came over to say, "Are you the lady who's writing about Farrakhan?" "Yes," I said. I suppose it was a dead giveaway; I was a lone white woman. He had invited a white woman to the church for this Sunday.

"Oh," he exclaimed, "you misunderstood me over the phone. I wanted you to come up front so I could introduce you. After all, so many of these people knew Gene, that's what they called him then. But it will be all right. You can come down to the church basement for coffee and meet people there."

In the basement, over coffee and buns, Father Brome seemed to have overestimated the enthusiasm of his parishioners to want to talk with me. He found only one. Perhaps he would have found more if he'd stayed, but he excused himself, saying he had business to attend to. That warmth I had felt in the chapel, when so many people had looked at me and smiled, now was dimmer. The feeling I've had so many times in recent years when I walked into a situation as the only or almost only white, attacked me again. Today it was subtle. No one looked angry or nasty. They just ignored me. No one who had not experienced it before would have recognized the invisible but obvious sign that said, "You're not welcome here." To whites who are unfamiliar with the particular warmth that black churches once extended to all, black or white, this reaction would have gone unnoticed, especially because churches were for so long segregated that whites simply didn't go to black churches. But times have changed. Blacks are now more openly suspicious of whites and more ready to make their suspicions apparent. When I first arrived at St. Cyprian's and sat through the services, it hadn't been clear what I was doing there, and people obviously gave me the benefit of the doubt. But then it became clear I was using their church for my own purposes, and that wasn't acceptable.

There was a chasm of difference between the coolness I felt in the basement of St. Cyprian's and the hostility I felt at the Mosque Maryam, but the feelings at St. Cyprian's were probably only more subdued and less aggressive than those at the mosque. The fact that it isn't easy to find a black who will not strongly defend Farrakhan to whites doesn't mean that blacks have any sympathy with his religious ideas; they don't. What it does mean is that they admire, perhaps secretly, his stance against whites. Not that they themselves would publicly express such ideas, but they will defend his or anyone else's right to do it. In that defensive posture the basic coolness emerges. And here I was, a white woman in his old church, trying to find people who would tell me about him, reveal things I might use against him.

The coffee hour that I was sure was always cozy and friendly soon ended, and people filed out almost before I could get my bearings. The priest's business seemed to have detained him permanently. Finally, alone in this large basement hall, reckoning he would not return, I tried to find my way out. The door the others had used was now locked. I stumbled around the church until I found an open door.

17.

Out on Tremont Street I walked around the church. I had expected, judging from the simple, well-maintained entry and interior of the church, to find similarly neat grounds. Instead the tiny stretch of ground that surrounds the church is untended and filled with debris, with what looked like months of neglect. It is hard to imagine that first generation of West Indian congregants permitting such neglect. Most likely there were once shrubs and flowers here. It appears that the church can no longer support itself as it did when the neighborhood was a staunch outpost for all the West Indians who were emigrating to Boston, when it was the center of life for that community. Although this congregation was then much poorer than it is now, it is almost certainly much smaller. Attendance in the Episcopal church is down everywhere. And Episcopal churches, like most formerly all-white churches, are now integrated, which means that some members of St. Cyprian's who have moved away from the neighborhood can choose to go to a nearby church instead of traveling. St. Cyprian's is still a lively church, but, like so many other Protestant churches, not what it used to be. Reaching the minister by phone always proved to be difficult, a sure sign of diminished activity.

I wandered down Tremont Street, a big six-lane artery that cuts through Roxbury. I crossed the street and stood at the corner where Toussaint-Louverture Hall had stood, the memorial to the Haitian general who had led the first successful insurrection against slavery but had died in a French dungeon. The *New York Times* had described him in 1928 as "that black Washington who is known to all school children with an eighth grade education in elocution," because of William Wordsworth's sonnet in his honor: "Though fallen thyself, never to rise again, / Thy friends are exultations, agonies, / And love, and man's unconquerable mind."

Louverture Hall was Marcus Garvey's Boston headquarters. John Beynoe believes he was inspired to become a lawyer by the oratory he heard at the hall, often by unemployed workers "who could preach like you never heard. I don't know how many of us were inspired by that little cocoon, that little Village, but a lot, I know."

That little "cocoon" in Roxbury that inspired John Beynoe was, in the thirties and forties, not much more than a thousand people, most of them from Barbados. Gene Walcott's father allegedly had come from Barbados when he emigrated to New York, where he and Mae had apparently lived for a short time before he disappeared. Farrakhan, though, has been known to say his father came from Jamaica.

I made my way along a curving street off Tremont, through parkland called Madison Park, across the street from a rather upscale middle-class housing development. A few blocks over, at 600 Shawmut Avenue, where Mae Clarke had raised her two sons, I was not surprised to find a row of shabby old red-brick, three-story housing projects. Shawmut Avenue now also had lots of old houses and stores, some boarded-up buildings and stores, and some houses being smartly renovated. It was a neighborhood in transition, like so many urban communities that have not fallen into complete decay, especially those adjacent to white communities, which this was. Roxbury was spared the blight that so many other big cities experienced in the riots of the sixties (and as late as the eighties in Miami and St. Petersburg in the nineties), but the small thriving businesses that John Beynoe recalls are all gone. "I could still run the distance of the six drugstores that were on Washington Street," he said. "And bakeries, and hardware stores. But as soon as the first stones were thrown, every storekeeper up and moved out." A few stayed, and a few new ones moved in, but, as Beynoe points out, "You wouldn't get a deal in any of those places."

At the corner of the block where Gene Walcott's family had lived there are still three imposing limestone churches. Mae Clarke and her sons walked almost a mile to St. Cyprian's, the church of their fellow West Indian Anglicans. Their clan preferred their own church to the local American black churches, whose churchgoers didn't much care for the Jewmaicans.

Was this expression, designed to defame the West Indians, one of the sources of the vicious anti-Semitism that would later become such a significant mark of Louis Farrakhan? Strange how this epithet that expressed the jealousy and envy—and contempt as well—of black Americans toward the West Indians was viewed by the West Indians not as a mere bit of foolishness by an inferior group but as insulting, as if they had been called vermin or some other such detested creature. One group of blacks chooses as its epithet for another group of blacks the same epithet that has served the real enemy, whites, so well over the centuries.

It is not generally imagined that one of the sources of Farrakhan's hatred of Jews was those early insults he may have endured from the American blacks with whom he went to school and played in the playgrounds. Goodness, he didn't deserve such treatment. He was born in America, and his mother didn't come from Jamaica! Furthermore, his mother was very poor for a while. She'd been a domestic just like so many other black women, American or immigrant (all working for Jewish women, it seemed). How could it be fair to brand him with that hateful name? But the idea that it was used against his community by other blacks, who believed they had more rights in this country than the immigrants, was a seed that may later have germinated into another: why should Jew hatred be used against other blacks? Why not direct it at the real target, the Jews themselves?

18.

I walked over Shawmut Avenue to Massachusetts Avenue, which is the boundary between Roxbury and Boston proper, a broad old street that runs straight through Boston and Cambridge, varying with the neighborhoods it traverses, including the Harvard campus it borders. This section of "Mass" Avenue was once upper middle class, a hard boundary with black Roxbury, but that boundary has become fluid. Some of the brownstones have been broken into small apartments, some are being renovated, some are boarded up—clearly a changing neighborhood. I was headed for Wally's Cafe, at Mass and Columbus Avenue, about a mile or so from Shawmut, a famous Boston jazz club that has been a hangout for musicians since the thirties.

On my way I stopped at the Mass Cafe for lunch, a little barebones restaurant with taped African music and African food—Eritrean and Ethiopian food, that is, along with bagels and cream cheese, pasta and teriyaki, espresso and cappuccino, wine and beer, and a soft drink dispenser. The young African couple who ran it obviously knew how to attract a crowd, though their English was still sparse. This lunch crowd on Sunday reflected the clearly polyglot neighborhood: a group of Africans, speaking enthusiastically in their own tongue, a few young white students (the Boston area has fifty colleges and universities), a few gay men, and a group of young blacks with no other distinguishing characteristic. Yes, they all said, they knew about Louis Farrakhan, they knew he came from Roxbury, but none of them had much to say about him. It made little impact on them that he had grown up only a few blocks away.

One man stood out—he was about sixty among this mostly twenties crowd, tall, coffee-with-cream colored, grey-haired and balding, good-looking, bulky but well-built. He was a regular here, he told me. He stopped in every Sunday afternoon to pick up a lunch and take it home. The food was good, but just as important, the cafe was in the Village where he had grown up and it was, in just a tiny way, coming home every week from where he now lived a good distance away in Jamaica Plains.

Having admitted he had known Farrakhan earlier, he spoke to me hesitantly, saying he didn't have time to talk. Yes, he'd known Farrakhan pretty well. But he wasn't sure he wanted to talk with me about him. At last he agreed to let me come to his home later in the week. He would talk with me provided I would promise not to reveal his name. We made a date.

19.

Wally's Cafe was a shadow of its former self, according to the bartender, Frank, who was Wally's grandson. Once it had been a huge swinging club—Dizzy Gillespie, Charlie Parker, Fats Navarro, Sarah Vaughan, Billie Holiday, the list was endless. It had started out across the street with a big dance floor and plenty of space, but the decline of the jazz audience with the rise in the sixties of rock and roll had forced Wally to move into these smaller quarters, an old-fashioned saloon with a corner at the back serving as a bandstand, a dozen or so tables, and a bar. The jazz had never stopped, not for a night, and there had never been rock and roll or any other nonmusic. But now most of the old-timers were dead. There has been a small revival of jazz in recent years, and even if it was all copycat music, the younger crowd couldn't tell the difference, so Wally's was once again popular. Every night lines formed around the corner waiting to get in, but it wasn't the same thing. This atmosphere was that of a dimly lit neighborhood saloon. There probably would never be a place for that jumping club again. But, Frank told me, even if the music wasn't exactly what you hoped, Wally's never stopped being a swinging place.

Frank had never met Gene Walcott. He hadn't been born yet when Farrakhan was on the street, but he'd heard about him from his grandfather and from the few old-timers still around. They talked fondly of the young guy who hung around the corner with them, kibbitzing with the musicians, and who had gone on to make his own name as a musician—the Charmer. Even if what he did wasn't exactly jazz, people sure loved it, and Frank had heard tales about how that calypso music was so much fun. No one around Wally's had understood what happened to Gene to make him quit that music and become a Muslim. It was a mystery they were still talking about forty years later, Frank said. What kind of a church was it where they didn't have music? All the Protestant churches they'd known about had choirs and organs and plenty of hymn singing. Those old-timers didn't know that Elijah Muhammad demanded that Louis X give up his music—no singing, no dancing, no organ music, no spirituals—in his church because it was too reminiscent of the white church from which he and all his followers had fled.

"He was wild just like all the others. He'll tell you himself. He drank and smoked reefer," one old-timer told me. "But people change. He changed. How do you know? But one thing is sure, you can take what he says and put it in the bank. It's as good as money. He's a prince of a fellow. I knew him until he went off like he did. Couldn't figure it, but never doubted him. He had to do what he had to do."

The other old-timers listened as their buddy talked, their faces blank. "What do you want to go on like that for?" one of them asked his friend. "I haven't got anything to say about him," another told me. They weren't unfriendly. I had a right to ask. They just had the same right to refuse to answer. They offered to buy me a drink to prove they weren't angry or hostile. I seemed like a nice enough girl, and they made it abundantly clear during the two hours I sat at the bar, sipping a drink and chatting, that anyone was welcome at Wally's, it was a friendly bar, but talking to a stranger about an old friend was out of bounds, and the fellow who had spoken was out of order.

Very quietly at one point, Wally's grandson told me to come back at one the next day, Monday. He was pretty sure the fellows who made a regular stop at Wally's early on a weekday afternoon would be more likely to talk to me. They weren't as old and rigid as this crowd, nor did they drink as much.

After my third visit to Wally's, when Frank and I had become buddies, he decided that those old friends of Farrakhan refused to talk with me because I was white. They were, he suspected, protecting Farrakhan from the potentially scurrilous pen of a white woman who was, in addition, Jewish, which didn't help. They were all too conscious of Farrakhan's reputation among whites and the way he was treated by the mainstream media, and they weren't about to provide them any ammunition. They may even have known of Farrakhan's own distrust of the media and felt they had to respect that. You could never be sure with a reporter how your words would be interpreted, even distorted.

Blacks aren't the only ones who don't trust reporters, after all.

Hardly anyone in America, black or white, has much respect for them. A survey by the National Opinion Research Center in 1996 found that Americans distrust journalists as much as they distrust Congress and the executive branch. Only about 40 percent of Americans respect journalists. That wasn't always the case; polls taken in the 1970s showed that people depended on the media to protect their interests and to counter the effect of politicians.

For blacks, distrust of the media is stronger than among whites. Consciously or not, they resent the constant depiction of their fellow blacks as criminals, resent, for instance, seeing Farrakhan so often depicted as a demon by the media, and resent the fact that so much of what is seen in print and on the small screen about blacks is negative. (They fail to recognize that most of what is considered *news*, especially by television people, is negative.) The fact is, research shows that blacks in general mistrust *people* more than do whites. NORC's Tom W. Smith says all the evidence shows unequivocally that this great disparity in trust between blacks and whites reflects the minority status of blacks. Their position causes them to doubt the goodwill of others. But even among blacks, it seems, and whites too, the less educated and those with lower incomes are most distrustful.

Blacks trust other blacks more than they do whites, though even that trust is hedged. Since most reporters are white, this doesn't help their cause with blacks. It has also led to controversy in some newsrooms, where editors consistently send their black reporters to cover stories about blacks. Most black reporters feel these assignments tend to ghettoize them and prevent them from advancing in their jobs, which is probably true. But it is just as true that black reporters can generally get more cooperation from blacks involved in a story and therefore can better serve the interests of both the black community and their bosses—which puts them in an unfortunate and uncomfortable position, part of the larger price always being paid for being black in America.

While blacks are usually more cooperative with black reporters, many of them expect "protection" from their black brothers in the media—that they won't report the whole truth if it reflects badly on blacks. For instance, Louis Farrakhan boldly told the National Association of Black Journalists meeting in Nashville in August 1996 that white publishers "skew the news," and that black journalists have a responsibility to be accurate and fair when they are writing about black leaders. "When you hear them beat the hell out of me, calling me an anti-Semite and a bigot, it'd be nice to hear a brother who applauds behind the door come and say, Farrakhan's not the man he's depicted to be. He's a lot better than that."

Most journalists, black or white, would question such a role for themselves. But many black journalists, especially the young, are torn. They don't know exactly what to think or do about Farrakhan, whom they know has a huge following in the black community but is indeed regularly savaged by their newspapers, sometimes even by fellow black writers, usually the older, more sophisticated ones. Few of these veterans have much sympathy for Farrakhan or for the ideas he represents.

But Farrakhan is, without question, the preeminent voice in the black community. One way or another he has to be addressed by black journalists, whether they agree with him or not. At the meeting of black journalists to which Farrakhan had been invited, the members gave him a standing ovation after he had severely insulted them. Why did all those people applaud Farrakhan, just as his audiences all over the country give him standing ovations when he insults and attacks them? Munroe Anderson of WBBM-TV in Chicago, one of the old-timers, said he hadn't quite figured it out. It was a mystery, but no more of a mystery than the one posed by all those blacks around the country who do the same thing. In part those audiences share a game with Farrakhan, a game called signifying—a trading of insults—and they don't take seriously what he says. But as Clarence Page says in his 1996 book *Showing My Color*, "There is always a danger in the game of signifyin' when the boundaries between playful aggression and real aggression begin to blur. The game then turns into an eyeball-to-eyeball challenge, unless someone backs down. But danger does not appear to trouble Farrakhan. That's part of his appeal." One may ask why so many people are not only tolerating Farrakhan's signifying but actually loving it. Perhaps the answer is not difficult. Perhaps so many blacks so enthusiastically applaud Farrakhan's harangues not because they love what he says but because they love the implication he conveys: he is showing up other black leaders who tend to sugar-coat their ideas. He's "telling it like it is," not for the words themselves, but to flatter their intelligence. "We all really know what gives." He isn't insulting them—he's really flattering them. So powerful is this message that even journalists who are supposed to be equipped, as Ernest Hemingway said, with "shit detectors," were seduced when he used his tactic on them.

There's only one problem with this explanation, and it may be a problem I see because I am white: my shit detector tells me that while Louis Farrakhan is skillful at making it appear he is playing a game with his audiences, and they prefer to see it that way, he believes what he is saying.

My shit detector also tells me that Farrakhan's audiences accept and applaud his "signifying" because it plays to their intense feeling of inferiority, their sense of invisibility that Ralph Ellison talked about in 1947, the pain of having internalized the contempt and hatred of whites. I grew up on Jewish jokes, a humor based on having internalized the anti-Semitism of the outside world, jokes that mocked and ridiculed everything Jewish. Blacks had similar jokes. But blacks also had signifying and playing the dozens. And while ethnic jokes (don't forget the Poles) traveled into the mainstream only to be banned by the thought police, signifying remains the private property of blacks. Even when it is so often hurtful and ugly, it is theirs, privately owned and operated. Black reporters such as Clarence Page, William Raspberry, and Carl Rowan have graduated from those games, which annoys the hell out of Louis Farrakhan. What kind of blacks are they? Clearly they are slaves to their white editors.

20.

Jamaica Plains is a long cab ride from Cambridge, where I was staying. It is, like so much of the Boston area, ancient-looking, and the section I was visiting could be said to look decaying. Middle-class whites were moving out. All kinds of people were moving in. I asked the cab driver to wait until I was sure I had the right address and Robert was there. He had agreed to talk with me and had given me his address on Sunday at the Mass Cafe, but he had no phone. Who knows what might have happened by Thursday? I needn't have been nervous. He was cordial and friendly, perhaps even pleased to see me. He took me up to the third floor of a huge old frame mansion that had been converted into low-rent apartments for recovering addicts. He'd lived there a long time, first as a recovering addict himself and then as the caretaker. He shared his four-room apartment with one of the tenants but was looking forward to getting a smaller apartment for himself.

Robert made clear that his past was not relevant, that except when it converged with Farrakhan's past, we wouldn't talk about it. Wasn't it possible, I wondered, that he was first attracted to Farrakhan precisely because he was an addict, and had heard about the Nation's success with addicts? Sorry, but that was forty years ago and not up for discussion. It seemed that this residence was recent, but Robert was noncommittal about that. It was pretty clear I wouldn't find out what had happened in between, and why should I? Robert would tell me what he knew about Louis X, as he had known him. Still, as Robert spoke it became clear that he was a bright, informed man, quite articulate, from an ambitious West Indian family, who had gone to Boston English High School at the same time as Farrakhan, though he had known him only as a track star. This whetted my curiosity. Who was this guy? He was a little stocky now, at age sixty-nine. He told me he belonged to a Christian sect that denied any racial associations, that he was a "human" only. And while he went every Sunday to the Mass Cafe in the Village, he no longer had any contacts there. That was a world in the past.

But long ago, in that other life, when Robert came out of the army in 1956 he did return to Roxbury, to the Village. He didn't say what he was doing, but he made it clear he was at odds with himself, like so many returning soldiers. One Sunday afternoon, with nothing else to do, he and a friend went to visit Farrakhan's mosque. Robert had heard Elijah preach in the forties when he came to Boston, but this second visit wasn't to last as long. When the routine attempt was made to search them, Robert's friend loudly objected. Why were they being searched? he wanted to know. No answer was forthcoming from any official. Instead a woman in the audience shrieked at him to shut up. They left.

A few days later Robert ran into Farrakhan, who was not yet the minister, who apologized for the incident. The woman who had been so discourteous had been disciplined, he said. A little like the army. He didn't say how she'd been disciplined, and Robert didn't ask. Farrakhan urged him to return the next week to hear Malcolm X speak. Robert and his friend did return to hear Malcolm, who was beginning to be famous.

"And then," Robert said, "they let me ask questions, and I got a full view of what their teachings were. They defied logic." Robert was still living not far from the mosque and continued to see Farrakhan occasionally. "I was a barber then, I cut his hair a few times. He was a very nice man personally. The only thing that was wrong was the ideas, the teachings. Did you read *Teachings [Message] to the Black Man*? People knew about rifles six thousand years ago? People could fly? And we're the result of a botched birth-control experiment? Sometimes when I listen to him on the radio or watch him on TV, I don't see how a cultured man can believe all that stuff. I think he's talking all that stuff because he thinks he can help people. But then you have to remember that Hitler had that same master-race stuff."

The Muslim Adam X, who replaced Malcolm X at the New York mosque after his death in 1965, was a long-time friend of Robert's and had been in Boston until that fateful year. Robert saw him periodically, along with Farrakhan, but as the years went by, while he continued to like and respect them both, as he listened to them he became more and more incredulous. "It would be as if I was listening to George [Orval] Faubus [the notorious racist white governor of Arkansas during the 1950s]."

I wanted to know how Robert explained the combination of ferocious racism and anti-Semitism we see in Farrakhan with his kindliness, generosity, and intelligence.

"You see, this whole thing is worse than mythology. In the first place, you take his name. He claims Farrakhan is an Arab name that he has traded for what he calls his original slavemaster's name. That's crazy. He has just exchanged one white man's name for another's, and that Arab man might been one of the many who were buying and selling an awful lot of black people. He doesn't have the vaguest idea of the truth of all this."

On the other hand, Robert says, "I don't know about this 'ferocious' racism. I don't know what they would do if they had power, which they don't."

I pursued Robert. "I just don't understand how all those different forces converge in the same man."

"Well, it's a good question. And when you look at just the one man, you can think, 'He's a little crazy.' But then, how do you explain all those people who follow him? Let me ask you a question. How do you think I felt as a young man—twenty years old—when I went into a mosque and listened to what these people were saying? I listened and I thought, 'Are these people stupid?' You know, years later, those two men [William] Shockley and [Arthur] Jensen came along [in the sixties], claiming that blacks were genetically inferior, and I have to tell you, after I thought about those Muslims, I wondered if maybe those guys didn't have something going for them. The kind of reasoning you hear from Farrakhan and his people is like nonhuman reasoning. I have spoken with people from many religions, and I have found that, of them all, only the Muslims and the Mormons don't make any sense. They don't hold water. I could have put together a better story than they did."

Robert proceeded to entertain me with a couple of theories of the beginning of the races that were certainly as reasonable as those that guide the Muslims and the Mormons, and just as amusing. They offered a pleasant break. Then Robert returned to reality. "It is such a shame about Farrakhan, because I can tell you the man has a heart of gold. He is a genuinely nice man. I remember once, years ago, when he was the minister of the mosque, we were talking outside the mosque and another man came along and said, 'Oh, yes, this is Louis, he is the big man in the mosque,' and Louis said, 'Oh no, you're wrong, I'm not a big man. I'm a very small man.' I don't think then that he had these delusions of grandeur. But you know, he had a very great love for Elijah Muhammad."

As we began to say goodbye, Robert said, "I hope none of this will be attributed to me." I assured him that I would not use his real name and that no one else would ever hear my tape. I finally asked him why he was so concerned with his anonymity. "You never know what those people will do," he answered.

I reflected for a moment on Robert's reaction to his old Village neighbor, and then on those reactions I'd heard from others from the Village—successful, upper-middle-class church people. I was reminded for just a moment of the European burghers in the thirties who supported Hitler, and then of Lisa Fittko, a woman I know who for ten years carried on a life-threatening struggle against Hitler, along with a handful of other mavericks. It was not a long, carefully considered thought, only a momentary reflection, but quite unavoidable.

Part Six

MAKING A LIFE

1.

So, having been rejected by the Juilliard School of Music in New York, the pinnacle of American music training, Eugene Walcott was instead offered an athletic scholarship to a tiny Southern teachers' college in Winston-Salem, North Carolina. On his way there, Gene was stunned to discover that he could not buy a ticket into a movie theater in the capital of his country, only shortly after he had lost a dear friend in the Korean War. He was still in his teens. This incident, he reported, brought down upon him the full impact of racism.

He hasn't reported the feelings he had when he went to board the train for North Carolina and discovered that he had to sit in the special section of the train reserved for blacks, a condition legalized by the U.S. Supreme Court in 1896 in *Plessy v. Ferguson*. The *Plessy* decision legitimized the notorious Jim Crow laws of racial segregation that began to appear in the South in the 1880s and that were only gradually overturned in the 1940s and 1950s, mostly by the dramatic 1954 case of *Brown v. Board of Education*.

Nor did Gene recount his feelings about his encounters with these Jim Crow laws. The deeper into the South one went, the tougher it got for blacks. They learned to say nothing, perhaps even smile sweetly.

The taste *I* had of that feeling never left me. At the same time Gene Walcott was on his way to Winston-Salem on that segregated train, I was a graduate student at the University of Illinois at

Champaign-Urbana, 137 miles south of Chicago. I lived about a mile from the campus in a modest, clean, rather pretty rooming house (as we called them in those days), the sort that so many students everywhere lived in then, and I thoroughly enjoyed my young white "townie" neighbors in the house.

Across the street from us was a black sorority house. The fact that it was all black and nowhere near the other sorority houses wasn't surprising. Blacks were permitted into the university but not into the dorms, certainly not into the white fraternity and sorority houses. And when blacks formed their own living associations, they were a good way from the white associations. But there were no other blacks, no local blacks, living on our block or even in our neighborhood. I didn't think much about it. Local blacks were segregated the way they were all over the country. But I had no idea where the black community of Urbana was.

One evening I had an invitation from a black friend to attend a concert given by Dinah Washington, then one of the favorite black jazz singers. Of course I accepted. It didn't occur to me to ask where the concert would be held.

We drove over the railroad tracks and into what I had heard about but never seen, a Southern black town. This wasn't a separate town, though it appeared to be; it was simply the completely segregated black section of Urbana.

I had been on the South Side of Chicago, where the blacks lived, and in Harlem. One got to those places by crossing a street, and some of the streets in those sections of the city had their special markings, especially of poverty but also of a culture unto itself. I had been in Chinatown in New York and Chicago, and I had been in a variety of urban ethnic neighborhoods, all of which had their own markings, but I had never driven down pitch-dark unpaved roads with no street lights or signs in a town that looked like the pictures from the Great Depression, a town that was just across the railroad tracks from and had the same name as the prosperous white town in which I lived.

It was years before I saw another example of a Southern black town. There were the same unlighted dirt streets with raggedy old frame houses, a few little stores, and a variety of churches. That was fifteen years later when I went to Selma, Alabama, in 1965, to march with Martin Luther King.

Gene Walcott had lived in a relatively poor, mostly segregated section of Boston. He was not among the majority of American blacks in 1950 who knew the South, who had been born there and fled, or whose mamas or papas had taken them there to visit the family long after they themselves had migrated north. Gene Walcott, whose family was West Indian, had seen none of the American South. But, though he now has strong reservations about the effects of *Plessy's* reversal, surely young Gene Walcott knew about it and resented all its implications.

2.

Had he walked away sooner from that Southern town, would Gene Walcott be the Louis Farrakhan of today? Would his mind have been less dizzied and warped so that many years later, when *Plessy* had been overturned and the stage set for the gradual integration of American society (a fantasy?), he would not, as a minister of the Nation of Islam, declare that he and the Nation resisted that goal? Had he gone back north sooner, would he, only a few short years later, have come to believe that only with complete racial separation could blacks live decently? How much influence did his exposure to the Jim Crow South have on his vulnerability to the appeal of the Nation? He rarely, if ever, refers to that Southern experience. If it didn't make a deep impression on him, he would undoubtedly be the first black who was thusly unaffected.

3.

Racial separation remains an integral part of the Nation's program. The call for it appears on the back page of every issue of the *Final Call* as part of "The Muslim Program," just as it did in Elijah's *Muhammad Speaks*. And Farrakhan has many times repeated Elijah's earlier lamentations about desegregation, declaring in 1990, for instance, that "throughout the South the economic advancement that we gained *under Jim Crow* is literally dead [my italics]." He told the national black magazine *Emerge* that year that blacks had been generally harmed by civil rights legislation because "women, gays, lesbians and Jews have taken advantage of civil rights laws, antidiscrimination laws, housing laws, and they have *marched on to a better life while the people who made it happen are going farther and farther behind economically* [my italics]."

Among "the people who made it happen," such talk is blasphemy. The roster of those people in highly placed jobs of all kinds is too long to detail here but includes members of the president's cabinet, congressmen, mayors, city and state legislators, sheriffs, and every manner of public official; successful professionals or businesspersons, and many people still toiling in the vineyards, in the remnants of the civil rights movement, in community organizations, rape and domestic violence centers, child welfare, help for the homeless, and in education. Scarcely anyone outside the Nation would deny the massive gains made by blacks as a consequence of civil rights legislation. One need only look in business and professional activities to find educated and accomplished men and women who would once have been buried in less than prestigious jobs at the bottom of the hierarchy—if indeed they would have been hired or been given the opportunity for an education—or the skilled workmen and women, secretaries and file clerks, and on and on, to see the benefits reaped from the civil rights movement.

A comparison of the 1970 and 1990 U.S. census reports shows that in all categories of professional work as well as among electricians and sheet metal workers, for instance, more black people were employed in 1990 than in 1970. A fact now fairly well recognized is that the increases among black women are greater than those among black men in almost every category.

Yes, for every corporation, business, or university in which blacks have prospered since the sixties, there seems also to be one where discrimination remains the order of the day. Even if so, that leaves only half the number that once discriminated.

Most grievously—and this appears to be the limit of Farrakhan's vision—another fact is also true: while a large new black middle class has emerged and swelled since the sixties, many other blacks have fallen far behind during the same time. An estimated third of the black population, who earn less than before or none at all, are less educated, more addicted to drugs, more incarcerated, and have more babies with absent fathers. The causes of this collective tragedy are widely debated, but the victims are often furious that they have been left behind by that forward march of the black middle class. This sometimes unfocused anger might be stoked by condemning the civil rights movement. It is certainly conceivable that, in the desperate situation in which they find themselves, unable to see a way out of their problems, some of the black poor might be led to see the civil rights movement as a fraud, even a cause of their misery; rather than try to find some means to make the legislation benefit them, they might instead reject the whole pot. This appears to be the goal of Louis Farrakhan.

But he also knows that many powerful whites and a handful of blacks, such as U.S. Supreme Court Justice Clarence Thomas, are uttering the same words, demanding the repeal of that affirmative-action legislation, insisting, like Farrakhan, that blacks would fare better without it. That would seem to put Farrakhan in an awkward position. Does he wish to be publicly associated with the white reactionary right? For instance, what is he to do when Congressman Newt Gingrich's 104th Congress and President Clinton, in August 1996, end what the president called "welfare as we know it," repealing that part of the Social Security Act that since 1935 provided Aid to Families with Dependent Children? Didn't this action effectively pull the economic safety net—in place for sixty years—out from under poor mothers and their children? Had this safety net harmed blacks? What can Farrakhan say about that?

The *Final Call* reports the news and comments editorially (it's often the same) on national and many local events affecting blacks, and often on events that are only peripherally related, but not one word of comment followed the signing of the so-called welfare reform bill, which aroused the public outrage and dismay of all those dedicated to helping the poor. Farrakhan solved his dilemma with uncharacteristic silence. He no doubt hoped he could keep quiet as he traveled to the Caribbean islands to bring his message of atonement, though he could hardly avoid the issue of poverty among these people who are among the poorest in the world.

"Poverty of the mind is the worst kind of deprivation," he told the people of Guyana, one of several Caribbean countries he visited in September 1996. "Money can be gotten if one has the right state of mind." The *Final Call* reported that in Guyana, long the home to massive interracial and political strife financed by the CIA, where the average annual income is $1,950, Farrakhan "called for Blacks to demonstrate discipline, hard work, and savings."

It was unclear whether Farrakhan simply hoped people would forget what he had written about welfare in 1993 and then repeated in speeches over the next couple of years, or whether he was standing behind those words. In *Torchlight for America* in 1993 he wrote, "I know that welfare is necessary as a safety net for society's poor . . . [but] Elijah . . . taught us that it's time for us to say farewell to welfare. Welfare means farewell to self-reliance and self-respect." Welfare, Farrakhan says, has led America to produce "its own destruction by *putting millions of people out of work* [my italics]. We don't believe in nonproductive human beings. This is why when our people come into the mosque of the Nation of Islam, we put them to work."

Perhaps there were some welfare recipients who thought that welfare had put them out of work. But even for the most illiterate or the most disturbed, that could hardly have been a tenable idea for more than twenty seconds, especially for those mothers of several children who had never held a job. But this wondrous fantasy was one of the primary ideas suggested regularly in Farrakhan's speeches.

Farrakhan's fanciful images on this question aren't very different from conservative ideas about welfare "reform," from blacks or whites—Newt Gingrich, Charles Murray, Glen Loury, U.S. Supreme Court Justices Antonin Scalia and Clarence Thomas, and President Bill Clinton, to name an assorted handful. They too talk about putting all those welfare recipients "to work." They too insist that the welfare system has created the terrible problems of the inner city.

Where would the welfare recipients work? The women in the hills of Kentucky, for instance, who make up a good portion of the welfare rolls—where will they find jobs? Many welfare reformers seem less concerned with poor families than with the growing resentment of the middle class and the rich.

But Farrakhan could care less about the middle class and the rich. He does seem really to believe that welfare is a path to hell, chosen by people who are either too lazy to make any other choices or too ignorant, that welfare must be destroyed in order to save those people's lives. That he is spouting the conservative line seems not to trouble his followers because so many of *them* also resent welfare recipients. It's not so much because they resent paying taxes to support them but because the welfare folk are an embarrassment; they engender that sense of guilt that so often afflicts people when others in their group have nothing.

With all his daring, Farrakhan knew the welfare scene would be a tough call. Whatever he might say about welfare because Elijah said it, he couldn't simply demand an end to welfare as white conservatives had been doing for so long. Too many black families existed on welfare, some of them for many years (though they were the smallest group, their number had grown immensely since Elijah's death). And Farrakhan understood perfectly well that most people, even many whites, knew that welfare recipients were unemployable because they lacked job skills, were barely literate, and had grown up with a whole range of deprivations in the inner city. While Farrakhan certainly had some grasp of the complexity of the welfare system and the society it engendered, he found it easier to ignore that complexity and blame the white system, on the one hand, and the people themselves, on the other. For many people, even reasonably well-educated young people, Farrakhan's approach is much easier than trying to understand the depth of these problems.

Even so, Farrakhan wasn't so naive to think he could get away with calling for the immediate end of welfare. So he backtracked. True, we had to get rid of welfare, but first we had to have "job retraining." (Retraining? For what jobs?) "I am pleased to see President Clinton moving in this direction with regard to welfare," Farrakhan said. Alas, soon after, the White House seemed to have forgotten completely about retraining, and with the resignation at the end of the president's first term of Robert Reich, almost the only advocate of retraining in the president's cabinet, and the reelection of a majority Republican Congress, the signs seemed all too clear that the dirty work of closing down welfare might end with no real plans to "reform" it.

Farrakhan had nothing to say. He had other fish to fry. After all, he wasn't surprised. In 1993, when he congratulated Clinton for moving toward retraining, he also wondered whether it wasn't all window dressing. "Can white America stand to see an employed, productive, dignified black America?" he asked. "Know that if America can't stand to see us make this kind of social progress, then the only solution is complete separation in a land of our own. Know that if we cannot get justice within this country or via separation, then the country is destined to go the way of ancient Egypt, ancient Rome, Babylon, Sodom and Gomorrah and the way of the British Empire."

Well, that's pretty rich talk, and superficially it's hard to disagree with, pretty hard not to applaud wildly in a college auditorium. The fact is that race is the defining issue in this country. When Farrakhan suggests that social progress may be realized in a "land of our own," it's evidence of his illusions, or at least his presentation of such illusions. But that the United States could experience massive social upheaval and decline if the gap between rich and poor continues to widen is not an unreasonable or a unique prediction. Unfortunately these words, along with so many like them, delivered all over the country to large audiences, are meaningless because the bottom line is that Farrakhan doesn't care about a better welfare system, job training, a job corps, or any real solutions to the problems of the black poor, here or anywhere else.

His interest is in building a great and strong Nation of Islam, with branches wherever there are black people. All those people needn't be members but just supporters, as occurred in the 1930s with Communist parties throughout the West. Supporters were called sympathizers by the Communists, fellow travelers by others. With a large band of fellow travelers and a core of members in Africa and the Caribbean, where he spent a good deal of time recruiting in 1996 and 1997, and a reasonably large membership in the United States, Farrakhan can begin to consolidate his influence—to gain control of the black peoples of the earth. A fantasy? Of course. But what would life be without fantasies? And, let's face it, some fantasies come true. The world is overwhelmingly what Americans like to call minority. And in that "minority" world is a great deal of chaos and pleading for a savior. As he traveled around parts of that world in 1996–1997, Farrakhan was often received like royalty.

4.

Once having gained control, how might Farrakhan attack the massive problems of blacks around the world?

We have a broad hint of how he thinks that might be done in almost every issue of the *Final Call*, in an advertisement for the "Three Year Economic Program." This is described as "the solution to unemployment, hunger, poor housing, and all the other detriments that plague our communities." The ad asks for a ten-dollar-a-month contribution, or nickels and dimes, if that's all you have. These contributions, the ad says, "made it possible to purchase the 1600 acre farm, but there is so much more we have to do."

A phone number is given for more information. The phone number is that of the Chicago national office, where someone takes your name and address and offers to send information. What arrives in the mail is a three-page brochure featuring Farrakhan on the cover beside a list of the program's goals: "farms, factories, businesses, banks, housing, hospitals, and schools." The brochure explains why the program is necessary. It says: "This is not just a program for Muslims. This is a program that will benefit the entire community. Everyone is invited to participate who is concerned about the conditions of Blacks in America, and American society in general.

"If all would contribute willingly and honestly all that they could to this economic plan we would soon have BILLIONS and enough money to begin to do something for ourselves, other than begging for that which we can get for ourselves."

Along with the brochure comes a one-page newsletter dated February 1997, reporting the purchase of 1,556 acres of land in northeast Georgia, called Muhammad Farms, a part of what was once claimed as a 4,500-acre farm owned by the Nation (read Elijah). The newsletter also details the farm equipment that has been purchased and the crops that have been planted and harvested in 1995 and 1996.

There's a bit of a problem here. David Jackson, at the *Chicago Tribune*, went to Georgia to look at Farrakhan's new farm for which he paid $1.35 million in November *1994*, putting down about $500,000 and borrowing $850,000 from the seller at 10 percent interest. According to the county records Jackson reviewed, "His land-holding company is scheduled to actually take title in 20 years."

The twenty years isn't remarkable, but Jackson's use of "his land-holding company" is a little worrisome. Shades of Elijah. Of course, it might be a land-holding company for tax purposes, too.

It would seem that Farrakhan and his real estate negotiators weren't terribly smart. They wanted Elijah's old farm so badly that they paid $1.35 million for 1,556 acres of what was actually a 3,800-acre farm that had cost the current owners the same amount eight years before. (Farrakhan claimed the original farm was 4,500 acres, but Jackson checked the county records.) Under the deal, the owners sold the timber rights to a box company and retained the right to a peanut-growing quota assigned by the Agriculture Department. Farrakhan promised a canning factory on the property. Jackson says the "canning factory" is merely a small cinderbox shed, littered with the debris of what had once been a tiny operation canning peas. There is also a dairy house, now rotted away, that is not even on the land Farrakhan bought but which he has said he hopes to purchase one day. And three 70-foot-high grain towers that Farrakhan pictured on his fund-raising materials are not on the land he owns.

It gets worse. The man who managed the farm for Elijah, ninety-four-year-old William Smith Muhammad, the son of an escaped slave who learned his farming from his father, told Jackson that the section Farrakhan had bought "has been stripped." "Much of it is choked with a chest-high weed called Johnson grass," Jackson reported.

But all these problems apparently are irrelevant to William Smith Muhammad. "Whatever Louis Farrakhan wants down on the farm, this Brother William is glad to do it," he told David Jackson. He calls Farrakhan his "beloved."

So there it is: the first step in a program to save the wretched of the earth—the most primitive capitalism with land he has been cheated at, just like blacks have been cheated since the end of slavery. Or perhaps Farrakhan's idea is more reminiscent of the cooperative movement, which began in the early nineteenth century and which included a number of religiously based cooperative communities, most of which lasted only a few years. But most coops have traditionally been single purpose—buying, selling, sharing implements, credit unions, grocery stores, and so on. One organization, the National Council of Farmer

Coops, has two million members. Whether a coop has attempted to build whole economic communities, including homes, farms, shops, offices, and so on, or whether they are single-purpose, the principles used have been pretty much the same. The Rochdale Principles, elaborated in England in 1844, provide, among other things, that each member contribute a certain amount of money but may have only one vote regardless of his or her contribution, and that a percentage of any money earned by the business be returned to the members in the form of savings.

The first part of these principles, namely that each member should contribute a certain amount, was adopted in 1964 by Elijah and has been reinstalled by Farrakhan. But the rest of the Rochdale Principles never seems to have been part of the Nation's economic plan. Perhaps Elijah hadn't heard about it and was simply improvising on the principles of capitalist accumulation. After all, Elijah did nothing if he didn't improvise. And in general, what Elijah did, Farrakhan does, even to the amount of the suggested contribution, though the value of the dollar has changed dramatically. Farrakhan is so dedicated, it would appear, to replicating Elijah's ideas, that when he rejuvenated the so-called Three Year Economic Plan in 1991 he retained that ten-dollar-a-month tithe that Elijah had instituted. Farrakhan also failed to mention any return to the investors or wages to employees. (That the Nation's property all ended up in the hands of Elijah's family adds a certain dash to this story.)

Consider this plan, as outlined by Farrakhan for the nineties. Ten dollars a month per person. With about 33 million blacks in the United States, it's not unreal to speculate that at least 100,000 might give ten dollars each month. That's a million dollars a month. It doesn't take an economic genius to figure out that, at the end of the twentieth century in these United States, a million dollars doesn't go very far toward creating economic breakthroughs. It won't come within tossing distance of solving any of the economic problems of the poor, or even the homeless, among whom are many blacks.

Ah, but Farrakhan is not thinking in terms of 100,000 people. In his brochure he says, "I am appealing to you—each and every one to turn your millions of dollars over to this . . . Plan." Now, that's different. But wait a minute. There are 33 million blacks in this country and Farrakhan is asking "each and everyone of the 30-40 million Black people of America—to turn your millions of dollar over. . . ." Just what does he mean? Surely he knows that only a tiny percentage of blacks together have "millions of dollars." And that the traditional civil rights organizations complain loudly that wealthy blacks tend not to be philanthropic. Still he persists. A few sentences later, he says it again, though closer to reality: "Send every penny, nickel, dime, dollar, hundreds of dollars or millions of dollars that you can spare to: . . ." One thing can be safely said about this program: Farrakhan needs to hire a professional fund-raiser.

Beyond his "three-year economic program," Farrakhan gives us not a single hint about how to solve the massive economic and social problems of the third world, of which he regularly claims to be a savior, let alone his own poor blacks. Does the reader sometimes feel he or she is reading fiction, as I sometimes feel I am writing it?

5.

Gene Walcott remained at that small black teachers' college in North Carolina for two years, drinking out of black-only water fountains in the town, riding at the back of the bus, stepping off the curb when he passed a white man or, much more important, a white woman. He must have figured that from this black teachers' college he would not get out of life what he wanted. Could he have imagined that only ten or so years later he would be denouncing the legislation that stripped Winston-Salem and the rest of the South of all those means by which whites humiliated blacks? In his wildest dreams as that young student in Winston-Salem, could he have imagined himself in 1990 sitting in Washington, D.C., in the editorial offices of the *Spotlight*, the weekly organ of the ultrareactionary Liberty Lobby ("pro-individual liberty and pro-patriotic"), wearing one of his hand-tailored suits, smiling his brilliant smile, his curly hair oiled to perfection, talking to its editors as he talks to the editors of so many publications that invite him to appear before their editorial boards to present his ideas? He tells these editors, "Not one of you would mind, maybe [the qualifier is necessary, even Farrakhan recognized], my living next door to you, because I'm a man of a degree of intelligence, of moral character. I'm not a wild, partying fellow. I'm not a noisemaker. I keep my home very clean and my lawn very nice. . . . With some of us who have learned how to act at home and abroad, you might not have problems. . . . Drive through the ghettos, and see our people. See how we live. Tell me that you want your son or daughter to marry one of these. *No, you don't* [my italics]."

That Farrakhan actually believed that the editorial board of *Spotlight* might want their sons or daughters to marry a good, clean, quiet black or even welcome one to live in the house next door, gives to the rest of this incredibly sad but despicable statement an aura of madness that characterizes so many of Farrakhan's words. This is the same man who, as a youngster, was an acolyte in an Anglican church and the violin student of a Russian Jewish teacher.

6.

In the 1950s every big Northern city and some Southern cities claimed their fame in the entertainment world. There was more work for white musicians and entertainers than for black ones, especially in the South, but most good musicians and entertainers found fairly regular work, though it meant almost constant traveling. Of course, black entertainers and musicians stayed only in hotels or rooming houses in black neighborhoods. In the South they sometimes had to rent a room in someone's house, a room that would otherwise be occupied by a member of the family. Even in the North, sometimes they weren't permitted to use the washrooms in the white-owned clubs. And it wasn't unusual for them not to be served in a restaurant outside the black neighborhood. Blacks often didn't get paid as well as whites. They were often misused, abused, and cheated by white managers and club owners. But those problems didn't discourage the artists; they went on working, though they might be bitter and angry. Many, perhaps most, used drugs to palliate the pain. Some died very young, one of the most notorious being sax player Charlie Parker, who died in 1955 at only thirty-four. Another was singer Billie Holiday, who died in 1959 at forty-four in a prison hospital, having been arrested for drug possession. Billie once said, "You can be up to your boobies in white satin, with gardenias in your hair and no sugar cane for miles, but you can still be working on a plantation. . . . We were not allowed to mingle any kind of way. The minute we were finished with our intermission stint we had to scoot out back in the alley or go out and sit in the street."

This was the environment into which Gene Walcott moved from Winston-Salem, a small, quiet, relatively sober town in the South. He no longer suffered the indignities of Southern small-town life. He was no longer a black scholarship student, a winning runner, in an all-black college. Now he was the Charmer, or Calypso Gene, a successful performer in the big world, in the sophisticated life of modern music. But for a black man in the fifties, indignities came with almost everything one did. Most bore them quietly. There seemed to be little choice, though there was a growing movement of reaction, small, uncertain.

7.

Gene Walcott was busy with his music career and not paying much attention to politics. In fact he'd never paid much attention to politics. If anything, he tended to take a greater interest in religion, though he had pretty much separated himself from the church of his youth. One day in Chicago in 1955, before he was due to go to work at Mister Kelly's, then one of Chicago's most popular clubs, a friend proposed they go to hear a speech by Elijah Muhammad. Gene hesitated a moment and then said, "Sure, why not." For an entertainer on the road who didn't much drink or use drugs, daytime, even in Chicago, could be pretty boring.

Gene was shocked and touched by what he heard. This man Elijah was talking about a different world, a world in which blacks would conquer the earth, a world in which black people would lead clean, holy, dedicated lives separated from the unholy, impure, wicked lives of whites, a world of worship that despised Christianity.

It wasn't yet clear how any of this might happen and how he might fit into it, but Gene Walcott was fascinated. He went on with his life, touring, touching base in Boston regularly. He was building his career, and he was married now to Betsy and had to think about a family. But the idea of joining Elijah's band of Muslims lingered at the periphery of Gene's thinking. It needed thought. It needed inspiration.

Home in Boston in the early fifties, he came upon Malcolm X, who headed the local mosque and who spoke regularly on street corners in Roxbury. Here was the inspiration he needed. Malcolm was filled with fire. He resembled Father Wright. Elijah was a man of wisdom and righteousness and, indeed, vision, but this young man on a Boston street corner had a light that shone as Gene imagined Christ must have shone two thousand years earlier, the Christ to whom he'd been drawn as a youngster. But Christ was the white man's god; Malcolm was a black one, though Malcolm was, like Gene, light-skinned, which always carried a special burden among blacks, a mark of Satan, some said, of slavery—no fault of their own, but there are so many people out there who blame the messenger, and this shared attribute no doubt made Malcolm even more attractive.

Malcolm took Gene under his wing and taught him all the tenets of the Nation and some of the tactics of building it. Before long Gene became Louis X, having decided to use his first name instead of Gene and having dropped his "slave name" and substituted the X that signifies the nonwhite anonymous name of a Nation member. Soon he was Malcolm's assistant, then head of the Boston Fruit of Islam. He continued to sing and write calypso-style music, but now it was for the Nation. His ten-and-a-half-minute song "A White Man's Heaven Is a Black Man's Hell" soon became the Nation's anthem, played regularly in all the Nation's public places, and on a record it sold well. Longtime music critic Nat Hentoff remembered hearing the record in 1960 when he went to a Nation luncheonette in New York to interview Malcolm. "The singer [Louis X] had a high, flexible attractive voice. Though the lyrics were decidedly hostile to all Caucasians, the voice was curiously—indeed, rather ominously—serene. The style was lyrical, sunny." Those traits of the young singer—lyrical, sunny . . . and serene—remain apparent today to a spectator at any public forum at which Farrakhan appears. His smile is undoubtedly the same sweet smile that earned him the title of the Charmer. But those traits also still appear "ominous" to some. The word evil has been used to describe his smile.

By 1959—he had been head of the Boston mosque for two years—Louis was such a shining member of the Nation that he was selected as one of a group to represent it on a television show put together by Mike Wallace and Louis Lomax. Louis X had written not only the national anthem of the Nation but a song, "Look at My Chains," and a couple of musical plays that, with the use of "actors" from the Nation, toured the country, playing in mosques and public halls. On Wallace's TV show, a section of one of Louis's plays, *The Trial*, was shown in a filmed version of a performance in Boston's Hancock Hall. In his *Black Muslims*, C. Eric Lincoln quotes from the unpublished typescript of Wallace and Lomax's show. Louis X played the prosecutor in this play that portrays a white man on trial for his crimes against blacks. One of the prosecutor's speeches charges "the white man with being the greatest liar on earth! I charge the white man with being the greatest drunkard on earth. . . . I charge the white man with being the greatest gambler on earth. I charge the white man, ladies and gentlemen of the jury, with being the greatest peace-breaker on earth. I charge the white man with being the greatest adulterer on earth. I charge the white man with being the greatest robber on earth. . . . So therefore, ladies and gentlemen of the jury, I ask you, bring back a verdict of guilty."

The "white man" is played by one of the Nation members wearing white grease paint, poignantly reminiscent of all the white actors who for years used grease paint to play blacks, Al Jolson being the most famous. Naturally the jury finds the white man guilty, and the judge sentences him to death. He is dragged off stage protesting all his good deeds for the "Nigra people."

Louis X wrote a companion play called *Orgena* ("A Negro" spelled backward), which was usually performed in tandem with *The Trial*. Lincoln describes *Orgena* as a satire on "Americanized" blacks in a variety of presumably despised roles, from the dope addict to a member of the "400 set," as he describes it, including an "educator." According to the play, Lincoln says, all these terrible people are the unwitting consequences of what "the whites have made of them since 'kidnapping them from their ancient cultures three hundred years ago.'" Of course the play ends happily with the restoration of the characters by the Nation of Islam to "the traditional dignity and intelligence they once enjoyed in their own civilization," Lincoln says.

Yes, those are the precise words in 1960 of the young professor at Clark College in Atlanta, words that remained unchanged in the 1994 edition, by which time Lincoln was teaching at Duke University and had developed a wide scholarly reputation. Without quotation marks, it's hard to figure out which words are Lincoln's and which are Louis's. It's not at all clear how much of the description of the characters is Lincoln's and how much is Louis X's. On the one hand, it's difficult to imagine a popular calypso singer using such smug, bourgeois terms for what appear to be a wide range of ordinary blacks. But reading Farrakhan's later speeches, in which such bourgeois ridicule of his fellow blacks is standard, it's easier to imagine. Perhaps this play was the first public display of that attitude, and Lincoln was only paraphrasing him. On the other hand, while Louis was fiercely antiwhite in his musical productions, he was not particularly ham-handed, which Lincoln's description of *Orgena* certainly was. But we may never know because the plays long ago became unavailable after Elijah forbade such frivolous activities. As in many early Christian groups, there would be no singing and dancing in the Nation. Elijah decided that when Louis's productions became very popular. Louis's songs and plays may have attracted some people to the Nation, which was certainly a fine thing, but they had apparently detracted from Elijah's projected image of the Nation as a world of restraint and sobriety.

The bit of *The Trial* we do have, and Lincoln's description of *Orgena*, makes us wonder about Elijah's sophistication in the uses of propaganda. Could he have failed to understand the success of Louis's propaganda? Or was he, as Louis implied in comments to *Sepia* magazine in 1975, a serious puritan, who asked Louis, "Brother, do you want to be a song-and-dance man or do you want to be my minister?" Or did Elijah simply not want anyone overshadowing him in any way? Certainly Louis's dramatic abilities did indeed overshadow the little man with the reedy voice who nevertheless managed to convince audiences with his messages of fire and brimstone and the end of the world for whites. And Elijah's behavior toward Malcolm is evidence he didn't care to be overshadowed.

No telling what Louis's path in the Nation might have been had he been given greater opportunity to use his talents for propaganda. Farrakhan in 1996 did perform a classical concert for his followers, and here and there he has restored music to the Nation. An occasional popular music review column appears in the *Final Call*; the Nation has produced and sells for only nineteen dollars "TA HA—The Final Call

Symphonic Music Video," written and narrated by the common-law wife of Elijah, Tynetta, of whom the ad says, "Mrs. Muhammad has never received any musical training, nor can she read or write musical notation. She states that her music is a gift from Allah." The Nation also occasionally produces an audiotape by a member-singer who sings the honors of Elijah or Farrakhan. And for only nine dollars one can receive an audiotape of the Muslim Song and March of Victory, apparently played during the Million-Man March, which I have to admit I overlooked.

8.

By the early sixties Louis X, minister of the Boston mosque, had risen to a star role in the Nation. He was one of a handful who were closest to Malcolm and Elijah, who swore fidelity regularly. Malcolm describes in his *Autobiography* the scene of one of Elijah's many public speeches around the country. "At the microphone would be the Nation's National Secretary John Ali, or the Boston Temple Minister Louis X. They enlivened the all-black atmosphere, speaking of the new world open to the black man through the Nation of Islam."

Louis's success was in no small part the result of his relationship with Malcolm that had grown over the years. He described it to the black writer William Pleasant in 1990: "First Louis Farrakhan (as Louis X) was converted by the Honorable Elijah Muhammad, but I came under the tutelage of Malcolm X. He was my mentor, he was a man that I deeply loved and deeply admire, and I really adored him as my father in the movement. We were very close at that time in our development. Betty [Malcolm's wife] hints, and even said to me once, that Malcolm took me off drugs. This is not true. Louis Farrakhan never was on drugs for Malcolm or anybody else to take me off drugs. As a youngster, I smoked a reefer or two, or three or four. I popped a few pills but that's as far as that went. I never wanted to perform high. I never liked drinking. I smoked a little, but I never went in for drugs, so that is false.

"Malcolm was endeared to me because of his tremendous strength and discipline, and I loved him because to me he was the strongest representative of the man I loved, the Honorable Elijah Muhammad. However, there would come a time when through envy and jealousy inside the movement, Malcolm began to wither in terms of faith and he began to become more angry and disillusioned. He felt that his leader and teacher, the Honorable Elijah Muhammad, was behind this jealousy and this envy and wanted to get rid of him, because Malcolm had become so popular that many writers had felt that Malcolm X was in fact the movement called the Nation of Islam."

The families of the two men, though in different cities, visited regularly. The two men confided in each other almost like brothers, though there was in each man, as there seems to be in many men, a reserve that left the door open for the friendship to end. Contrary to conventional wisdom, though Malcolm had been the hustler and criminal and Louis the nice middle-class boy, it was Malcolm who was the more trusting. He was shocked to learn he had been kept in the dark by Louis when he, Malcolm, revealed (what he thought was news) to a group of East Coast ministers his discovery that Elijah had secretly fathered several children with his young secretaries, and that when that news leaked out in Chicago there had been a steady withdrawal of people from the Chicago mosque. Malcolm found that these ministers had known the dirty gossip for several months, without discussing it with Malcolm. Farrakhan implies he knew nothing about Elijah's philandering until he heard this "very slanderous accusation" from Malcolm.

Malcolm said he had already begun to feel some disquiet, some jealousy among the other ministers, an unease that Farrakhan also described. "People adored Malcolm, even though they were afraid to say it. So . . . envy caused people in the Nation to start sniping at Malcolm. And it was reflected in *Muhammad Speaks* when Malcolm would do great things, and would never get published in our own paper but it would get published in other papers. Malcolm was a sensitive man. He began to feel this. And then, of course, he began to feel that the Honorable Elijah Muhammad was *behind* what he was feeling. And to a measure that was true."

Malcolm was pretty certain that after his meeting with the other ministers, his closest friend Louis had betrayed him by reporting the event to Elijah. In 1990, with Malcolm and Elijah long since dead, Farrakhan admitted to Pleasant that he had indeed reported to Elijah, though he claimed he had warned Malcolm he would. "Now, some may call that opportunistic, I don't know, but I am a loyal man to my father. The Honorable Elijah Muhammad was more than any father, and of course Malcolm was, too. But if I had to choose between Malcolm and . . . Elijah . . . , my choice would be . . . Elijah . . . , who was Malcolm's mentor and teacher. *That's my decision!* but I made it." Tough decision, it would seem—but not for a man on the fast track, aligning himself against the man who is clearly on the way out. That couldn't have been so tough. On the other hand, this decision didn't force Louis into a choice between his two mentors. The choice Louis had to make was between informing on Malcolm or simply keeping his mouth shut. It appears that the other ministers involved chose the latter path. Only Malcolm's best friend informed on him.

After Malcolm was forced out of the Nation by Elijah, in his wrath he went to the media with the story of Elijah's adulteries. Louis again chose to act against Malcolm. "Elijah was the fountainhead of our moral conduct. A lot of Muslims didn't believe [Elijah could do that]. They thought Malcolm was lying on Elijah. I *knew* it to be the truth, but I also knew that the slant Malcolm gave it was designed public-wise to say that Elijah Muhammad was really an immoral man, an immoral teacher, and that Malcolm was a much more suitable man to lead Black people than was his teacher Elijah Muhammad."

In Louis's eyes, Elijah was apparently exempt from his own teachings about infidelity and morality. Or perhaps it seemed more advantageous to overlook the problem.

"Many of us *would* have hurt Malcolm if we could have," Farrakhan told Pleasant, "but the Honorable Elijah Muhammad in truth told me *and us to leave Malcolm alone!* . . . As an obedient servant of the Honorable Elijah Muhammad the only thing we *could* do was fight Malcolm in the public through words—as Malcolm threw mud on the Honorable Elijah Muhammad, we defended and threw mud back on Malcolm."

Soon the Nation's newspaper, *Muhammad Speaks*, which Malcolm had created only a few years earlier, was filled with denunciations of Malcolm by a variety of ministers who called him a traitor. These denunciations were intense, but they stopped short of calling for Malcolm's death. Only his closest friend dared go further. Louis said, among other things, in *Muhammad Speaks*, "The die is set, and Malcolm shall not escape. Such a man as Malcolm is worthy of death." In another issue he said, "Such a man as Malcolm is worthy of death, and would have met with death if it had not been for Muhammad's confidence in Allah for victory over the enemies."

Thirty years later, under circumstances I have earlier described, Louis (now Farrakhan) claims he now sees those threats as a mistake. But he insists he otherwise played no part in Malcolm's death.

Whether Malcolm was killed by members of the Nation independently avenging his revelations about their leader, or whether he was killed on orders by Elijah, or whether Louis X was directly involved in his death or, as he now claims, simply a regrettable instrument of his death, or whether he was killed by the FBI, as is claimed by many inside and outside the Nation, including Farrakhan, is unlikely ever to be proven. Even Malcolm, feeling the sword over his head, was confused. At one point in his *Autobiography* he said, "As any official in the Nation of Islam would instantly have known, any death-talk for me could have been approved of—if not actually initiated—by only one man."

Later he changed his mind and told his biographer, Alex Haley, that the attempts on his life were not at all typical of the Nation. "I know what they can do, and what they can't, and they can't do some of the stuff recently going on. . . . I think I'm going to quit saying it's the Muslims."

As for Louis X's role, when Malcolm was shot he was across the river from Manhattan, about two hundred miles from his hometown of Boston, in Newark, the home mosque of the Muslims who were convicted of shooting Malcolm. What was Louis doing there? He was, he says, filling in for the local minister who was in turn filling in at the New York mosque in Malcolm's absence. It had, of course, been planned for him to be there at that time—an unhappy coincidence. He may have known absolutely nothing of the plan by members of the Newark mosque to kill Malcolm that night. He told a radio interviewer in 1995 that he was sitting in a Nation restaurant when he heard the news over the radio. He left the restaurant and walked, "reflecting on this man who was my teacher, my mentor. Though I disagreed vehemently with Malcolm's characterization of the honorable Elijah Muhammad, I was not happy that such a man was murdered."

This was a sentiment for 1995, the year in which Farrakhan begged for forgiveness—not for murder, of course, but for inciting to murder (an act that could have put him in jail for a long time had the government chosen to indict him). But as noted earlier, his public apology to Malcolm's wife gained him much goodwill and new followers. That he could have voluntarily taken that step years earlier, perhaps erasing the doubts of many, seems not to have occurred to him. As late as 1993 he was still talking about how Malcolm deserved to die. In his Saviour's Day speech that year he said, "If you want to live, you leave that man [Elijah] alone where we are concerned. When Malcolm stepped across that line, death was inevitable."

Giving up that line and instead taking some responsibility for Malcolm's death, which he was finally forced to do a couple of years later, would have meant eating humble pie, of which he had done quite enough. However he defines his relationship with Elijah now, it appears that Farrakhan spent years groveling before him, taking orders, being his shill, finally absorbing the biggest insult of all when he was denied the leadership of the Nation that he had rightfully expected— and then he had been forced to grovel before Elijah's son. Some might say it was merely a case of an employee taking orders from the boss. But this was no ordinary boss. He claimed to be divine, and Farrakhan seems to have believed him. And Farrakhan's was no ordinary job. Now, in his own divine role, Farrakhan has continued the intensely authoritarian tradition established by Elijah.

Despite his claims for humility and for his willing years of obedience, Louis Farrakhan has never been a man to eat humble pie easily. He has nurtured, since he was a youngster, a powerful ego and sense of pride. Malcolm may have attained great glorification, but he was, after all, dead, no threat at all. More important, he had left the fold to which Farrakhan was still completely faithful. So why on earth should Farrakhan admit to anything as dirty as having something to do with Malcolm's death? While he did, on a couple of occasions over the last thirty years, admit he may have helped create the atmosphere that led to Malcolm's death, and did express regret over his death, he continued to emphasize that Malcolm was a traitor and deserved to die.

Then in 1995 the FBI foolishly became involved in the silly plot against Farrakhan's life based on the belief he had killed Malcolm, a plot that made national news. Only then did political wisdom force Farrakhan to come forward and publicly declare a version of the truth. Perhaps it's true that *all* he did was incite his fellow Muslims to murder, or perhaps it's true that he helped plan it. Or perhaps the FBI took advantage of the hatred he had stirred up and murdered Malcolm, who was clearly a public enemy to J. Edgar Hoover, as Farrakhan told William Pleasant in 1990. Along with so much about the inner workings of the Nation of Islam (and of the FBI), the true story will probably never be known.

One strand of this story that Farrakhan hasn't talked about is the impact of Malcolm's emerging ideas. How much of his death could be attributed to the fact that he had repudiated Elijah's attitudes toward race, that he had invited whites to join his organization, that he had adopted an orthodox Islamic creed that made Elijah's version of Islam look like a bigoted, absurd tale, and that he had rejected most of the Nation's authoritarian ways? Malcolm might not have been killed that day had he not refused to conduct the body searches routinely made at any Nation gathering. He said, "It makes people uncomfortable." It reminded him too much of Elijah, he told Alex Haley. So in his effort to create a democratic atmosphere, he enabled the guns that killed him to enter the Audubon Ballroom that day. In his new life he had happily joined the hazardous world we all face when we don't conduct our public meetings or church services as if someone in the crowd might kill us.

Farrakhan remembers that all too well. No one gets into any public place in which he speaks, anywhere in the world, without first being subjected to a search by the Fruit of Islam.

But when Farrakhan talks publicly about the death of his old friend and mentor, he makes no mention of that dreadful memory or of how Malcolm's emerging ideas threatened the very foundations of the organization that he had done so much to build and to which he still clings.

9.

While Farrakhan's role in Malcolm's death will never be known, it has always been clear to everyone looking that Malcolm's death was the single most important event in Louis X's life with the Nation. Within just a few months he rose from minister of a modest mosque in his hometown to minister of the second largest and most important mosque in the country, in New York City. He took over Malcolm's role in the Nation.

He soon appeared to all to be Elijah's natural heir. Wallace, Elijah's eldest son, who would under normal circumstances be expected to inherit the mantle, had pretty much dissociated himself from his father. He had supported Malcolm in many of his ideas and had, with Malcolm, become a traditional Islamicist. He and his father had been feuding for years. He had been in and out of the Nation, having been excommunicated by Elijah for his relationship with Malcolm. He told his father, "I find your helpers, your followers, and the family withering like dying flowers, and the righteousness that you projected to us so beautifully and so purely and so plentifully is no more the chief ingredient in the activities of your administration."

Later, when the pressure against Malcolm was at boiling point, Wallace went to the *Chicago Defender* to report that his life was being threatened by "officers" of the Nation. He named certain members of his family and of the Nation's staff. "There have been beatings, lies, and hypocrisy. . . . They are just as bad as the Belgian devils who once ruled the blacks of the Congo. . . . Perhaps they are as bad as the whites who now rule our people of South Africa . . . because their crimes are against their own people." He said his father's goal was to be "the strongest black man on the face of the earth." Wallace may have had a few fanciful delusions about his father, which wouldn't be entirely unexpected for the son of Elijah, but there may also have been considerable truth to his accusations.

Still, Wallace was a strong man; Elijah's other sons had no leadership quality.

The man who was Elijah's closest assistant after the death of Malcolm, the National Representative of the Nation, the man who kept things going while Elijah was growing sicker and sicker in his Arizona retreat, the man who believed in the words and ideas of Elijah even as his own son denied his father's validity, the man who was Elijah's right-hand man for nearly ten years—this man, Louis X, should have inherited the leadership of the Nation, should have been anointed as the new representative of Allah.

But Elijah had a long history of double-dealing, at the least. He was a family man, wasn't he? Well, so he cheated on his wife a few times, had a few babies on the side. Still, could he share the family wealth with an outsider? Besides, this Louis X was just another toady. His son Wallace—now there was a man with guts. Just look at his record; this was a man who could do things. Oh sure, he'd insulted his father and had had to be excommunicated; but boys need to feel their oats. Now he was a man. Once he had his finger on the pulse of the Nation, he'd know what to do. He'd continue to make it profitable. Whatever he did was okay with papa. Despite all his talk about the divine, Elijah was, after all, a practical fellow. The most important thing, in the long run, was that this uneducated, dirt-poor boy from the Deep South was able to build, by his own brilliance, this sizable empire to leave to the large family he had made. No small accomplishment. Louis X? He'd get along.

10.

To say that Elijah's decision was a bitter blow to Farrakhan is this year's understatement. Farrakhan had, in his eagerness to please his boss, succeeded in stamping the Nation with precisely the mark that Wallace described to the *Defender*. There are a number of accounts of violence by members of the Nation in the years that Farrakhan was in command, though they have not been traced directly to him. But people who talk and write about Farrakhan regularly imply that, just as he had incited some Nation members to kill Malcolm, so he had incited more violence against supporters of Malcolm and violence within the Nation. Northwestern University political scientist Adolph Reed, Jr., is one of those. He reported in a 1991 *Nation* article a firebombing in 1970 of a Philadelphia bookstore that refused to remove a poster of Malcolm X from its windows after threats from local Muslims. Reed also reports several other violent episodes in the early seventies for which there is either direct or indirect evidence of Muslim involvement. The worst, in 1973, was the butchering of seven people, including five children, members of the Hanafis, a separate Islamic sect, that lived in a residence owned by famed basketball star Kareem Abdul-Jabbar, in Washington, D.C. The Hanafis held the Nation responsible for the massacre in what Reed describes as "a simmering theological dispute . . . [that ended in] an attack of which only zealots or hardened killers are capable."

Reed also claims that in the seventies "Muslim operatives [could] be seen hanging out with denizens of the underworld, but sectarian zealotry often condoned a strong-arm style." Reed offers no evidence that the Muslims were hanging out with criminal types, but history provides him with ample evidence for the violence so often found among zealots. That there may have been violence practiced by Muslim zealots in the early seventies, in an era of social unrest, is a strong possibility.

Reed implies that Farrakhan incited the violence in speeches in which he criticized blacks for what Reed calls their "putative moral weakness." In 1971, as he traveled the country as Elijah's representative, Farrakhan was already speaking to whomever would pay to hear him, saying the same fearsome things he was saying now, the same things he was beginning to suggest in the late fifties. Reed quotes Farrakhan as telling a student audience in Fayetteville, North Carolina, with reference to Ralph Abernathy's pledge to pursue Martin Luther King's "dream": "Talking about dreaming somebody else's dream! Don't you know that when you're dreaming, you're *asleep? Wake up,* black man!" And Farrakhan then proceeded, in what became his famous style, to call his audience "drunkards," "dope fiends," and "foul, frivolous woman."

Whether Farrakhan's incredibly hostile addresses to his audiences—which are seen by some blacks as merely "signifying"—incited the violence of some Nation members in the 1970s, or whether these acts were self-inspired, is not clear. What is clear is that the same kinds of denunciations no longer seem to have the same effect.

For instance, in 1984, during the presidential campaign, when Farrakhan had departed so strongly from Elijah by supporting the black candidate, Jesse Jackson, he used his famous "Death to him" tirade against Milton Coleman, a black reporter for the *Washington Post.* Coleman had revealed, on February 3, almost casually, near the end of a story, Jackson's famous slur of New York City as "Hymietown." The Anti-Defamation League protested Jackson's anti-Semitic crack. Farrakhan turned his rage first against the Anti-Defamation League and then against Coleman for having revealed the slur.

At the Saviour's Day celebration later that month, a forum Farrakhan has often used for such purposes, he warned the ADL, "If you harm this brother, I warn you in the name of Allah, this will be the last [black] you harm. We are not making idle threats. We have no weapons. . . ." As had been occurring for several years, there followed a bitter exchange between the ADL and Farrakhan. In one of those exchanges, Farrakhan's famous remark that Hitler was "a very great man" first appeared in response to a remark by Nathan Perlmutter, ADL's director, about Farrakhan's "beerhall demagoguery." Despite Farrakhan's threats against the ADL and the earlier threats against Coleman, no physical violence was directed at the organization or the reporter.

In a radio broadcast two months after Coleman's story appeared, Farrakhan issued another formidable warning: "We're going to make an example of Milton Coleman. One day soon, we will punish you by death, because you are interfering with the future of our babies— for white people and against the good of yourself and your own people. This is a fitting punishment for some dogs." The *Post* hired a bodyguard for Coleman, but there was never any indication he was needed. Once again Farrakhan had threatened death to someone whom he considered an enemy, creating the impression that he and his followers are fiercely dangerous people. But it's all façade. There is no follow-up.

11.

Had there been a dramatic shift in the Nation's attitude? Had Farrakhan's words once incited violence among his followers, but later did not? Or was the violence in the seventies by and among Nation members largely unrelated to Farrakhan? In fact that violence occurred during a period of intense unrest around the country, when no one was watching the shop at the Nation of Islam. The image of kids hurling erasers at one another when the teacher is absent is perhaps too mild for this situation, but Elijah was very sick and living in Arizona, and Farrakhan was second in command, a little like the substitute teacher.

Who starts those eraser fights? The tough kids, usually. In this case the tough kids in the Nation were often reformed criminals who had spent time behind bars. What happens to them when there is no one giving orders, no one symbolically standing before them warning them to be good? Did Farrakhan have control? Some, probably. There may have been more violence if he and other ministers had not had a minimum of control. But it seems clear now, after all these years of Farrakhan's tight control of the Nation, that his explosive, provocative, death-dealing words—often strangely accompanied by strong, even harsh admonitions to his people against violence—do not lead to violence, if they ever did.

Was Malcolm a special case? The words were the same. Malcolm was a traitor, so was Milton Coleman. But Coleman was a traitor to the black people, not to the Messenger of Allah, the leader of the Nation of Islam. The death threats may have sounded the same, but their importance could scarcely be compared.

The Nation has been blemished by accusations of violence since its beginning, despite the fact that for most of its more than sixty years it has been largely free of violence. Apart from the couple of alleged cases of religious sacrifice in the earlier years, and the violence of the early seventies, there is little evidence of serious violence by black Muslims either inside or outside the Nation. But Farrakhan admits some. He says in a booklet published as early as 1983, called "The Meaning of FOI," "The old military training of the FOI was wrong in several respects. [It] must be thrown out of the window because that was not a training to save our people. You were often being trained in the manner of the army of the devil. . . . You looked upon yourself as an army of killers. And that's why if you didn't have no devil in front of you to kill, several of you turned on each other, threatening each other, jumping in each other's chest . . . they didn't really respect the mercy in the law of God. They wanted to be a law unto themselves. And before you know it, many brothers became insensitive to one another and then it was easy for a brother to kill another brother.

"And if you really want to know the truth, that's why Allah permitted the Nation to be destroyed. Anytime you lose the love of the brotherhood, you will absolutely destroy the house. So we're not set up as judges; we've got a judge. . . . So my dear and beloved brothers of the FOI, our role is a role of Saviours. . . . That's our job, brothers. So let's put up the old weapons of this world and pick up the weapons of the next world—and that is truth." Whether the brothers have picked up the weapons of the next world, it appears they have put down the weapons of this world.

12.

Reading the *Final Call* today, one finds highly selective reports of violence, usually reports of alleged attacks by police or other law enforcement agencies against members or other blacks. Partly this is because the space is limited and there is a strong effort to report on international as well as national events, mostly about blacks but not always. Black-on-black violence is never reported. The paper regularly takes up the causes of well-known blacks who are said to have been wrongly jailed for political reasons, among them, for instance, Elmer "Geronimo" Pratt, a former Black Panther party leader who was convicted and sentenced to life imprisonment in 1972 for the murder of a white schoolteacher, and in early 1997 was granted a new trial. Violence in Africa or Latin or South America or even Bosnia is regularly reported with other news from abroad. In all its reporting of violence, however, the *Call* is surprisingly objective—as if violence were such a delicate subject among blacks that it has to be handled very carefully and avoided if possible.

For instance, in a case of violence by the police against its members, the August 20, 1996, issue of the *Call* reported on the event in a cover story with the headline "Under Siege! L.A. Cops, FBI and AFT Confront Unarmed Muslims at Mosque." Page 3 and a number of pages following contain a long, detailed description. Hardly a siege, but one can sympathize with an editor's impulse to dramatize the event. It was certainly an attack on the Nation. Three photos on the cover and several inside show the media, the police, and an assortment of law enforcement officials in front of the Los Angeles mosque. The story, by Rosalind Muhammad, West Coast bureau chief for the paper, and generally a good reporter, opened: "Hundreds of Los Angeles County Sheriff deputies, Inglewood police officials and federal authorities, 'itching for bloodshed,' seized and surrounded Muhammad Mosque No. 27 in the city of Inglewood during the August 8 eviction that mosque officials called illegal." If this sounds like a melodramatic lead, read on.

It appears that this attempted eviction on August 8 was the culmination of a protracted legal battle with the owner of the property. According to the *Call*, he had continued to breach agreements with the mosque. Nonetheless he had managed to obtain an eviction order to which the mosque's lawyer had responded by filing an injunction requesting a hearing, which had also been set for August 8. On the morning of that day, ignoring the impending hearing, the county proceeded with the eviction. First it cordoned off five city blocks as hundreds of representatives of the county police, the FBI, and the Bureau of Alcohol, Tobacco, and Firearms showed up, fully armed and demanding that the Muslims leave with none of their property. Most people who are evicted are permitted to take their property, and the police help them carry it into the street. These people were told to leave without anything.

Furthermore the police, according to the paper, refused to look at the documents offered to them by mosque officials, entitling them to remain on the property until a deal could be made with the owner.

There was no violence; the police just roughed up and maced a few Muslim officials, including the minister.

The Muslims backed off and went to municipal court, where that fated hearing was scheduled to take place. The judge refused to conduct the hearing and recommended that the parties try to resolve the matter in an informal meeting in the recreation room of the courthouse.

On their way, the minister walked along with the building owner, whom he knew pretty well, since the Nation had been in negotiations with him to buy the building since 1994. The minister told the owner about the macing.

The landlord, one Alan Jonas, is then quoted as saying, "I told them not to hurt you all."

Meanwhile the bailiff in the courtroom had asked the minister to tell his followers, members of the Fruit of Islam who had gathered in and around the courthouse, to leave. Instead the minister had them line up single file in two columns outside the courthouse building.

But when the minister heard Jonas's words and saw cops, in riot gear, rushing toward the area in which the FOIA was assembled, he got scared. He shouted, "This is a setup! Let's get the hell out of here," and the FOI quickly disbanded.

At a few points in this long and detailed story, one may question the reporter's objectivity, as happens in news reports everywhere. And one also wonders, with all the news out there, should the paper be giving so much space to this one story? But the fact is that the mosque had been rather dramatically attacked. And it does feed the paranoia of the Muslims: it is one of the few cases in which there was contact between the police and the Muslims.

But what is this story all about? Read by an outsider, it's a story that leads us to assume a long history of Muslim violence in Los Angeles County. Why else were the ATF, the FBI, and a small brigade of county cops at this eviction? Perhaps for this eviction of an entire organization you might expect to see ten cops. Maybe a few more. Maybe you think the Muslims could give the cops a hard time, so they beef up their forces a bit. What are they going to do, have a shootout over an eviction? Well, maybe. If the people in this organization are believed to be armed and dangerous and won't move. Remember Philadelphia, in 1985, when Mayor Wilson Goode, who just happened to be black, approved a police operation to bomb out a group of black back-to-nature folks who wouldn't move when the city wanted to evict them. Them and all their neighbors too. Eleven bodies, including four children, were found; sixty-one row houses were destroyed, and 250 were left homeless.

A minister emeritus of the Los Angeles mosque said, "They were on red alert. They had one gun in their holster, one in their back, another in their boot. They came armed to the teeth and ready to enforce something else in a very brutal manner." Even if that minister was exaggerating, the presence of these armed fighters at this eviction raises a question or two. Did county officials figure they were going into Waco, Texas, again, or did they forget about those consequences?

I could find no evidence of violence by Los Angeles Muslims either in or around the mosque, among themselves or with strangers. In fact, it is forbidden among all Muslims to carry firearms, and violence is strongly condemned. So what is this about?

Perhaps it has to do with fantasy. Perhaps Jonas had warned the police about those "dangerous" Muslims. "Don't hurt 'em," he said, "but you should be careful about them." A county police supervisor might not be well informed about the Muslims. Mostly Nation members keep to themselves, except to sell their papers on street corners in the ghettos. It seems that Jonas had reneged on his offer to sell the property and owed the Muslims $60,000 for repairs they had done for which he was to have paid. They claimed he had cheated them in a variety of other ways, had refused to accept their latest rent checks, and had instead obtained an eviction order. Meanwhile the Nation still hoped to buy the building and recapture some of its costs. They secured an order for a judicial hearing to air the problems. Strange coincidence: the date for the hearing was the same one on which Jonas's eviction order was to be carried out.

What was to be done? Jonas appeared to be no longer interested in selling or in paying his debts either. He wanted an eviction. The events suggest that Jonas may have called the police and warned them to expect difficulty executing that eviction order. After all, those Muslims can be frighteningly violent. Farrakhan's speeches are filled with violence, aren't they? The people in the media say so all the time. So it was a logical step to call out those forces for an eviction. And it was a logical step later, when the Muslims' lawyer asked the municipal court judge to listen to the arguments, for him to refuse to hear the case.

13.

In Rosalind Muhammad's story is one paragraph that gives one a momentary jolt. It places this story, and everything else in the *Final Call*, in question. At the top of the second page, not far from the beginning of the story about "the siege," Rosalind Muhammad or her editor, James Muhammad, has quoted the Los Angeles minister: "The Honorable Louis Farrakhan told me to announce to the media that not 30 days will pass before an earthquake will strike the state. . . . Then they will see the power of our God Who will not let this injustice go unchallenged."

Do Farrakhan's followers (especially his editors and writers) understand that this is his boilerplate gibberish? Or do they, as good Muslims, believe him? It doesn't make much difference. This is his newspaper, and he will do what he likes with it.

Yet reading the *Call*, it is obvious that in this, as in so many aspects of Farrakhan's life, he is torn. On the one hand he would like to have a respectable newspaper serving the world's blacks, and somewhere he understands that to do this he must meet certain standards of accuracy and objectivity. So he allows his journalists to do a reasonable job of accurately reporting the news—as well as they are able, considering that many of them do not seem to be trained or experienced journalists. And he uses the dispatches of several legitimate, well-respected, if strongly left-of-center, international news services, particularly International Press Service (IPS) from Paris and Pan African News Agencies (PANA) from Dakar, Senegal. The result is the only national newspaper regularly reporting on news of blacks around the world and doing it fairly accurately. Which is not to say that the paper always reports all the news or that it is never biased.

Despite its clear prejudices, one does get from the *Call*'s foreign pages, especially the African pages, a strong sense of a continuous struggle for control in the African nations. The picture of Africa painted by the American media, focusing on bloodbaths, is quite different from the *Call*'s. In addition to its reports of armed struggle, the *Call* also discusses negotiations among parties in the struggles and a variety of subjects involving the life of the peoples.

Unfortunately one sometimes needs a scorecard to figure out who the military dictators are, since Farrakhan's exquisite shit detector for Americans seems to fail him periodically for Africans. Sani Abacha, Nigeria's bloody military dictator, is given a pass for brutal murder and described as bringing democracy to Nigeria, while Zaire's President Mobuto Sese Seko, who was engaged in a greater fight for his survival, is revealed with all his dictatorial warts, including a report by "Swiss media" that he has "more than $4 billion in Swiss bank accounts." Between the two men, however, there is a crucial difference for Farrakhan. According to one of the most reliable sources of information about Africa, the Washington-based TransAfrica, Mobuto was originally paid and trained by the Central Intelligence Agency, and was assisted by the CIA in the coup in which he took over Zaire in 1965. This after a series of events that included the assassination of Patrice Lumumba, the former head of what was then called the Congo, an act in which the CIA was strongly suspected. Over the years since, in three attempts to overthrow Mobuto, the CIA has come to his aid.

All of this occurred during the cold war, when Washington believed it had a big stake in controlling the emerging African states. Sani Abacha, on the other hand, staged his military coup in 1993, after a long series of bloody wars and coups, when the United States no longer feared Soviet influence in Africa and therefore was no longer supporting military dictators. In fact the Clinton administration threatened to place sanctions on Nigeria after Abacha murdered some dissidents, a role so new to the United States that it was scarcely credible.

So, while American media parade the gorgeously garbed Mobuto and his wife through Zaire's capital after his latest stay in the south of France, this time to recover from cancer surgery, the *Call* is providing a detailed report of the economic problems of that country. And while the establishment press and the State Department widely condemn the murders of nine Nigerian dissidents, including the famous poet Ken Saro-Wiwa, the *Call* is running a story about Nigerian government accusations against foreign oil companies for "engaging in series of underhand practices . . . that include tax evasion, spurious contracts, unfair treatment of Nigerian workers, abuse of expatriate quotas and lack of accountability."

A brief paragraph at the end of this story notes that "Nine Ogoni [tribe] leaders . . . which led a relentless campaign against Anglo-Dutch oil giant Shell, were executed in November, 1995, after they were tried and convicted of murder of four of their kinsmen. Human rights groups insist that the killings of the nine were political executions because they had blamed Abacha for permitting Shell to devastate their land."

So while Farrakhan, in his speeches as well as in the *Call*, refuses to hold Abacha accountable for the dissidents' murders, he wants to be sure his readers know those dissidents were engaged in a "relentless campaign" to force the oil companies to clean up their operations. That Abacha may have been forced into his own battle with the oil companies by the reactions in Nigeria and around the world to the executions is surely a possibility. But one can see his difficulty and understand Farrakhan's position. Foreign oil companies account for most of Nigeria's income.

Clearly Farrakhan's coverage of Africa's dictators may require a scorecard for any ordinary reader, and the message is not always clear, but in Farrakhan's book he is punishing the dictators whom he sees as American puppets (and they often are) and rewarding those who are independent of the United States.

The *Final Call* is Farrakhan's major voice; it is more complete, broader, than his television or radio shows or his speeches. He needs somehow to put his mark everywhere in the paper, but he also needs other people praising him and reinforcing his ideas. Thus alongside the efforts of honest journalists there appears in the *Call* a variety of columnists who write fifty-seven varieties of Farrakhan's ideology, from outright bigotry to mystical numerology.

My favorite of these columnists is the "Messenger of the Messianic Millennium, by Rev. James Luther Bevel." Bevel's photo, an otherworldly picture of his head with his turned-around collar against a solid black background, graces the heading as several of the columnists' photos do. He looks like an ancient sage with his bald head, grey fringe and beard, and piercing eyes. I suspect Bevel is now in his seventies, but he could be younger. He is no less eccentric now than he was when he worked for Martin Luther King on the staff of the Southern Christian Leadership Conference. There was lots of room for eccentricity in the civil rights movement, and Bevel was considered one of the brilliant practitioners.

When I first saw Bevel's name and photo in the *Call*, I tried to find him. I had last heard that he was living and preaching on the West Side of Chicago. I wondered how he had made the journey from a Christian minister allegedly working for integration to a shill for Farrakhan. I was unable to find him.

Bevel is my favorite for entirely perverse reasons. He was at the heart of one of the scariest hours I've ever spent. In Selma, Alabama, in 1965, at ten o'clock on the tense night before the scheduled March to Montgomery, he sent a white boy of about sixteen and a white blind girl, neither of whom had ever been in Selma before, out to a chicken shack about a mile away to buy food for a couple of dozen people who had just arrived from Chicago. He gave them some vague directions. When several of us objected to these two being sent on this errand, the Reverend Bevel's response was, "They're white, forget it." By the time the couple returned more than two hours later, none of us was hungry any longer.

One paragraph from the January 14, 1997, issue of the *Call* sums up Bevel's current view: "In order for Black people to develop spiritually, intellectually, culturally, and constitutionally and to develop scientific industry, they must be members of a nation [the Nation] that is totally dedicated to the development of their total potential under their administration. This is the only way to gain a common body of knowledge and apply it for scientific purposes."

In a sense the *Call* is a much cruder, much more obvious version of, shall we say, the *Wall Street Journal* or the Manchester, New Hampshire, *Union Leader*, or dozens of other papers that use most of their columnists and their editorial writers to broadcast the publisher's ideology. Almost every newspaper uses at least its op-ed pages to support the views of its publisher. But the *Call* is much less sophisticated.

There's another side to this desire for glory—or power—that Farrakhan seeks through the *Call*, which is beautifully illustrated in his printed threat to Los Angeles County of an impending earthquake. An earthquake? Louis Farrakhan knows damn well he can't cause an earthquake, just as Bill Clinton knows he cannot reform Medicare. And he knows that the people in Los Angeles County know it too. But it's not the earthquake, stupid, it's the tenor of violence so often implied in Farrakhan's public pronouncements.

The news of the eviction at the Los Angeles mosque may not have made the national news, but it certainly reached all the followers and members of the Nation, indicating to them that only an organization as powerful as the Nation would get that much attention from Los Angeles law enforcement. And that kind of attack certainly warrants the Minister's threats.

14.

Looking at the evidence of Nation behavior, it all seems to point to a group of people who have decided to shun violence, partly as sheer pragmatic politics (it keeps them out of jail, where many of them have already spent time) and partly because it sets them apart from the rest of the inner city. It enables them to act as an example, surely an excellent recruiting tool. When a group of FOI go into a housing project, under a contract with the housing authority, and manage to bring the drug and crime rate under control without the use of violence, it must be an incentive to many in the project to check out the Nation. And the continuing presence of those neatly, conventionally dressed young men, standing on street corners and hawking the *Final Call*, is surely a sign of the nonviolence of the Nation of Islam.

Sadly Farrakhan has managed, with his fiercely racist tongue, to convince many people of the contrary, that the Muslims are a violent group. That isn't the message received by those in the inner city; for them his radio speeches, for instance, are inspiring and capture their feeling of anger. And they know, in their daily lives, what violence really is.

The people who are frightened or appear to be frightened or angered by Farrakhan's tirades are either white or very sheltered middle- or upper-middle-class blacks. These people usually include those in power, like the Los Angeles County police. Such people often believe that the Nation should be given no encouragement, certainly not rewards by government. As a consequence, the occasional contracts awarded to it for a variety of services—health clinics, guard services, and so on—have eventually been withdrawn at the request of a politician.

For example, despite Farrakhan's regular ravings about the heinousness of homosexuality, the National Institutes of Health in 1996 awarded an alleged $570,000 to the Nation's Abundant Life Clinic in Washington, D.C., for the treatment of AIDS patients and for clinical trials on an AIDS drug. After all his remarks, did Farrakhan expect there would be no political flack in the wake of this grant? Of course he did. He thinks he can say anything and get away with it. But New York Republican Pete King, Farrakhan's most formidable congressional foe, wrote to Health and Human Services Secretary Donna Shalala requesting a "detailed account" of the clinic's funding with advice to "sever its financing." King also wrote to the Internal Revenue Service requesting that it "do something" about the clinic's funds. The funds were soon frozen.

King's press secretary, Daniel Michaelis, told me that King is indeed trying to "put Farrakhan out of business" by convincing federal agencies to withdraw all funds from the Nation. "Farrakhan's really done more than any single person to strain race relations in this country," Michaelis said. "He's not only anti-Semitic, he's anti-Catholic, anti-American, anti-white. He's no better than David Duke or those 'armed wackos,' as he calls them, the militiamen."

Michaelis declared that the first Clinton administration "had been reluctant to tackle Farrakhan" but that, as a result of Representative King's pressure, a good deal had been accomplished. "This is one of the first things we will put before Andy Cuomo [the head of Housing and Urban Development in Clinton's second administration]. I don't expect it to be a difficult matter to convince him to withdraw any funding [for security services] that might still be going on."

As of January 1997 the Abundant Life Clinic was managing to survive. "We are not going to allow this difficulty to interfere with patient care as long as we can maintain it," said the Nation of Islam minister of health, Abdul Alim Muhammad. "But at some point if we can't pay rent, we can't see patients. And it looks like they are literally trying to force the clinic out of business."

A spokesman, Muhammad Muhammad, told me, "We're living on the spirit of God, he's more than money." God and donations, it seems, though Muhammad refused to talk about contributions from the Nation itself.

When events such as this occur, Farrakhan makes his usual threats, often attributing the damage to the Jews. (He sometimes claims that Pete King, an Irish Catholic, is Jewish.) While it is clear Farrakhan has incited no violence since taking over the Nation in the late seventies, he has nonetheless created in the minds of most whites and some blacks an image of a fiercely violent, hateful Nation. That image exists not only among ordinary whites—thus heightening, as King claims, a sense of racism—but also to those in power, thus diminishing whatever efforts the Nation might make to improve its own position.

In one city after another across the country, King and other politicians have prevailed on HUD to cancel contracts with the NOI Security Agency, the Nation's security guard company that had obtained millions of dollars of contracts with HUD or with local housing authorities to guard housing projects. King and his allies claim that the Muslim guards are lazy, criminal, and have beaten up tenants. Some independent investigations have agreed with King's assessments. David Jackson and William Gaines, two reporters at the *Chicago Tribune*, in

1995 raised serious questions about the performance of the Nation's guards, some of whom were alleged not to be Muslims at all but simply ex-cons fitted out with a white shirt, a bow tie, and a crew cut.

In Washington, D.C., Gaines and Jackson reported, several guards were arrested in battles with the police. The Nation responded to the arrests with a $33 million civil rights suit. In Baltimore, on the other hand, a spirited demonstration by tenants claimed that the Nation's guards had been the first to rid their project of drug dealers and gangbangers.

Knowing that politicians often have a strong influence on their constituents, especially those who are beholden to them, as public housing tenants are, I tried to find out what had happened in Washington and Baltimore. Chiefly I tried to interview building and tenant managers. Not one was willing to talk with me. After all, they had jobs to protect.

In King's view it was essential to take those contracts away from the Nation. They were, he believed, the major source of funds for the Nation and therefore must be canceled. King appears to know very little about the Nation or its finances.

It may be true that the Nation's guards were lazy and abusive. Some of them may have sat around while gangs easily entered the building, as Jackson and Gaines report. It would scarcely be the first time a private security company received such criticism or was fired after several complaints. But it is highly unlikely that such complaints against an ordinary security firm operating in a variety of states across the country, far from New York City or Washington, would arouse the wrath of the good congressman from New York. Pete King could care less what happened in the guard cages and corridors of Rockwell Gardens in Chicago or in projects in South Central Los Angeles or Pittsburgh. He has enough to worry about in New York. What he cared about was that the Nation of Islam had, in Baltimore alone, a one-year security contract for $4.5 million, and similar contracts in a number of other cities.

Common sense would persuade us that these cancellations, causing huge holes in the budget of the security agency and thus of the Nation, occurred because the Nation's main spokesman and his assistants seem to believe it is more important to strike fear into the hearts of whites and their leaders than it is to build the Nation. But while

Farrakhan certainly has a diabolical side, he also has a variety of other intentions, often in direct conflict. He does want to build the Nation. He does want to provide jobs to his members, including jobs as security guards. He does want to build a respectable health clinic in Washington and in other cities. He just can't win for his own need to lose.

Still, for all his racist ranting, can it be true, as Pete King's representative claimed, that "he's done more than any single person to strain race relations in this country"? Are Farrakhan's and his assistants' obvious, vulgar, often ugly attacks on whites, Jews, Catholics, and others really a greater strain on race relations than the steady onslaught on blacks and other minorities by the Republicans for twelve years? Was Farrakhan's claim, made in some college auditoriums, that Jews own the media more effective than the Willie Horton television ad used by George Bush in his 1988 campaign? Did Farrakhan's claims about Jewish conspiracies made in Symphony Hall in Phoenix create more strains on race relations than Ronald Reagan's television speeches about welfare queens? I wonder.

The difference, of course, is that Farrakhan was attacking whites, whites in power and Jews he thinks dominate power. Republicans were attacking blacks—not all blacks, of course. They put one of them on the Supreme Court to prove they weren't racists. But the black they put on the Supreme Court represented, and made clear that he did, all the racist ideas of those who did him that favor. So strongly did Clarence Thomas despise blacks on welfare that he spoke out openly against his own sister who at one point had had to accept welfare.

On almost every issue, for twelve years, in a great variety of ways, in North and South, in their politics and in their legislative work, the Republicans made clear to the American people their contempt for blacks. The effect on blacks was to cause a great deal of pain, partly because being treated badly always causes pain. But in addition, the fifteen years before had led them to hope for something different from a resumption of what they had become used to before the 1960s.

For whites, the message of the Republicans wasn't painful, it was cheerful. Blacks actually were as bad as whites thought they were, so they didn't have to suppress their thoughts as Democratic administrations, and even President Nixon, had urged them to do. It took a while for whites to rise up in anger against those extravagant hopes expressed by blacks, and the so-called privileges they had been granted by Democratic legislation in the sixties. But they did.

So, by the nineties there was a strong sense of racial cleavage in America, with scarcely any help from Louis Farrakhan. There was more poverty, crime, teenage pregnancy, and general despair among poor blacks, while the gap between the poor and the rich grew wider every year. Mirroring the anger of poor blacks was Farrakhan, by the mid-nineties supported by the majority of blacks because he expressed their anger too. He has indeed put a strain on race relations. Whites don't appreciate when blacks get angry at them. They have shown that for three hundred years. But has Louis Farrakhan done more than anyone else to strain race relations in the United States? The charge is more sad than ludicrous.

15.

There was a time when it appeared Farrakhan might be reconciled with whites, might welcome integration, might want truly to make peace among the races. For three years after Elijah died in 1975, Farrakhan (who had only recently taken that name) went along with all the new ideas of Elijah's son. He didn't agree with anything Wallace (then known as Imam Warith Deen) was doing with his father's bequest, but he nevertheless remained on the scene and cooperated, even going out across the country to try to explain the shifts in Nation policy, especially to members who had been Elijah's faithful followers and were dropping away every day, forming a variety of organizations, all of them destined soon to disappear.

Wallace brought Farrakhan to Chicago from New York, ostensibly to assist him in the process of changing the Nation. But the more likely reason—one advanced by most of those familiar with the situation—was that he feared a rebellion in East Coast ranks, led by Farrakhan.

The question that doesn't seem to get asked by those writing about Farrakhan is why he went along with the total dismantling of the Nation, beginning with the change of the name to the World Community of Islam in the West, the change of the name of the Harlem mosque to the Malcolm X mosque, the rejuvenation of Malcolm's reputation, even the change of his own name from Louis to Abdul Haleem, and the demand that he take regular classes in the Koran and the Arabic language to which Warith subjected his ministers, and on and on—a thorough transformation. Why did he lend himself to the process? Why did he announce that, in this new Nation, Elijah's ideas about the presentation of the male self had been abandoned? Why did he tell audiences that "It doesn't matter what a man wears or how long his hair is. If he wants to wear a beard, let him wear it," as he said in Los Angeles? Surely he must have sensed his leader turning in his grave. Was he such a total opportunist that he was willing to be the right-hand man of the person who was in the process of dismantling the organization and all the ideas to which he had devoted most of his adult life? Were his religious ideas so shallow that he could readily preach a whole new set of ideas to please his new boss? Were his ideas about racial separation so trivial that he could give them up when it seemed advantageous?

Was he so corrupt that he was willing to play mouthpiece for a $50,000 gift from Warith plus a hundred-dollar pay raise for serving as minister of a new, obscure mosque in a walk-up apartment near a North Side Chicago housing project? A far cry from his previous ministry. On the other hand, while he was ministering to this tiny, inauspicious mosque and doing Warith's biddings, he and his family were living in a spacious house in an upper-middle-class integrated community in Chicago, courtesy of Warith's money.

Northwestern University professor Adolph Reed suggests that in fact Farrakhan was not so cooperative, that he "constituted himself on the right flank as guardian of the Messenger's orthodoxy, ready to challenge deviations." If he was indeed challenging Warith, why didn't Warith just fire him? Warith's behavior in transforming the Nation into his kind of Islamic organization did not suggest a reluctance to do what he needed to do. His whole adult history reflects a man who does what he wants, even if sometimes unprincipled.

Perhaps Reed is right. Perhaps Farrakhan really was having a private struggle with Warith that was known only to a few people, and Warith was afraid to fire him because he had been such a powerful force in the Nation. People might leave even faster than they already were. Many former members of Elijah's Nation were setting up rival groups, some of which exist today, though they could not be considered serious rivals of even the smallest storefront church. Farrakhan's public role for three years contradicts Reed's view. He was, as he had been previously, the National Representative of the Nation, only now he was explaining this new Islamic organization that was open to everyone, including whites, and would no longer adhere to all those rules that had for so long been considered holy in the Nation.

There's still another view to be heard, that of African-garbed Conrad Worrill, chairman of the Department of Inner City Studies at Chicago's Northeastern University, chairman of the National Black United Front, longtime leader of the Black Nationalists in Chicago, and an early supporter of Elijah, whose byline appears regularly in the *Final Call*. Worrill describes Farrakhan's years with Warith as "just sitting around with nothing to do." Ministering to a small mosque and occasionally giving a public speech might well strike a busy person as just sitting around. It might have struck Farrakhan that way too.

Considering the contrast between the Farrakhan before the death of Elijah, the Farrakhan of the next three years, and then the Farrakhan of the years after, it is astounding that the interim years lasted as long as they did. Farrakhan claimed to have been "lulled to sleep" by Warith's ideas. Lulled to sleep by ideas that were contrary to everything he believed, ideas promulgated by the man who, after rejecting his father, was given the job Farrakhan deserved? More likely Farrakhan was simply biding his time, trying to figure out what to do with himself. There he was, in his mid-forties, with no salable skills and no desire to do anything but what he had done so successfully for most of his adult life. Certainly he couldn't return to show business. It was another life. It would mean virtually starting from scratch, something a man with a big family and big ambitions couldn't even consider. Staying with Warith was a new life too, but it was relatively easy and financially comfortable. He might not wish to do it for very long, but for a while it gave him time to think.

Came the third year it was over. He couldn't take it anymore. He told a confidant (Jesse Jackson claims to be that confidant, as does Abdul Karim Hasan, a longtime Nation colleague): "I won't be a prostitute for anybody anymore. Why should I do it for anybody else when I can do it for myself?" Farrakhan may not have intended that his words be taken literally. He rarely does. But it would be hard to do otherwise. He proceeded to create an imaginary character for himself, take it out on the road, and sell it to anyone he could convince, mainly members of the former Nation. Did he feel he was being a prostitute? Or was he simply using extreme words to Jesse Jackson, hoping to arouse his dismay, the way he loves to do?

What exactly was Farrakhan planning to sell? Well, he would sell what he'd always sold—his charismatic personality, his ability to influence people. In exchange, under Elijah, he had won love and admiration and, of course, some money and some power. But not enough, as it turned out. When he sold his services for Warith, never believing in what he was doing, he was awarded with hard cash. Like a prostitute. Now he was planning to sell the same qualities to spread his own ideas, as he had done under Elijah. But this time he had no illusions. This time he would get paid, though the money was less important than the power. Not the kind of power he'd had under Elijah, which was only an illusion. This would be the real thing, complete power.

16.

The first thing Farrakhan did was to tell off Warith publicly. In what would be his last sermon under Warith, delivered in Chicago's Mosque No. 2, the Nation's flagship mosque that Elijah had bought in 1972 with a $3 million "loan" from Libya, Farrakhan burst forth with all that had apparently been gnawing at him. He condemned his boss for refusing to acknowledge Elijah: "You got a nerve not wanting to speak . . . [his] name, and he built this house. He gave you everything you have."

Then Farrakhan went into retreat for three months. There were rumors of threats on his life, which couldn't be dismissed. Would the followers of this new democratic organization threaten to kill Farrakhan because he had insulted Warith and then deserted ship? Warith certainly claimed to want a democratic organization, but lots of his followers had been Elijah's too, and Warith was his son. Malcolm had, after all, insulted Elijah, and look what happened to him. Warith insisted he had nothing to do with these rumors of threats against Farrakhan. All the descriptions of Warith paint him as a man devoted to the peaceful democratic practice of Islam. But how many such men have we known who have made that claim but have been slaughterers?

On the other hand, did Farrakhan spread those rumors himself, further insulting Warith and justifying his own removal from the public eye? It wouldn't be unimaginable.

Whatever the reason for the retreat, from it emerged a new Farrakhan. Gone was the confusion. This man had had a rare religious experience. His leader, his mentor, Elijah Muhammad, who was still living somewhere in the earthly sphere, had paid him a visit. He had come to assign Farrakhan to a divine mission. He was to be Elijah's representative to resurrect the Nation of Islam just as it had been under Elijah. Farrakhan never explained what Elijah had to say in this divine visit about his son Warith. In fact, Farrakhan explained little about that visit. It was too metaphysical. If Elijah was Allah's messenger, what did that make *him*? He didn't begin calling himself God. That came later. For now he was simply a man with a divine mission.

17.

Why Farrakhan remained with Warith Muhammad for three years despite the huge differences between them is more easily explained than why he has, since 1977, created the myth of the ever-living Messiah, Elijah, who is constantly on call for advice, whom he venerates as a God, and whose representative he is. There have been many, many moments over the last few years, as I listened to Farrakhan speak and read his newspaper, when I felt he truly believed his own myth, that Elijah actually did talk to him. If that were true, my curiosity would be irrelevant. He had a religious experience, some would say. Others would describe it as a psychotic episode, in which a dead hero reappeared as a vision.

Yes, I have had a few moments when I believed that actually happened, which would explain everything that has happened since. But most of the time I have felt with all my being that this whole drama has been staged by one of the shrewdest opportunists in recent history. I come to that conclusion not because I don't believe such experiences of faith can occur, but because this one was so nicely timed to solve Farrakhan's problems. There he was, having told off Warith and nowhere to go. In that sense it's understandable, but my problem is: where was Farrakhan's heart and his head when he created this myth to venerate a man who had treated him so badly, who had, after all, given him a mighty shaft? Doesn't it stick in his craw every time he glorifies that man, every time he begins a sentence with "The Honorable Elijah Muhammad taught us . . ." to explain almost everything in the world, much of which are his own ideas? How can he proclaim that all his thoughts and feelings come from that man who so badly betrayed him?

At the beginning Farrakhan's motive was obvious. If he could rally Elijah's faithful to him, he would eventually have the power and prestige that Elijah once had. Sure, it wasn't the kind of thing one likes to lie down with at night, this creating a myth about a man you resent. But showmen often have to do that. My question is, why didn't he, over the years, when he was being so successful, phase out the myth? Why did he continue to appear to idolize that man, to treat him like God? Was he too insecure to take off on his own? In his own eyes, was his fate too tied to Elijah's? Or is he just crazy enough to believe the stuff he says about Elijah? Farrakhan still talks about that visit from Elijah and others since. Elijah's Nation has been resurrected despite Warith's attempts to destroy it. Elijah is still the head man, if only in spirit, and Farrakhan is still his right-hand man, running the show, just as he did for so long, a little like the pope or the president of the Mormons.

The system works. If it ain't broke, why fix it? Still, one wonders what goes through the Minister's head when he is lionizing his former boss.

18.

By himself Farrakhan was pretty helpless. He had no sizable funds, no means to reach the people, and only a tiny base in Chicago. He had been there only three years with an apartment-size mosque, and had only recently tried to win support for his opposition to Warith's ideas. He could have gone fishing, as Malcolm used to say, speaking on street corners and talking to people on the street. But that was for the little guys, the fishermen. Farrakhan was no longer a fisherman, hadn't been for a long time, and had no taste for it. Besides, that process could take forever. He needed to get this show on the road.

So he went for help to the Black Nationalists in Chicago. In their own philosophy they had much in common with the Nation. In general, the modern Black Nationists emerged from the Black Power movement initiated in the late sixties by Stokely Carmichael. But, as noted earlier, black nationalism has a long history in America, and the modern version remains dedicated to essentially the same goals of nineteenth-century nationalists: independent institutions for blacks. Many young people in the sixties, inspired by these ideas, emigrated to Africa, and Africa remains an idealized homeland, though visions of a large emigration have long since disappeared. Today they have numerous organizations with slightly different goals and tactics, but modern Black Nationalists remain essentially loyal to one another.

In the seventies, still fresh with the vigor of Black Power, there was much more unanimity. To some extent the Black Nationalists then looked for inspiration to Elijah Muhammad, though they largely rejected his religious dogma and authoritarian rules. Their strong sympathies were for Malcolm X, and on a number of levels they supported Malcolm's Nation.

Most of that support was withdrawn after Malcolm's death, when many Black Nationalists believed that those within the Nation itself had murdered him. Just as important to the Black Nationalists was their emerging view that the Nation was not the "people's nation." It had been run like a private fraternal organization, and then, with the death of Elijah, they discovered that even that idea was too broad. "It was," Haki Madhubuti says in *Claiming Earth*, "a family religious-business run and controlled by Elijah Muhammad."

Madhubuti is more forthcoming than his Black Nationalist colleagues about their sentiments toward the Nation during the years before 1977, when Farrakhan approached them. By the time I interviewed them in 1994, most of them had reservations about discussing Elijah with me. It might reflect badly on Farrakhan, who by that time had covered himself with Elijah's mantle. Most of them were no more sympathetic to Farrakhan's authoritarianism and religious dogma than they had been to Elijah's, but they were unwilling to attack Farrakhan. He had become the foremost leader in the black fold. He had earned a wide reputation among blacks and was under attack by whites. The attitude that prevailed among most blacks, foremost among them the Black Nationalists, was that Farrakhan's attacks on whites and Jews were largely deserved. Even some Black Nationalists I interviewed in 1994 who had strongly attacked Farrakhan's bigotry—one called him a fascist—by 1996 had undergone a conversion. Farrakhan had attracted three-quarters of a million black men to his rally in Washington, D.C., early that year.

But in 1977 the memories of Elijah Muhammad were fresh. And the murder of Malcolm was equally fresh. So the Black Nationalists hesitated even to talk with Louis Farrakhan (then called Abdul Farrakhan). But finally they agreed to listen to his spiel.

Stories differ over what happened next, but all of them resemble the one told by Madhubuti. Farrakhan approached Madhubuti in 1977, just as he had approached other Black Nationalists, to sketch out his plan. He didn't reveal to them that he had been visited by Elijah; that would simply have led him right back out their doors. He told them instead that Elijah had been too "exclusive and secret."

"His goal," according to Madhubuti, "was to involve the 'Nation' with the larger Black community. His vision . . . was much in line with that of many in Chicago's Black political and cultural community."

Madhubuti then asked about fifty people whether they would meet with Farrakhan. Twenty-seven agreed to come, including people from the media, from the entertainment world, and from education, politics, and community organizations. Without explanation, Madhubuti claims that the "internal 'warfare' . . . between various 'Black Muslim' factions at that time" forced him to hold the first several meetings with Farrakhan in his home, something he had never done before. The implication is that Farrakhan's and perhaps others' lives would be endangered by meeting in a more public place—an implication that seems to have no substantiation. Was it paranoia operating, or was Madhubuti's house a more intimate, more conducive atmosphere in which Farrakhan could tell his story?

At these meetings Farrakhan, the Charmer, told his small but influential audience that he would make the Nation into something entirely new: "more political, more involved in the larger Black Community, less self-righteous and all-knowing, one that would keep its communication lines open and work as part of a Black united front.

The new NOI, he said, would follow the teachings of Elijah Muhammad but would be more creative and insightful in its interpretation of
Islam in relation to the Black community"—the kind of message this
group would welcome.

When the first question addressed to him concerned the murder
of Malcolm X, Farrakhan told the group the same thing he has said
ever since: he had no direct or even indirect hand in Malcolm's death,
though he may have helped create the climate that led to it. This may
have been the first time he told that story. Madhubuti recalls Farrakhan's remarks: "His answer, one that few of us will forget, was given
in a voice and tone of complete sorrow and resignation. He was obviously prepared for the question. He talked of the history and his personal connection to Malcolm, whom he described as his big
brother-teacher and as the man who helped to prepare him. . . . His
explanation, coupled with his formidable persuasive powers, put most
of our minds to rest on that question."

The group met again several times and then pooled their resources and went to work to help Farrakhan rebuild the Nation. They
scheduled his first public speech at the auditorium of Madhubuti's
school; it was a packed audience. For the next few months Farrakhan
held meetings at the school, the Institute of Positive Education. Madhubuti charged him $99 a week.

Within a year, as Farrakhan's success grew, he began to look more
and more like the Farrakhan whom Elijah had known and loved—if
not quite enough. Madhubuti and most of his colleagues were dismayed. This was not what they had been promised, and this was defi-
nitely not what they wanted. They watched as body searches at
meetings were reinstituted, along with the Fruit of Islam. What truly
drove Madhubuti and his friends away was that "We tired rather
quickly of being invited to share the dais while Farrakhan gave *the*
word for three hours each Saviour's Day." No one upstaged the Black
Nationalists like that. They "distanced" themselves, as Madhubuti described it.

For a few Black Nationalists, Farrakhan is still a hero. One of the
best known, Conrad Worrill, sits patiently by while Farrakhan speaks
for hours, but Worrill gets his hearing with a far larger audience by
writing regularly and prominently in the *Call*. Others were pretty
angry at having been so badly used. They kept their eye on Farrakhan

but, angry as they may have been, kept their opinions to themselves. He did share, after all, many Black Nationalist ideas. By 1981, however, when Farrakhan began to publish the *Call*, it was clear he would offer nothing that resembled a "creative and insightful" interpretation of Elijah's ideas but instead would repeat them verbatim. Farrakhan was "a leader who cannot, and should not be dismissed or minimized by the assessment of others outside of the Black community who have ulterior motives," Madhubuti said in *Claiming Earth*, but some problems were beginning to be hard to overlook.

In 1993, at the annual Saviour's Day meeting, Farrakhan declared, "Every prophet had a community of zealots that, when you rose up against that prophet, the people would rise up and kill you. . . . If you want to live, you leave that man alone where we are concerned. When Malcolm stepped across that line, death was inevitable."

A warning to those who might rise up against him? Using that famous dead man to raise his own stature? Once again cursing the man who was still a hero to many? Farrakhan was risking himself anew. The organization he had rebuilt in these sixteen years was largely composed of those faithful to Elijah at all costs. But here and there could be found some, like the Black Nationalists, who remained faithful to Malcolm, though his "canonization" was still to come. If Farrakhan's organization was strong enough, as he expected, he would intensify his own position by once again calling up the anger against Malcolm for having betrayed Elijah. If the organization was strong enough, it would not matter if he lost those who were loyal to Malcolm. Daring and self-assured as he has been for all but a few years of his life, he obviously decided he could take that risk. And he got away with it.

19.

Gradually Farrakhan put out the word that Elijah had directed him to rebuild the Nation, and the old structure began to take shape again. The secrecy of the Nation being what it is, the number of mosques that have returned to the fold since the late seventies is not revealed, nor is the individual membership. Scanning the *Call*'s columns, where much attention is given to the mosques, one is led to believe there are ninety-one mosques across the country, but that's an illusion. Mosques numbers 67, 75, 80, and 91, along with assorted numbers between 2 and 27, are clearly active. I may have missed a couple between 27 and 67, or some mosques may not be mentioned in the newspaper, though in the nature of things that seems unlikely. These numbers are the ones assigned by Elijah and retained since his death. Many of the older mosques did not survive the death of Elijah, caught as they were in the conflict that followed Warith's leadership of the Nation. There were any number of attempts to set up separate groups, some of which have survived, so the mosque numbers we see scattered throughout the pages of the *Call* represent some of the original mosques, but how many one can't tell. And we don't know how many there were originally.

One does get a partial but interesting picture of the nature and growth of the Nation from the "FCN" (*Final Call National*) weekly page. In its own peculiar way, as it reports the best *Call* street sales of the week, it indicates the growth of the organization. Hawking the paper has always been a requirement for members, almost an initiation for new members. First of all, it is a source of income, though after the expenses of the paper are met, the income from the *Call* cannot represent a huge contribution to the Nation. The paper sells no outside advertising, which represents the bulk of the income for most publications. Income derived from the *Call* is solely from its circulation, both mailed subscriptions and street sales. It is entirely possible that other sources in the Nation are subsidizing the *Call*. Just as important, however, the paper is the Nation's primary contact with the black world, the main vehicle for attracting new Nation members, the main means of publicizing the speeches of Farrakhan and other leaders as well as upcoming events, and the main outlet for marketing its books and tapes, mainly taped speeches by Farrakhan, Elijah, and other ministers, and the books of Elijah and Farrakhan, clothing, uniforms, the Salaam Restaurant, the University of Islam, T-shirts, personal care products, and so on, all of which provide a good portion of the Nation's income.

Salesmen receive a commission on their sales of the *Call*, and for many young men this is an important source of income. David Jackson of the *Chicago Tribune* reports that William Smith Muhammad, down there in Georgia, at ninety-four, "survives by selling fruit and *Final*

Call newspapers from the 1952 International van that sinks into the mud outside his [one-room] trailer with a goat tethered to the wall outside." William Smith, in his tiny town of Bronwood, Georgia, surely has no hope of ever having his picture in the *Call* with other salesmen, but many others are encouraged to get out there on the street corner, even when the take isn't terribly good and the weather is pretty bad, in the hope they might be recognized in the FCN Progress! that appears each week.

The page starts with photos of Farrakhan, the Supreme Captain, and the Assistant Supreme Captain (Farrakhan's sons), and a brief salute to the top salesmen that ends with "On behalf of the publisher, Minister Louis Farrakhan, we thank Almighty God Allah. . . ."

Then six small photos portray the top regional sales captains of the month, and eight group photos show the "most improved" group with inset photos of the top salesmen of the week. Some of these groups represent mosques, but the majority are study groups, not ready to be full-fledged mosques but still doing well at selling papers. Since such a concept as proportional representation seems absent, the top fellows are all from large or medium-sized cities. Or perhaps the Nation simply hasn't penetrated the small towns. In one issue selected at random, for instance, the top salesman, with 1,700 papers, was from the West Side of Chicago. But Chicago is the national headquarters of the Nation. Isn't it likely that the largest number of papers would be sold there? Still, it's not quite as bad as it sounds. In another randomly selected week, the winner, with 900 papers, was from Indianapolis, the twelfth largest city in the country, with a relatively small black population (432,000 blacks among 5 million whites as of the 1990 census).

But this progress report is curious. For most of the groups shown in a couple of randomly selected issues, no top salesman is listed. No numbers are given. The groups are described as "most improved" (in the region). Brooklyn, for instance, apparently sold more papers in this particular week than in the preceding week, which was true in both the random issues I checked (September 1996), but it seems that no one sold enough papers to warrant a tribute to the best salesman. What does it take to get that?

The lowest sales figure for the top salesman is five hundred. In other words, a salesman doesn't rate "top" status unless he sells at least five hundred papers a week. So it is unlikely that, hard as they may try, the young men in Peoria can ever compete with their counterparts in the big cities.

But in the case of the mosques and the study groups, what does "improved" mean? Actual numbers might be embarrassing, so the *Call* says simply that all those mosques and study groups are improving. Does this encourage folks to get out there and sell the paper? Listen, a man living in our "fifteen-minutes-of-fame" era who doesn't have much going on in his life can't help but be thrilled to get his picture in the paper. And we're not talking about any paper now. This is the *Final Call*, the paper published by the great leader Minister Louis Farrakhan. The faces in these pictures look happy, satisfied, and proud. Minister Farrakhan has treated them with respect and admiration by putting their pictures in the same paper in which his own picture appears so frequently.

I have mentioned only men because there are no women in these pictures. Women in the Nation are not expected to go out on street corners or, worse yet, from door to door, hawking the paper. That isn't proper work for the Muslim woman, not the image of the Muslim woman the Nation wishes to project.

This is not to say that the image of women in the Nation is a negative one, shades of Saudi Arabia or Iran. The skeleton image of womanhood is based on Islam, but like everything else in the Nation, the use of Islamic doctrine depends on what is practical for Farrakhan (mostly for Elijah before him). The *Call* prints many photos of women, from fashion models (Nation fashions, of course) to Minister Ava Muhammad, who is not only a minister but a lawyer for Farrakhan and, incidentally, quite beautiful. There's a heavy emphasis on Farrakhan's wife and daughters and his minister of protocol, Claudette Muhammad, all of whom are handsome, elegantly dressed women but who appear not to have voices. One searches in vain for a few words by the women in Farrakhan's life, especially when one sees so many photos of them looking so stately.

20.

Another Nation secret is the circulation of the *Call*. That information, according to all the staff members I managed to talk with, is "confidential." On the street, talking to Muslims, they claim half a million. Who can dispute them? They aren't audited by Standard Rate and Data, which reports on newspaper sales, because they don't need to supply an accurate count of their circulation to advertisers. The Nation's advertising space is used for its own products.

Now, if one could talk with the *Call's* printer, one might find out how many copies are printed. But that is another secret the Muslims will not reveal. "It is not necessarily information that we would want to give anyone," the *Call's* production manager told me. I was researching black businesses, I said, and wondered whether the Nation used a black printer. There are no black printers, the production manager told me—which effectively ended that conversation. Even if I located the printer, who could be anywhere in the country, he might not reveal his customer's print run, which wouldn't be so unusual.

If the *Call* used second-class mail privileges—the fastest and best—offered to magazines and newspapers by the U.S. Postal Service, its circulation figures would be immediately available. Publications using second-class mail must publish their circulation annually. But in 1996 the *Call* no longer used even a third-class nonprofit permit.

So we are stuck with the word-of-mouth claims that the *Call* sells half a million papers a week. Consider the 1,170,869 daily national circulation of the *New York Times*, with its massive reputation and promotional efforts, and its sales to any and everyone who will buy it, white, black, Hispanic, or Asian. Compare that picture with the *Call*. Its audience is almost exclusively black. That automatically limits its potential audience to only a tenth that of the *Times*. And most of this audience is likely to be at least sympathetic, let alone loyal to Farrakhan. That would seem to limit circulation further. Seen in that light, the *Call's* claim of half a million seems huge, hard to believe.

Apart from numbers, consider the *Call's* possible impact. Take the Million-Man March. Farrakhan's call to the October 1995 march, made over nearly a year's time, was all but ignored by mainstream media and by many black newspapers. The major outlet for Farrakhan's appeal was his newspaper, through a regular page-size ad. Of course the march was also announced briefly during Farrakhan's hundreds of radio and television programs, on the Internet, and by sympathetic black radio commentators and disc jockeys, especially as the event drew nearer. And word of mouth helps a lot. But none of those notices could compare with the weekly, emotional impact of that ad.

No organization planning an event a year in advance would sneer at that much exposure.

When the mainstream media occasionally mentioned the march, it was with obvious skepticism. Was this man off his rocker to believe he could attract a million black men to Washington? For a Day of Forgiveness and Atonement? I was skeptical myself. But I was reading the *Call* and listening to the radio. I did have moments when I thought, if he indeed had half a million readers, considering the appeals he was making, and all the radio announcements and organizing that he and his people were doing all over the country, regularly reported in the paper, he might very well draw a big crowd. Farrakhan even went to the Ebenezer Baptist Church in Atlanta, King's father's church, and told his audience: "In our immaturity we missed the value of Dr. King. And the civil rights movement missed the value of Elijah Muhammad, Malcolm X and other national leaders. However, time and circumstances have caused us all to mature. Maturing is part of the struggle, and when you mature you see the value that you missed yesterday." The *Call* reported, "The Minister said march planning would be incomplete if it was not first 'sanctified' by and at Ebenezer Baptist." After the meeting at the church, Farrakhan and his entourage laid a wreath at King's grave. Now, that's what you call maturing.

What seemed clear in advance was that Farrakhan's march would draw a crowd, perhaps even more than the 250,000 who marched on Washington in 1963 for civil rights. That march was also widely publicized, though over a shorter time.

But that 1963 march had the support of hundreds of organizations, including huge unions, churches, white and black, the entire black press, and many white liberals in the media. While Farrakhan aroused support among some Christian churches and a variety of community groups, there was also considerable opposition—Chairman of the Joint Chiefs Colin Powell, who said he wouldn't lend respectability to Farrakhan's name; Jesse Jackson, who said practically the same thing but in the end was forced by overwhelming support not only to change his mind but to speak. Many Christian ministers despise Farrakhan. (Many of them despised King for a while too.) The major black civil rights organization, the NAACP, an organization dedicated to interracial harmony, supported by white (including Jewish) money, withheld its support for the march, though it wasn't united and some members attended. It didn't help to win NAACP support that Farrakhan's chief organizer of the march was Benjamin Chavis, the man the NAACP had fired citing misuse of funds, sexual harassment, and too close a relationship with Louis Farrakhan.

Given all these circumstances, imagine the expressions on the faces of the media people when the Boston University Center for Remote Sensing, studying aerial photos, estimated the march crowd at 837,000. This followed the initial estimate made by the D.C. Park District—400,000. The Nation and many blacks sympathetic to Farrakhan were still using a figure of two million over a year later.

The only demonstration in this country ever to approach the Boston University estimate occurred in 1970 in response to President Nixon's bombing of Cambodia and the killing by the Ohio National Guard of four protesting students at Kent State University.

Skeptics nonetheless viewed the Million-Man March not as support for Farrakhan but as a demonstration of black male solidarity and protest that just happened to be organized by Farrakhan. It could not serve as evidence of the effectiveness of his tactics, especially of his newspaper. But on the first anniversary of the march, at the area surrounding the United Nations in New York, still another huge crowd responded to Farrakhan's call to come and bring the message to the world. Was this demonstration also only incidentally Farrakhan's accomplishment? Were these people also coming to demonstrate in spite of Farrakhan's leadership? In fact, this second march was not Farrakhan's idea. He bought it, of course, and helped organize it, but the real spur behind it was the Messenger of the Messianic Millennium, Reverend James Bevel, who is never without an idea. A demonstration at the United Nations called by Jim Bevel? There might actually be a few hundred people there.

21.

I have not exhausted the strengths of the *Call* as Farrakhan's vehicle—for human rights appeals, for human interest stories, for all kinds of advice and spiritual uplift, for "philosophical" discussions, for news of Africa, Latin and South America, the Middle East, for news of blacks in trouble all over the country, even for occasional fashion news, for announcements of speeches by the Nation's ministers, for the expression of bigotry and hatred, and for photos of all kinds of people.

What is so astounding about this newspaper is that, in the face of dwindling circulations of many newspapers and magazines, this one is clearly growing. After being able to publish only sporadically, once every couple weeks, once a month, for many years, it was finally able to go weekly in the spring of 1996, not coincidentally a few months after the Million-Man March. The issues steadily grow fatter, filled with more news and photos than the year before, particularly as Farrakhan travels extensively among majority black countries, where it appears from the *Call* that he receives royal treatment, even offers of billion-dollar loans from Libya. The *Call* is a newspaper filled with a dramatic sense of life and excitement that far outpaces the mainstream press. The news in the *Call* is more often than not good news.

One can imagine subscribers eagerly awaiting the arrival of the *Call*. It is printed in a larger typeface than most publications, and though most of its photos are clearly amateurish—too dark, too fuzzy, and so on—in these photos are the faces of black people doing things, like chubby Sister Chloe Muhammad, with her winning smile, dressed all in black, standing amidst her bookshelves in her Maryam's Bookstore at the far southern tip of Chicago. The story about Sister Chloe is headlined "Maryam's Bookstore, A Place for Knowledge, Wisdom and Truth." Imagine that copy on the feature page of your local paper. Knowledge, wisdom, and truth?

But one must not for a moment overlook the fact that in this rather brief, quarter-page story that includes a 3x4-inch photo, the good Minister Farrakhan is mentioned five times. One of those mentions is to inform readers that customers are often attracted into the shop by the voice of Farrakhan booming from a loudspeaker outside.

22.

As I write this I am incredulous at the words I am about to say: the greatest measure of the sense of life and excitement in the *Call* comes from an intensity, even a love that one feels being exuded in this newspaper. This despite the few pages that exude bigotry, fear, and hatred, which are a constant presence. An example of what I am calling love is to be found in the February 11, 1997, issue.

This story concerns a near-fatal rape and assault of a nine-year-old black girl on January 4, 1997, in the Cabrini-Green projects in Chicago. At the same time another child, this one a blue-eyed blond, a six-year-old "beauty queen," a tiny Miss Colorado, was brutally killed under mysterious circumstances in the home of her wealthy parents in Boulder, Colorado. That story was hot news. Inevitably all the mainstream media ran major stories on this strange little white child whose mascara was as thick as one would expect on a highly rated beauty queen and who, it was implied, was the victim of a rather crazed stage-door mother and perhaps a father as well, both of whom refused to talk to the police. The story crowded out other news for several days. The terrible fate of the black child, Girl X, as she was called, just didn't rate the same coverage. On the same day the *Call*'s story appeared, a brief story in Section 2 of the *Chicago Tribune* described how Girl X's condition had improved sufficiently so that she could be moved from the hospital to a rehab center for long-term care.

When I saw the headline in the *Call* about "Girl X," I held my breath, expecting a long tirade against the white media for its treatment of the two stories. Instead there was just one paragraph quoting a Cabrini resident saying, "That white girl . . . got lots of media attention and all types of investigative techniques are being used to find her killer, but that's not being used on this girl." Beyond that quote, the mainstream media was not mentioned.

The story gave a complete and compassionate review of events as of press time, with quotes from the police and leaders in the community, from gang leaders who insisted that this attack did not bear the signs of a gang attack, as claimed by police and others, and discussion about raising funds for the family and moving them out of the projects. The general tone of the story was an outpouring of sympathy for the child. A readout in bright green on the first page of the story was a quote from Farrakhan: "For a young girl to undergo this, it is the same as murder. In fact it *is* murder."

The *Call* couldn't resist this murder. Farrakhan is quoted several times in the story with such comments as "We have to put a stop to this kind of behavior. . . ." The *Call* also reported that Farrakhan visited the child in the hospital on January 31—almost a month after she had been attacked. What took him so long? And a Valentine's Day benefit party at the Nation's Salaam Restaurant, on Chicago's South Side, was announced only in the February 11 issue.

Opposite the assault story was one featuring a young woman who had herself been assaulted when she was young and had put together a women's organization in response. Speaking at Mosque Maryam and asking for support following an address by Farrakhan, Beverly Reed said of him: "For the first time—since I was eight years old—I felt protected and I felt a man cared about and would protect me from assault." Farrakhan had spoken "forcefully about how to stop rapists from destroying the souls of women," the *Call* said.

All this coverage, even if a little late, has the feel of deep concern for this child, quite unlike the coverage in the *Chicago Tribune* of the same day. The *Tribune* story is not unsympathetic, but it cannot match the *Call*, where a headline in red bold type blasts across the page: "MURDER *of the* SOUL!" and a subhead in black reads, " 'Girl X' Rape, Poisoning Sparks Outrage in Black Community—Pg. 3."

So it's a little late. So what if the local media have been briefly reporting this story since it occurred. So what if a local black radio show has raised thousands of dollars for the family. This coverage by the *Call* has the ring of concern and compassion that you just don't get—don't expect—from the mainstream media for anyone, except maybe a six-year-old Miss Colorado, certainly not for a poor little black girl from the projects. Murder of the Soul!

23.

The *Call* is a newspaper that speaks in several voices, many of them amateurish, some of them angry and hostile, some of them downright foolish, some of them highly intelligent and informative, some of them even professional, altogether offering a strong message direct to the black world. This is not the *New York Times*. Or the *Nation*. Or *In These Times*. It also isn't the *Chicago Defender* or the *New York Amsterdam News*. With its garish use of color, bold type, tabloid size, and occasional off-the-wall stories about outer space, it might be mistaken for a supermarket rag. But it's not even a close relative.

Even to the most casual observer, the *Call* is the mouthpiece of Louis Farrakhan, the religio-political leader of the Nation of Islam, though he would hotly deny that label. He would insist that the *Call* exudes the feeling it does because of its heavy emphasis on God, or Allah. That emphasis certainly is there. "Murder of the Soul"? Clearly there are many who view Farrakhan as a religious leader and some who see him as God's direct representative on earth. That such a figure could create an organ of opinion and news like the *Call* is, after all, not so surprising. Such a person could presumably do anything and do it better than anyone else.

This biographer of Farrakhan doesn't share that view. To me, the *Call* is not the work of a religious leader or of God's direct representative. It is the product of a man of extraordinary wit and the ability to charm and disarm, to lie, to deceive, to distort, a man with an incredible understanding of the uses of propaganda, an exquisite feel for ordinary people and a special compassion for poor minority people, and, most important, a belief that he is destined to gain great power somehow, somewhere, maybe over the rainbow. Or perhaps he already believes he has great power. Perhaps his continuing effort to prove his power is not, as I suspect, a sign of his yearning but his belief that he's already there. Perhaps he confuses publicity with power. Certainly one cannot deny the depth and range of publicity he has received. And while publicity is a symbol of power all too often in American culture, it is mistakenly viewed as power itself. Has Farrakhan made that mistake? It's not easy for me to make that judgment. And I strongly suspect it's often not easy for Farrakhan himself to make that judgment.

24.

Farrakhan's conception of himself is where his problems begin and end. For instance, he wants very much for the *Call* to be a respected newspaper because that would enhance his reputation with that segment of the black world he yearns to attract to the Nation—educated professionals with good salaries. But if he gave the *Call* any more professionalism than it has, he would have to stop using it for his own messianic, egomaniacal purposes, and he can't afford to do that. He has to make it appear to the public that he is God, or at least godlike, either because he believes it or because he so painfully yearns for it to be true. On a segment of "60 Minutes" in April 1996, he told Mike Wallace of his belief that "they" are planning "to do with me what they did with Martin Luther King and Malcolm X, bring them down and then assassinate them." But, he assured Wallace, "I am not Martin Luther King. I am not Malcolm X. I am living in a different time frame. If God is with me, which he is, you'd better beware."

For the same reasons he cannot greatly exceed his present status. He can attract more poor blacks to his fold, even a few middle-class people. He can further expand the audiences he has already begun to build in Africa, the Middle East, and the Caribbean. He can excite and thrill more and bigger audiences with his speeches. He can even gain more radio and television time. And many of his earlier enemies will now defend him because, since the Million-Man March and the anniversary gathering in New York revealed his depth of support among blacks in this country, it doesn't make political sense to oppose him. With a few exceptions, journalists, academics, clergy, and politicians have figured out that criticizing or denying him may only redound poorly on them and lose for them their own audiences. When he went to Africa and the Middle East and met with and praised Sani Abacha, Qaddafi, and Saddam Hussein, and criticized the United States for embargoing Iraq and Libya, the United States government, especially Representative King, threatened him with a variety of charges and suggested that he be required to register as a foreign agent. Farrakhan adamantly refused, insisting he had a perfect right to visit any country in the world. Some black leaders questioned his judgment. C. Eric Lincoln, for instance, said he had "squandered" the great opportunity he had created for himself in the Million-Man March. Shrewdly, Farrakhan responded to the criticisms by saying, on "60 Minutes," "Everyone who stepped back from me, they didn't run away. They're just watching from behind a tree." In time this turned out to be true. It is difficult to reject a black man who tells Mike Wallace, in response to Wallace's statement that Nigeria is "the most corrupt country in the world," "You're not in any moral position to call thirty-five-year-old Nigeria the most corrupt country in the world with as much hell as this country, in its 226 years, has caused its darker-skinned people. It killed off most of its Native Americans. Yes, there's corruption in Nigeria, sure, there's corruption everywhere, but the history of this country is written in bloodshed. This country is more corrupt than Nigeria." Black leaders would find it hard to turn their backs on that.

That daring, that "truth-telling," along with his now-recognized ability to draw and inspire crowds, will inevitably enlarge Farrakhan's reputation in the black world. But he will not be able to reach beyond, into the wider spaces of this country where the real power rests. He will not be able to reach the minds and hearts of open-minded whites as some black leaders have done—Frederick Douglass, Booker T. Washington, W. E. B. Du Bois, Roy Wilkins, Martin Luther King, Colin Powell, Andrew Young, Jesse Jackson, Maynard Jackson, Julian Bond, Thurgood Marshall, to name only the best known, a roster that may soon include all the young ones on their way up.

Farrakhan is too angry. He lacks what all those men had: a generosity toward the great wide human race. He is, bottom line, too black, too separatist. He may sometimes dream of joining that pantheon of men who used to be called race leaders, but then he would be faced with the memory of those three years under Warith Muhammad: whites and blacks hand and hand together, tolerance, goodwill, ignoring the Jewish demons, democracy in the ranks and democracy in the leadership too. Ugh. That's not Farrakhan's way. And then there's that whole question of economics that plays such a large role in his presentation of himself. He clearly has no future in that cooperative realm.

Despite all his accomplishments, big and small, Farrakhan may be destined to end much like his mentor, though we can hope he doesn't spend so many years as a near invalid. His fame and fortune are limited, on one hand, by his peculiar attachment to Elijah, the Messiah, and Elijah's peculiar mixed brand of Allah and Christ that Farrakhan has strengthened; and, on another hand, to his obsessive hatred of the Jews.

25.

As the nineties passed, it seemed sometimes to penetrate Farrakhan's thinking that he had created these limitations for himself, and he sought a more temperate presentation. But that effort was regularly overcome by his anger. Because whatever else Farrakhan is, he is a black man filled with the wrath of the biblical Jewish God. Man has forsaken him, embraced evil, and he will not forgive him. Whites have worked for centuries to destroy the souls of blacks, and blacks have been too cowardly to save themselves. He will struggle and die on their behalf, but he's not certain he will make any difference.

That he is also a con artist, a charlatan, a demagogue, and an egomaniac is, in the end, beside the point. Those traits help make his world go round from day to day. They characterize the man who was, at the time of this writing, in early 1997, the most influential man in the black world. Undoubtedly he will become much more influential in a world that thrives on lies and deceit, and on the threat of violence and terror. To blacks Farrakhan appears to shine in that world with his straight talk. He is the original rap artist minus the scatology. How long this image will play on the black stage and whether he can make vital personal changes that will take him beyond his present state are unknowable, but changes seem unlikely.

While American blacks pay homage to this man, their problems remain untouched, perhaps worsen. It seems clear that for the foreseeable future, without effective black leadership, the white leadership will go on bemoaning the conditions of the inner city while steadily withdrawing assistance. I dare not predict how long Farrakhan's response to the white leadership—telling blacks to hitch up their bootstraps and clean up their habits—will play in the black world.

Also uncertain is Farrakhan's fate if his reputation in the black world continues to grow and expand. He is viewed by many as paranoid in his fear of assassination. He may be, but he lives among a great variety of paranoids. Some choose to murder doctors who do abortions. Others burn to the ground the churches of religious groups they consider dangerous. The list is long and terrible and ranges from lunatic bomb-throwers to highly efficient representatives of the U.S. government. Farrakhan's fear should not be lightly dismissed.

Nor, because his career is so likely to be limited, should he be dismissed. We take for granted the power of those who run the mainstream newspapers and magazines in this country, but we have never credited nor fully understood the power held at various times by owners of black publications. The *Crisis*, edited by W. E. B. Du Bois for the NAACP, was only the most famous. Black newspapers and magazines have long had a profound influence in the black world, if only as an antidote to the mainstream media. If Robert Abbott, the founder in 1905 of the *Chicago Defender*, were alive today, he could excoriate Farrakhan for his racism, but he would also tell him stories about how whites and conservative blacks too held Abbott's feet to the fire when he ran front-page photos of lynchings in the South.

While I certainly do not intend to diminish Farrakhan's hatefulness, it is important to recognize that the black leaders who preceded him all shared some of his racist feelings, and all made some of those feelings known. The main difference, as I said, is that those men also had strong feelings of tolerance and forgiveness, the kinds of feelings that led to invitations to Robert Abbott, for instance, to serve on a wide variety of city boards, black and white.

Since the sixties, when it appeared that segregation would soon be a thing of the past, the role of the powerful black newspaper has fallen into Louis Farrakhan's hands. This is partly by default but also because he doesn't believe in integration; he believes in the power of the all-black press (which, by the way, earlier black newspapers never were and are not today).

In this era of greater and greater racial divide, even in what appear to be more and more interracial settings, and in this time for many blacks that resembles the turn-of-the-century South, overwhelmed with despair and cynicism, it isn't entirely surprising to see a highly intelligent black man using a variety of long-discarded tactics—chief among them the daring newspaper of advocacy and the blatant use of racism—in an effort to recreate the role of the flaming race leader.

To date it isn't clear how many of the lessons of history Louis Farrakhan has learned. Until that picture emerges, we can't dismiss him.

As I said, I haven't much faith in his being able to learn and apply the lessons of history. Is he, in that respect, so different from the rest of the world? Isn't that why there is always a market for those who write history? Will the historian who tells Farrakhan's story twenty years from now have anything new to say?

INDEX

A NOTE ON THE AUTHOR

Florence Hamlish Levinsohn is an independent journalist who specializes in politics and urban affairs. She is the author of *Harold Washington: A Political Biography* and, most recently, *Belgrade: Among the Serbs*. She has also edited six books, including *School Desegregation: Shadow and Substance* and *Financing the Learning Society*, and has published poetry, short stories, and plays. Ms. Levinsohn lives and writes in Evanston, Illinois, and is the mother of two daughters and a grandmother of three.